LÉON BLOY: A STUDY IN IMPATIENCE

LÉON BLOY:
A STUDY IN IMPATIENCE

Albert Béguin

CLUNY MEDIA

Cluny Media Edition, 2018

For more information regarding this title
or any other Cluny Media publication,
please write to info@clunymedia.com, or to
Cluny Media, P.O. Box 1664, Providence, RI, 02901

Cluny Media edition, including new matter, copyright © 2018 Cluny Media LLC

Translations by Edith M. Riley

All rights reserved

ISBN: 978-1944418823

Cover design by Clarke & Clarke
Cover image: Paul Cézanne, *The Black Marble Clock*,
1869–1871, oil on canvas
Courtesy of Wikimedia Commons

CONTENTS

Introduction	1
Historical Sketch of the Life and Work of Léon Bloy†	13
CHAPTER I Initiation into Suffering: Identity and its Conquest	25
CHAPTER II Poverty, Money, and the People of Israel	75
CHAPTER III The Symbolism of History, and the Soul of Napoleon	137
CHAPTER IV A Prophet of Our Catastrophe, and His Impatience	193
Bibliographical Note	245

† This chapter has been added by the author for the English edition.

"It is characteristic of love to be impatient,
and extreme love is extremely impatient."

To Stanislas Fumet,
in fellowship of impatience

September 19, 1943

Introduction

Léon Bloy has not yet been given the place that should be his among the witnesses of present-day France. Some day, in shuddering retrospect, it will be recognized that in our age the honor of humanity was upheld only by the silent sufferings of millions of humble victims and by the work of a few poets. These poets, or at any rate the greatest among them, all realized the state of the world. Born into a society which they found tyrannical or loathsome, they had to free themselves from a clogging heritage of error, injustice, and meanness; in solitude that might well have daunted them, they raised their cry of suffering, their angry protest, or their song of hope, which now, as never before, was a "hope against hope." Profoundly different as they were in character, in language and in their attitude towards life, they were at one in their relation to the age: *opposing* to the modern world a voice which would have *imposed* itself on any other world. A race of lonely giants, their testimonies were so powerful that in the end they redeemed the spiritual poverty by which they were surrounded. Most people are aware that the poetry of Baudelaire and the life and writings of Rimbaud have an importance outside literature, for they were the first to see how much the human soul had been forfeiting. Claudel and Péguy, despite the attempts made to smother them under a misleading reputation, now appear as the two great renewers who, after a long period of intellectual mediocrity and aesthetic trifling, gave back to art its *true* value as knowledge—and no longer a magic Promethean knowledge but a confession of faith, prayer and truth. Today writers like Georges Bernanos and a number of the younger poets are finding the audience justly earned by their insight into events and their vigorous claim to reinstate all that has been disowned.

Léon Bloy, however, is still more or less unknown, and it is scarcely realized that he was one of those who had the clearest vision of the dreadful night descending upon the earth, and at the same time one of the most robustly positive of writers in this age of negations. For this lack of perception there are several reasons but no good ones.

In our present distress and, indeed, because of it, his work cannot fail to become intelligible and to meet a need. At the time when he was writing, his views on the history of mankind might seem exaggerated, and it is not at all surprising that an age of blind, earthbound optimism saw in him a monster. A solitary voice upraised amid a general belief in the steady progress of the species and in the early advent of a golden age that was to put an end to centuries of instability, Bloy proclaimed that an abyss was about to open beneath the feet of mankind. With stubborn fury, for forty years, from 1877 to 1917, he did more than prophesy; he called down the wrath of God upon the paltry convictions and the precarious equilibrium of a complacent society which put its trust in science and bourgeois virtues, seeking the kind of tranquility that comes from silencing one's soul and forgetting God.

We know now that his prophecies actually fell short of the reality; and we are dazzled by the spectacle of a human intelligence which, because it judged only from the standpoint of the Absolute, was able to form such a clear idea of the future course of history. Yet that very intelligence, so much the reverse of all that generally

LÉON BLOY: A STUDY IN IMPATIENCE

goes by that name, exposed Bloy's work to a succession of misunderstandings, of which some were born of blindness and weakness, but others were the wretched defenses put up by those who did not want to hear. It was not difficult to find in Bloy's writings the arguments needed for his own condemnation. Who but a monster of shameless assurance could brook being called "the thankless mendicant" and profess that his friends were those who gave him money? What a lack of good feeling in the pamphleteer who could presume to cast doubts upon the genius and sincerity of such honorable men as Paul Bourget and François Coppée! And what a bottomless pit of personal spite and social resentment must lurk in the heart of this writer without a public, that he should dare to repeat, with no casuistical reservations, the "Woe unto the rich!" of the Gospel. But better weapons than vituperation were devised against him; among men of letters, as among the "right-thinking" in religion, a systematic ignoring of the offender is a favorite form of revenge. Since this gadfly spoke of himself as "in fellowship of impatience with all the rebels, all the disappointed, all the thwarted, all the damned of this world," one way of dealing with him was to thrust him back among his friends, the poor. This expedient was handled with the infallible technique which a century of journalism had worked out for reducing truth to silence, and the truthful to poverty. And, since this incomprehensible being accepted the ordeal, repeating in strange fashion: "Everything that happens to me calls for adoration," concerted injustice was given the dexterous form of one last lie: they began to praise Bloy for his style (which is, indeed, of extraordinary magnificence) and, in order to keep his message from getting through, they swathed him in the legend of the perfect artist, the spellbinder, the wielder of words and images which should be admired without paying too much attention to the obscure ideas hidden beneath this splendor. When criticism, admirably subordinated to the interests and instincts of a society on the defensive, refrains from insulting Bloy by classifying him, with his personal enemies Veuillot or Bourget, among the "traditionalists" or the "reactionaries," it tries to neutralize his revolutionary force by placing him, between the Goncourts and Huysmans, among the subtle craftsmen of "aesthetic writing."

But no device can go on indefinitely distorting the sense of a work so prodigiously alive; and we may well ask ourselves, here and now, whether the strangeness of Léon Bloy—I mean the fact that he is a stranger in this century—should not, instead of giving us the right to judge him severely, induce us to judge ourselves. If such a man seems so out of place and so surprising in our midst, can we be quite sure that this is due to *his* freakishness rather than our own? May not we, rather than he, have been to blame for the solitude forced upon him? Why should Bloy have necessarily been wrong when he defined his position as "the abominable disgrace of having no snout in a society which, has no God"?

To be truthful, once that question has been raised there is no means of evading the answer: Bloy's vehemence, his famous rages, the luxuriance of his language and his imagination, the strangeness of his opinions—all these spell neither romantic extravagance nor the chaotic outbursts of an unhappy genius. That voice, booming out with such amazing vigor, lends his profundity of spirit a means of utterance which, in its wealth of resources and its virulence, is a measure of the vast distance between Bloy and his age.

Is there not something unmistakable about this living anachronism and the accents of this voice? Are they not the destiny and the obstinate cry of a Prophet? No title suits Bloy so well as this one, which he more than once repudiated. His solitude is a prophet's solitude: "I go before my thoughts into exile, at the head of a great procession of silence." His anger is a prophet's anger, since, according to an entry in Bloy's diary, a prophet is "first and foremost a voice to call down Justice. His cries will have power to hasten the devastations." And his worship, again, is that profound desire for God which brings the great Israelites face to face with their Lord, whom the people refuse to see: "I have become a kind of mystic poet, immured in the sempiternal contemplation of invisible harmonies,

LÉON BLOY: A STUDY IN IMPATIENCE

ravaged by all the furies of desire for God, and consumed body and soul by all the famines of earth and heaven."

Bloy is a prophet by reason of his situation. He is also a prophet in the commonplace sense of the word, through his accuracy in divining the future. But he is more essentially a prophet in the particular sense in which André Rousseaux conferred that title upon Péguy, so different from Bloy and yet, as we shall see, a man of the same spirit. In this acceptation of the word, the Prophet is not so much one who foretells future events as one who has a true understanding of things. Behind them, behind the facts of history, the texts revealed, the behavior of men, behind his own destiny and that of his people, he sees their true significance. He does not provide a commentary upon them, after the manner of the modern intellectual; nor does he explain them by causes, effects and laws, as the historian and the psychologist claim to do. He is like Claudel's character Coeuvre, in *La Ville*: "You explain nothing, O poet, but through you all things become explainable." For all his efforts are concentrated upon deciphering the created world (the world of nature or of history), conceived as a divine manuscript, and upon creating transparence where we, with our clouded eyes, see only opacity. At the end of its labors, such a mind has nowhere laid bare any rational plan; led by intuition, it discovers that the whole unfathomable quintessence of the mystery lies in the very spot where we could see nothing but a superficial fact; and, at the bidding of intuition, it worships the presence of that mystery, now run to earth.

All Bloy's singularity comes from this concentration of his attention upon reading the history of God in human history, and from the infinite pain and grief with which, day after day, he beheld the creature refusing to understand what everything should have taught it. If he is a man apart, it is not through any eccentricity of genius or natural peculiarity of character, but' because no other man ever took all his bearings so constantly with reference to the Absolute and none was so incapable of paying any attention to relative demands. "You judge me as a human being," he wrote in 1896, "regardless of the fact that I am outside all human standpoints, and that this is my strength, my only strength. The plain truth, the truth that shines forth in all my books, is that I WRITE ONLY FOR GOD." From every stage of his work, passage after passage could be quoted revealing, more or less ingenuously but always in the same spirit of love, this orientation of his spirit towards one single Object: "There is nothing true but what is Absolute." "Except God, everything is indifferent to me." "Nothing is necessary, nothing, nothing, except God." "I am first and foremost a worshipper, and I have always considered myself lower than the beasts whenever I have set out to act otherwise than from love and through the promptings of love."

This extraordinary fervor of spiritual craving finds expression again and again in Bloy's books. Take, for example, the following comment on Caïn Marchenoir, in whom the author drew his own portrait, in *Le Désespéré*. "That tragic soul pictured Paradise itself as an eternal tempestuous ascent towards the Absolute"—an image taken up again and developed into a splendid Vision in one of the finest chapters of *Celle qui pleure*.

But this aspect of Bloy, as a man of unparalleled vehemence, imbued with the sense of his extraordinary vocation, should never be allowed to obscure that other face of his, not opposed but complementary to the first—a face full of humility and transparent joy. This was the Bloy of the later books and the letters to Jean de La Laurencie; but long before that he had proclaimed the identity of suffering with joy, and of anger with contemplation, which was one of his greatest discoveries.

"I thirst," he wrote in 1900, "to be looked upon as a poor man, very lonely and full of love. You do not know my weakness or my ignorance, my downright abjectness or my fiendish SADNESS, and you know nothing of the JOY that is in the depths of my soul." And in 1895: "If I did not feel my misery, how could I feel my joy, which is the eldest daughter of my misery and bears a frightening resemblance to it?"

LÉON BLOY: A STUDY IN IMPATIENCE

Above all, there is the last sentence of *La Femme pauvre*, which should not be lost sight of for one instant since it is the living hearth-fire of Bloy's inward life: "There is only one sadness; it is the sadness of NOT BEING SAINTS."

A mind directed towards the Absolute and piercing all its veils, a soul living in the expectation of Divine Justice and yearning for it even more than for Mercy, such was the vocation peculiar to Léon Bloy. And that is the source of the mystery which shrouds his being.

What he himself said of *Le Salut par les Juifs* could be applied to his work, as a whole: rather than a book, it is "the outline of a book." Bloy *was unable* to say everything, for, in lighting up the depths, he recovered a view of things which human thought had lost for centuries. After the Fathers of the Church, and the simple believers at the full tide of the Middle Ages, there was no one who still had the secret of grasping reality without splitting it up into compartments; no one with the type of understanding that sees Brings only in relation to the whole of what is, was and will be. The modern mind, since the Renaissance, and even since the last phase of the Middle Ages, has turned away from that contemplation which, while embracing a whole system, is organized round a single center—the only possible center being the Redemption. Bloy goes back to a universe comparable to that of early Christendom, and this is what makes him obscure to us, who are only the first generation of his readers. We may take it that he is inaugurating a perfect and salutary renewal of our powers of vision, and the process will hardly be completed without the compulsion of events, when the bankruptcy of our errant civilization at last becomes so glaring that our eyes are violently opened. Such a spiritual revolution could only be roughed out by the painful labors of the Pilgrim of the Absolute. It will probably take his successors centuries to finish off the cure begun by this oculist of the soul, whose purpose was nothing less than to make it natural for us to see the invisible world.

"I have always said the same thing," he wrote at the end of his life. In this single thing, repeated under a great variety of figures and images, lies the essential clue to the strangely anachronistic sayings of this man who was "dazzled by the Face of God." Pascal—for whom Bloy had no love, but to whom it is permissible to compare him in spiritual stature—said that "every writer has a meaning to which all the conflicting passages of his work ultimately go back." In Bloy's case we are on the track of this meaning as soon as we realize how he harped upon the overwhelming discovery with which he was favored in early maturity; that, having entered upon the contemplative life through suffering, he loved it and asked for it, not through a romantic cult of sorrow but because he saw in human torments an echo of the agony of Jesus Christ, "crucified until the end of the world" and tortured by the delays to which man's obstinate refusal subjects the coming of the Kingdom of God; and that, for this reason, every increase of horror meant for him that God was at hand, that this was the beginning of the great tribulation which should precede the final kindling of souls by the Holy Spirit, and the fulfilment of time. Bloy lived like the Church herself—*expectans expectavi*—waking for that to happen which should put an end to all happenings. And he was unable to curb his great anger against everything which, by postponing the hour of his hopes, prolonged the sufferings inflicted by men upon their Redeemer. "The angers which burst from me are but the very faint echoes of a Curse from on high, which I have the surprising misfortune to reverberate," he wrote one day. And in a letter dated 1905 he added this profound definition of himself: "You think that in me religious feeling is a special form of rebellion. It is just the opposite. Mad as this may seem to you, I am by nature obedient and tender-hearted. That is why I write ruthlessly, having to defend Truth and bear witness to the God of the poor. That's all. My most vehement pages were written by love, often with tears of love, in hours of unutterable peace."

LÉON BLOY: A STUDY IN IMPATIENCE

This prophet was a poet. But a poet who, more than most, was conscious of the inadequacy of earthly beauty. "In our fallen state, Beauty is a monster," he writes. He knew that human words are inadequate and only serve to note the existence of the ineffable. This comment of his with reference to the Scriptures may also be applied to poetic language: words, in their diversity, all have the same substance, which defies human expression; they are "iridescent veils before the same tabernacle." Hence his exertion as a writer painfully conscious of the insurmountable gap between what he expressed and what he wished to express, namely "the sight of God"; he knew well enough that man has lost it, and yet he could not do otherwise than strain after it with all his heart. This accounts for the difficulties of his toil, and the disappointment which he often admitted, as, for instance, in a letter dated April 14, 1886, to Louis Montchal:

> I never manage to put my soul into what I write, and I have an ideal of love, of life and of eloquence which only serves to reduce me to despair, since it is inaccessible… I am condemned to this stupid trade of writing, which is certainly not my true vocation. I was born a warrior, a crusader if you like, in an age when war is dishonored and crusades are impossible… If by some miracle I became rich, I should drop literature and make myself the servant of the poor. I should find it much more beautiful and useful to have a leper, whose sores I was clumsily dressing, spit in my face, than to devote my time to the inept pursuit of adjectives and participles.…

Nevertheless, great writer that he was, with his inexhaustible vocabulary, the cadence of his sentences, the patristic Latinity of his eloquence, and the profoundness of his imagery, Bloy had to find a justification for his art: "It is indispensable that Truth should appear in Glory. Splendor of style is not a luxury, it is a necessity." His great longing called down the Glory of God upon earth, and his need for verbal invention matches his need to detect the presence of mystery, not in order to say what it is but to say where it dwells—which is everywhere. His studies in symbolical exegesis (as a follower of Abbé Tardif de Moidrey and a forerunner of the great commentaries of Claudel) had taught him the multiple significance of words and the allusive value of symbols. Looking below the surface, he set out to discover what each thing typified and what place it occupied in the plan of God; to fit it into the endless succession of analogies which forms the secret fabric of the created world and extends mysteriously into the invisible.

Thus, painfully tracing through a thousand forms "the history of the Three Persons of the Trinity"; continually recounting the Passion; eternally impatient for the final Descent from the Cross, which, in the temporal world, will dispel the desolation of man and set a term to the unfathomable "conflicts of Mercy with Justice"; Bloy, at whose every step mysteries increase and multiply, opens for our contemplation *abysses*—his favorite word—not of darkness but of dazzling light. They can be reached only by ceaselessly dispersing the false brightness of a superficial understanding. Where everything seemed simple, Bloy makes us aware that everything is incomprehensible and forces us to marvel.

Thus nothing could be further from the truth than to suspect that a personal lack of balance lay at the root of this continual "disarticulation" of appearances, which was Bloy's way of arousing stupefaction and bringing out the hidden lineaments of the real. There was never a mind more sturdily balanced than this vigorous intellect which turned the disruption of accepted stabilities into a method of thought and a demand for attention.

The four essays which follow do not set out to give a portrait of Bloy or a complete commentary on his work. They are not intended as a piece of literary criticism and, as a rule, I have refrained from passing judgment on Bloy's views. It seemed to me sufficient—and more in keeping with my own limitations—to approach the secret

LÉON BLOY: A STUDY IN IMPATIENCE

of this man's work and his soul by four converging paths, chosen as being those which the happenings and questions of our own day have made specially accessible to us, as well as specially necessary. The transcendent spiritual light shed by some of Bloy's great books upon the principal mysteries of the Faith remains veiled for the time being; only little by little, I think, will it be possible to grasp the fullness of his message and decipher the profoundest of his symbols. On the other hand, the exegeses of history and of the state of humanity, sustained by Bloy's inward knowledge, are becoming clear to us in the light of events. We can no longer remain blind to his wonderful views on Suffering, Poverty, the scandal of money, the destiny of the people of Israel, history as an instrument of Providence, the amazing figure of Napoleon, or the war of the nations. It is to us, moreover, that this witness of Suffering ultimately addresses the profession of Hope in which his train of thought always culminates, his life having been spent in "making hope out of despair, and eternity out of a lump of clay kneaded in my hand." Writing that there was never "a more incurable hoper than I," Bloy added: "As if it were not enough to hope for myself, I hope for my friends and even for the whole world, despite the continual blows and buffets of my relentless fate. My most beautiful dream, the constant dream of my days and my nights, is to find so much deliverance that I can become the liberator of others" (to Louis Montchal, June 16, 1886).

The four chapters of this book all lead in similar fashion to the threshold of the ineffable and, without proceeding to explore them, afford a prospect of Bloy's most inward meditations, upon the Trinity, the Earthly Paradise, the Virgin, and the final coming of the Holy Spirit. Their presence is a postulate which we are continuously called upon to accept, it being borne in mind that the difficult analogies by means of which Bloy seeks to unriddle Scripture or History have their foundations in these depths of contemplation.

But at the present time, when our thoughts are urgently summoned to confront an immediate and collective anguish, the essential truths which it was Bloy's mission to unveil (in so far as a human mind is capable of it) come nearer to us and are more helpful when the medium chosen is an interpretation of the common destiny of man. The opening study, on Suffering, seeks to adapt our viewpoint to the perspective of Bloy's spiritual life. The next one brings us face to face with those Christian pronouncements whose rediscovery is most vital today: on poverty, on money, on Israel. In the third essay, with Bloy as guide, the fortunes of Christendom and of France are followed through the ages, special attention being given to his commentary on Napoleonic history. In conclusion, his meditations during the war of 1914, full of ideas which seem to have a direct bearing on recent years, afford an insight into what Bloy calls "the optimism of Justice"—the clue to the nature of his impatience.

With the continual rediscovery of a few unchanging assertions in all the different languages used by Bloy for their expression, it has hardly been possible to avoid repetitions, since all the paths taken lead to the same points. I do not think I need apologize for quoting Bloy very fully, and for frequently comparing his thought with Péguy's. Although these two Frenchmen neither knew nor recognized each other, their agreement and their differences naturally suggest an immortal dialogue.

Historical Sketch of the Life and Work of Léon Bloy

Born in 1846, the year in which the Virgin Mary appeared to the shepherd children on the mountain of La Salette; fighting as a volunteer in the war of 1870; taking an active part in the literary life of Paris during the vogue of symbolism and naturalism; and, in his old age, living through the war of 1914 as an onlooker—Léon Bloy, who died in 1917, ranks as one of the most important writers of modern times. Although his work long went unrecognized and it is only recently that he has been given the place which is his due, his personal influence was considerable. By way of indication, it will suffice to recall that Bloy was instrumental in the conversion of Jacques Maritain, the neo-Thomist philosopher, for whom he stood godfather; and that in point of time he was the first of the writers who helped to bring about a Catholic renaissance in France. Charles Péguy, Paul Claudel, Georges Bernanos, and François Mauriac came after him and, if they were not his disciples, at least it may be said that he prepared the way for them. But apart from their historical significance, the intrinsic importance of his writings is considerable, both on account of their literary value and because their spiritual viewpoint has quickened French Catholicism with a new depth. His first teachers were the great traditionalists of the nineteenth century, Joseph de Maistre, Bonald, and Barbey d'Aurevilly; he did not continue in this direction, however, for he was to come under the stronger influence of Abbé Tardif de Moidrey, a great exegetist, and of Ernest Hello and Blanc de Saint-Bonnet, who helped him to activate his sense of symbols. Thanks to that intellectual training and thanks to his own spiritual gifts, it may be said that Léon Bloy was the first great French Catholic, for two centuries, to turn resolutely away from Jansenist tendencies, as Claudel and Péguy, for instance, did at a later date.

Léon-Marie Bloy was born at Périgueux on July 6, 1846, as the second of seven children of an engineer. His mother was of Spanish extraction. From his childhood he was in conflict with his environment; unruly, refusing to submit to a strict upbringing, torn between his father's avowed atheism and the mysticism of his mother, he had from an early age the sense of an unusual destiny and knew the pains of loneliness. His schooldays came to a premature end after his fourth year at a lycée, and in the years that followed he refused to consider any sort of career. He drew, painted, filled his mind with voluminous reading on historical and religious subjects and reached the embryonic stage as a writer of tragedies. A self-portrait at the age of seventeen has been preserved, with the comment Bloy wrote beneath it: "The makings of a handsome face."

In 1863 he left his family and went to Paris, where he proposed to study drawing. For several years he had one office job after another, never staying long in any of them. Letters dating from that period (not yet widely known) show him in a state of violent spiritual revolt, "hating Jesus and hating his Church." It was in 1869 that he first met Barbey d'Aurevilly at a bookseller's; he followed him, got into conversation with him, sought his company, and came very much under the spell of the Norman novelist. Barbey, who officially ranks as a Catholic writer but whose religious life soon seemed to his disciple to be lacking in depth, probably placed him in touch

LÉON BLOY: A STUDY IN IMPATIENCE

with various priests. From then onwards Bloy kept up an active correspondence with several of them and in particular with Dom Guérenger (author of the *Année liturgique*).

Soon after his conversion Bloy, in 1870, joined the irregulars fighting on the Loire. Later on he gave an account of that hard campaign in an excellent collection of short stories called *Sueur de Sang*. After the final defeat of France he went back to his family for a time, working in the office of a Périgueux solicitor and teaching one of his younger brothers. But he could not stand provincial life very long. In 1873 he was back in Paris as book-keeper for a railway company—a post in which he was not destined to remain any longer than in his earlier jobs. His first attempts at journalism date from the same period; but there again a few initial successes were soon followed by reverses. Bloy's animation and the splendor of his language appealed to editors, but the violence of his invective made them uneasy and they soon dropped him. In an unpublished letter written in 1883 to Madame Hayem, a friend of his, he described his adventures during those years, ending up:

> Here I am then, no good for any of the activities of this earth. I don't fit in anywhere. Journalism, which should have secured me a livelihood, is closed to me for the very strong reason that I cannot write four lines without endangering the equilibrium of the planet. Disowned by the Catholics, who find my enthusiasm and flamboyance unpardonable; spewed forth by the non-Catholics, who cannot digest my Catholicism; always wrecked in advance by my inability to acclimatize myself to this world; with no private means and no resources; I have sworn brotherhood with afflictions whose real immensity can be measured only by Him who knows the exact extent of our capacity for suffering.

But, while he was plumbing the depths of that adversity which was to be his lot from then onwards until extreme old age, Léon

Bloy in 1877 experienced a threefold upheaval. It was in that year that he met Abbé Tardif de Moidrey, who was engaged in reviving the symbolical exegesis of the Scriptures and had devoted his life to the Apparition of La Salette; thanks to him Bloy's whole spiritual life came to be centered in a constant reading of sacred writ. The same encounter led to Bloy's discovery of La Salette, to which he made a pilgrimage with Abbé Tardif (who died there suddenly in 1879, just when he was planning to go with Bloy to Jerusalem). The Discourse of the Virgin Mary to Mélanie revealed to Bloy a direct intervention on the part of Providence in the course of terrestrial history, and it was in meditating upon this mystery that he conceived the idea of an exegesis of historical events, as a parallel to the exegesis of the Scriptures. But at the same time there was a new element in his private life which, though exposing him to the greatest spiritual dangers, ended, after he had passed through an agonizing ordeal, by setting his feet more firmly in the path of mysticism: this new element was brought into his life by Anne-Marie Roulé, whom he later immortalized in the character of Véronique, in *Le Désespéré*. She was a prostitute for whom he conceived a most violent passion, in which sensual attraction was coupled with a noble love of the spirit. He converted Anne-Marie, who was borne by the current of his enthusiasm into the practice of contemplation and a religious life of perhaps exaggerated fervor. Having now reached the nadir of material adversity and having vainly sought to transform the tie which bound him to Anne-Marie into a chaste love, he tried to flee from temptation by taking himself off for a retreat at La Trappe, with the intention of remaining there. It was a failure: the Prior in whom he confided told him after a time that religious orders were not for him, and Bloy returned to Paris. All these dramatic events are known to us from the letters to Véronique (published in 1936 by Jacques Maritain); from the account which Bloy gave of them at a later date in his letters to his future wife (published in 1922), and from his correspondence (some of which is still unpublished) with Ernest Hello, Barbey d'Aurevilly, and Louis Montchal.

LÉON BLOY: A STUDY IN IMPATIENCE

Meanwhile Anne-Marie Roulé was living in a state of increasing religious exaltation; she saw visions and heard celestial utterances which she communicated to Bloy. This is what is known as "the secret of Léon Bloy," to which he made not infrequent allusions, without ever revealing exactly what it comprised. Anne-Marie would seem to have announced that the End of the World was at hand and that he, Léon Bloy, would play the part of a privileged witness, or even the role of the prophet Elijah. His inner life was very largely determined by these revelations, to which he never ceased to lend the utmost credence, living in expectation of the coming of the Holy Spirit and of his own martyrdom.

In 1882, after five years of this extraordinary strain, Anne-Marie Roulé went out of her mind and had to be shut up in an asylum, where she lingered on until her death in 1907.

But Bloy had not stopped working. In 1884 he published the first of his books to get into print. Written as far back as 1879, *Le Révélateur du Globe* is a summary of a book by the Comte Roselly de Lorgues on Christopher Columbus, but a summary which goes far deeper than the original work. It was Bloy's first attempt to give history a symbolical interpretation, and already his gaze embraced an extensive panorama of the ages, to which the book owes a number of splendid passages. Before this book, Bloy had written one on Marie-Antoinette, *La Chevaliére de la Mort*, completed in 1877 but not printed until 1891. That work and *Le Fils de Louis XVI* (1900) show his fidelity to the legitimate monarchy and to the teachings of the traditionalists; but there is far more in these books than a mere "political" attitude. Although Barbey d'Aurevilly gave them his backing, they had no success.

Between 1882 and 1890, that is to say between the end of the Véronique period and the date of his marriage to Jeanne Molbeck, Léon Bloy *did* enjoy a kind of celebrity in Paris, but it had little to do with the true qualities of his work. He became well-known as a formidable lampooner, being at that time mixed up in all sorts of quarrels between men of letters. He was to be seen among the frequenters of that famous rendezvous, the "Chat Noir"; and it was in the paper launched by that circle that he published those lightning attacks which not long afterwards (in 1885) were printed in book form with the title *Propos d'un Entrepreneur de Demolitions*. It was during this period, too, that on several occasions, having been challenged to a duel, after the custom of that milieu, he refused to fight, as a matter of principle—an attitude which greatly shocked his associates. In 1885 he launched a small weekly, *Le Pal*, of which he was the sole editor and which only ran to four numbers.

At that time he was living with a woman called Berthe Dumont, who died of tetanus in 1885 and of whom he has left a portrait in Clotilde, the heroine of *La Femme pauvre* (or rather in the Clotilde of the first part of that novel; for in the second part it was his future wife who served as model). This fresh calamity was followed by several years of profound dejection and Léon Bloy's biographers have so far only been able to piece together a very fragmentary account of the episodes and tribulations of that time of affliction.

In 1886, however, he published his first great novel, *Le Désespéré*, which gave rise to a somewhat obscure affair between two publishers and which, though it scored a considerable success (but only thanks to the curiosity excited by some of its superficial aspects) led to no improvement whatsoever in the author's material circumstances. This book, the best known of all Bloy's works, gives an incomplete and misleading picture of him. It is weighed down by chapters of merely topical interest and by violent attacks upon most of the writers of the day: among the grotesque or odious characters in Bloy's terrible portrait gallery, Alphonse Daudet, Catulle Mendès, Jean Richepin, Maupassant, Paul Bourget, and a number of lesser lights are easily recognizable under false names. But in *Le Désespéré* Bloy expressed something much greater than his bursts of anger and indignation; he put the whole of his personal life into it, the devastating memory of Véronique, the drama of his mystical impatience, the joy of his discoveries and, above all, of his great visions of history. It is an involved, many-sided book, written in a

LÉON BLOY: A STUDY IN IMPATIENCE

language clogged with its own richness, but a book whose substance is inexhaustible.

In May 1890, at François Coppée's, Léon Bloy met the daughter of Christian Molbeck, the Danish poet. Touched by the writer's wretched plight, attracted by the impression of force which he gave her, speedily converted to Catholicism by him, she married him a few months later. For Bloy this marriage was a blessing, despite the torments of a poverty which was no longer unshared. Jeanne Molbeck's presence had a calming effect upon him and, to judge by numerous entries in his diary, she seems very often to have put him on the track of profound discoveries.

From this time onwards Léon Bloy's work steadily increased in stature, amid sufferings in which he came to recognize the very mark of his vocation, repeating when things were at their worst: "Everything that happens to me calls for adoration." Bloy, his wife, and their four children were at times reduced to almost unbelievable poverty, despite the help which friends tried to give them and despite an amazingly abundant literary output. The two little boys born of this marriage died in infancy, victims of the appalling conditions in which the family lived. Two daughters, adored by their father, survived their privations and are still alive, one in Paris and the other in Prague. Apart from two visits to Denmark, as a lecturer in 1891 and in the hope of escaping from want in 1899–1900, Bloy hardly ever left Paris. In his last years, when he could afford it, he let himself be taken into the country for "summer holidays," of which he had a horror.

From 1905, however, his material sufferings and his inward ordeals (for the eager expectation of martyrdom continued to torment him with the same impatience) were alleviated by the presence of a devoted band of friends, mostly his juniors, who gathered round him, attracted by the warmth and light given out by his works. Alfred Vallette and his wife Rachilde, who ran the *Mercure de France*, displayed a fidelity which was the more remarkable since they were very far from sharing his Christian beliefs. Pierre

Termier, the distinguished geologist, bestowed upon him a wholehearted friendship which often went to the length of personal sacrifice (he wrote an excellent little book on Bloy, and the influence of his friend can be discovered even in his learned works). Clerics like Abbé Cornuau and Frère Dacien, the great painter Georges Rouault, the young composer Georges Auric, and a number of others, including Philippe Raoux, Jean de la Laurencie, and Réne Martineau, belonged to the circle of his intimates. But Léon Bloy's favorites were his godchildren, Jacques and Raïssa Maritain, and Pierre and Christian Van der Meer de Walcheren.

These beloved presences brought Bloy some relief from the torments he suffered in the war years from 1914. He died on November 3, 1917, at Bourg-la-Reine, in the house previously occupied by Charles Péguy. The two great Christian writers had never met.

To return to Léon Bloy's literary work—*Le Désespéré* was followed by only one other novel: *La Femme pauvre* (1897), a powerful masterpiece. It contains various echoes from the author's life: the story of Berthe Dumont, Bloy's betrothal to Jeanne Molbeck, the death of a child. But, transposed to another plane, they become symbolic elements in the complex and infinitely rich texture of the work, which is the most profound expression Bloy ever gave to his inner life. This novel had been preceded, in 1893 and 1894, by two collections of tales: *Sueur de Sang* (containing his memories of the war of 1870) and *Histoires Désobligeantes* (terrible stories whose meaning is hidden under a show of brutal realism).

The lampooner in Léon Bloy, far from being dead, was responsible for *Léon Bloy devant les Cochons* (1894), *Je m'accuse...* (1900), which was a violent diatribe against Zola, *Les dernières colonnes de l'Eglise* (1903), and *Belluaires et Porchers* (1905), besides a number of scattered articles.

But Bloy was now devoting more and more of his time to a meditation which found expression in three series of works: historical

LÉON BLOY: A STUDY IN IMPATIENCE

studies and commentaries; books on the Christian mysteries and their temporal incidence; and a succession of volumes of his intimate diary.

As a historian, Léon Bloy, after having been attracted by Christopher Columbus and Queen Marie-Antoinette, developed a passionate interest in Byzantium, which inspired a number of very fine passages in his two novels. Coming back to this subject in 1906, he published *L'Epopée byzantine*, in which he analyzed the works of Gustave Schlumberger and made them a pretext for expressing his own views on history. He next gave his attention to the character of Napoleon, and, after years of reading and research, published in 1912 *L'Ame de Napoléon*, one of the most perfect of his books and perhaps the one to which new readers of Leon Bloy should turn first. Joan of Arc, too, had long attracted him and he had begun to write about her shortly before the outbreak of the 1914 war, which had a powerful influence upon his book. It appeared in 1915 under the title *Jeanne d'Arc et l'Allemagne*.

Léon Bloy's works of pure contemplation are never so far removed from his polemical works that no trace remains of his violence and his fighting temperament. Nor was the historian in him completely obscured when he wrote them; indeed, he always centered his meditation in some reality of this terrestrial world, as he had learnt to do when reflecting upon the words of La Salette. It is the sense of human history, the signs of the intervention of Providence in that history that are always the mainspring of his reflections. But La Salette had taught him another thing: that nothing can have any meaning save in relation to the End of Time. Thus in every one of his great books he takes the path which leads to eschatology. The one among them on which he lavished the most time and pains was *Le Symbolisme de l'Apparition*, begun at a very early date, taken up again at intervals and published posthumously in 1925. With this book on La Salette may be coupled the one which Bloy himself published on the same subject in 1908—*Celle qui pleure*. Side by side with vehement outbursts against the suppression of the message of

ALBERT BÉGUIN

1846, it contains some of Bloy's finest dissertations on the mysteries of the Faith. And when in 1912 he published the manuscript of a *Vie de Mélanie* (the shepherdess of La Salette), he gave that biography a preface which is probably the most profound of all his writings. *L'Exégèse des Lieux Commons* (first series published in 1902, second series in 1913) is only superficially a humorous book; beneath the banalities of everyday life and the precepts of a bourgeois wisdom whose absurdity he lays bare, Bloy seeks to bring to the surface the secret knowledge and true mystery which, for his eyes, are to be found in the language farthest removed from faith. *Le Salut par les Juifs* (1892) is a meditation on Israel which gradually swells into a vision of apocalyptic times. Another wholly admirable book, *Le Sang du Pauvre* (1909), is a cry of revolt against social injustice and at the same time a contemplation of the mystery of Poverty. From 1892 onwards Bloy kept an intimate diary in which, besides noting down the little daily happenings of his life, he recorded what he had been reading and the thousand and one reflections inspired by contemporary events or the liturgical texts for the day. In 1898 he decided to publish this diary, but not without subjecting it to a process of polishing and revision which transformed it into real literature. This editing (in any case much less appreciable in the later volumes) did not rob the diary of any of its freshness. It is impossible to imagine a more poignant description of a life which seemed dedicated to misfortune and marked by an extraordinary persistence of suffering. The titles which Bloy chose for these volumes of autobiography are revealing: he began by giving them names which he had bestowed upon himself; later in the series these names were superseded by titles more applicable to the commonalty of human beings, and this transformation reflects the upward progress of the author's inner life. The first volume was called *Le Mendiant ingrat* (diary for 1892–1805, published in 1898). This was followed in 1904 by *Mon Journal* (covering the period 1896–1900, including the very important visit to Denmark), in 1905 by *Quatre ans de captivité à Cochons-sur-Marne* (1900–1904, life at Lagny-sur-Marne), in 1909

LÉON BLOY: A STUDY IN IMPATIENCE

by *L'Invendable* (1904–1907), in 1911 by *Le Vieux de la Montagne* (1907–1910) and in 1914 by *Le Pèlerin de l'Absolu* (1910–1912). Then came the two volumes written during the war: *Au Seuil de l'Apocalypse* (1913–1915) and *La Porte des Humbles* (1915–1917). During those same war years Bloy had also taken the events of the day as a subject for meditations of great amplitude. These compositions, which contain some of the finest work of the great prose-writer, were collected in two volumes: *Méditations d'un solitaire* (1917) and *Dans les Ténèbres* (published posthumously in 1918).

This rapid enumeration of Bloy's works would be incomplete if no mention were made of the numerous volumes of correspondence which have been published during the last thirty years, without having brought to light anything like the whole of Bloy's output as a letter writer (we have only a fragmentary knowledge of, for instance, the very important correspondence with Louis Montchal, Barbey d'Aurevilly, Ernest Hello, and a number of priests with whom Bloy was in touch at the most dramatic moment of his youth or in the fervor of his conversion). Reference has already been made to the letters to Véronique and to his future wife. Others whose richness and importance entitle them to special mention are the letters of his youth (published in 1920), the letters to his godsons, Jacques Maritain and Pierre van der Meer (1928), to Pierre Termier (1927), and to Jean de la Laurencie (1927). It would, moreover, be difficult to overrate the interest of Bloy's correspondence with Abbé Cornuau and Frère Dacien (1926), with Philippe Raoux (1937), with René Martineau (1933), and with Georges Khnopff (1929). A number of books about Bloy, and in particular those by Leopold Levaux, Joseph Bollery, Hubert Colleye, Stanislas Fumet and the collection known as the *Cahiers Léon Bloy* also contain unpublished letters to various correspondents.

The number of posthumous publications, of new editions of Bloy's books, and of works about him is sufficient evidence that the impression made by this man has steadily deepened in recent times. It is possible to mark the growth in his stature, the increasing clearness of his message, the widening of his circle of readers. Gradually the image of the picturesque pamphleteer fades, to make way for that of the great contemplative, and the Pilgrim of the Absolute assumes his true dimensions in Time. They are those of a prophet, and at the same time the very human dimensions of one who lived and suffered in the world of men.

CHAPTER I

Initiation into Suffering: Identity and Its Conquest

> Since childhood I cannot remember a time when I did not suffer in all kinds of ways and often to an unbelievable degree. That simply proves that God loves me very much.
>
> I have meditated long and often on suffering. I am now convinced that nothing else is supernatural in this world. All the rest is human...
>
> – To Barbey d'Aurevilly, December 11, 1873

"In his poor heart man has places which do not yet exist, and suffering enters in order to bring them to life."

This wonderful sentence occurs in an important letter which Bloy, at twenty-seven, wrote to his friend Georges Landry. The whole outward destiny of the writer and his spiritual life could be summed up in that saying. Bloy's existence, as reflected in his diary, his correspondence and the testimony of his friends, was an uninterrupted succession of afflictions; but each intensification of his suffering marked a step forward, a discovery and, literally, a new *birth*.

ALBERT BÉGUIN

No form of misery was unknown to Bloy: material poverty, anguish of soul, lapses and relapses into sin, the bitterness of carnal passion and of a pride that could not be stifled, the injustice of men, setbacks and humiliations of every sort, the cruel rending of his own flesh by the death of his two sons—and, even more terrible, the agony of spiritual impatience a hundred times disappointed. His supreme trial was undoubtedly the withholding of that martyrdom which he had not ceased to crave; he had to recognize, on his deathbed, that this claim too must, be renounced—that he must take the common road into "the great chaos of death."

But, though terrible cries were forced from him by these exceptional tribulations and though few men's sufferings have been so vocal as his, there is no point in recounting once again the details of that pitiless progress. It may be left to Bloy himself to depict, with all the power of his language and for his own ends, the dreadful stations of his Calvary and the insults heaped upon him by a society which resented his accusing presence. He alone has the right to use the incidents of his life (as he did) to express what he had to say, each specific circumstance becoming in his eyes an eloquent image of the common lot of mankind. Those who overlook the deep significance of his confessions have often made too much of the picturesque pathos to which such uncloistered adversity may lend itself. The point is not so much to visualize the squalid surroundings in which one of the greatest minds of our day was reduced to living as to understand by what inward paths Bloy was led to the assertion, at each intensification of his afflictions: "Everything that happens to me calls for adoration, for nothing is outside the divine plan"; and, above all, it is important to realize the exact meaning of that great saying, which is one of joy rather than of resignation.

Suffice it to say that Bloy's misery was very real and that we have no right either to cast doubts upon it or to suspect him of exaggeration. There will always be people ready to fly out at the temerity of a poor wretch who ventures to say that the established order of modern society has condemned him to an unjust fate; and such

LÉON BLOY: A STUDY IN IMPATIENCE

people have not failed to reproach Bloy with the scandal which his complaints were in danger of provoking.

> How inconsiderate and shameless to disturb the peace of good, devout souls or of firm believers in social progress by revealing what injustice their polished world conceals and to what degradation it may force a man! Why such an outcry, anyway, as if nobody else was in difficulties towards the end of the month? Other men have lost their children and have maintained a dignified silence. Besides, there was nothing to prevent Bloy from earning his living "honorably": he could have gone on with his job as railway clerk instead of throwing it up to become a Trappist...which did not last long anyhow. The editors of right-thinking newspapers were all prepared to employ his fine talent if only he would moderate his language and keep his scorn for the enemies of religion, instead of which he had the deplorable habit of picking holes in the "good sheep" and inopportunely denouncing their hypocrisies. And then, think of his royalties! A little prudence and a little thrift would have saved him from having to beg for help right and left. Not to mention that it takes a fair amount of impudence to write to a reputable scholar that his name is Termier because he is predestined to pay Léon Bloy's "terme" [his quarter's rent], or to come out with this abominable pleasantry: "You can write and tell your 'young engineer' that...having become Léon Bloy's benefactor, he can stay as he is and have his fling. 'This gentleman is with me,' I shall say one day on the threshold of Paradise. That will be enough."

In reply to these charges, it will not do to urge that want is never in the wrong against a society which denies the existence of such a thing, the better to persuade itself of its own perfection, or which tries to hush it up for the sake of propriety. It will not even do to suppose that, though Bloy's outward misery was no greater than that of many poor wretches who kept their misfortunes to themselves, he must have been more sensitive to suffering. No, what *should* be said is that a man of his stamp was destined not to suffer more than others but to suffer *better*, since he had early discovered what suffering is and had then spent his whole life in getting to the bottom of this mystery, until he was able to write, a few months before his death: "I have not suffered misery; I wedded it for love, when I might have chosen a different mate."

It is by following Bloy through his apprenticeship and his exegesis of Suffering that we shall come to understand why, having loved it so deeply, he nevertheless proclaimed a legitimate revolt against the injustice of which he felt himself the victim. This paradox, like so many others in him, is not insoluble.

There is, however, another common mistake which falsifies the interpretation of his work. Some have been inclined to see in his love of Suffering a romantic heritage, and he has been reproached with crying louder than his pain, out of lyricism, for the pleasure of letting his voice ring out. This kind of comparison is the daily bread of historians of literature, whose special job it is to neutralize every effectual work and all the life of the spirit by employing a system of classification in which everything ultimately resembles everything else, having been reduced beforehand to a set of formulas and patterns. Bloy did not, of course, stand outside his own age, and what life and long meditation taught him was not without some likeness to certain intuitions of his romantic predecessors. But, apart from the fact that these similarities relate to spiritual truths which are the common stock of humanity and which have been rediscovered from age to age throughout the Christian era, it is natural that poets of the same period should interpret experiences belonging to the mental capital of their contemporaries. Every historical situation gives the mind a particular bent. It is only gradually, however, that this becomes crystallized, and—contrary to what is too often supposed—it is not unusual for its first manifestations to take the form of literary themes or phrases, which are somewhat strained, before

LÉON BLOY: A STUDY IN IMPATIENCE

a great mind comes upon the scene and gives them full scope. Bloy may be regarded as having gathered up a part—and the best part—of the romantic heritage, but as having enriched it with an understanding practiced in penetrating to the confines of mystery.

Romantic clamor, moreover, is not always so theatrical and hollow as some would make out, and the deepening of the sense of human suffering by the great poets of the nineteenth century opened up the path along which Bloy was to advance much further than they had done. One has but to recall the Hugo of the *Contemplations*:

> Perhaps you fashion unknown things in which
> The pain of man mingles as element...

Or, above all, Baudelaire:

> Other than this, nothing so truly bears
> Witness, O Lord, to human dignity:
> The passionate sob that echoes down the years
> And dies upon the brink of Thine eternity.

To be sure, considerations of human *dignity*, which mattered for Baudelaire, are not among Bloy's preoccupations, and he sees something different from the movement of earthly laments rising towards God to *die* on the threshold of his kingdom. With his eyes fixed on the fact of the Incarnation, he can see that the sufferings of this world cross that threshold and, inversely, that Christ's agony radiates love upon the creature's pain. Yet, for all that, there is something of Baudelaire's mentality in him, and who could fail to recall *The Albatross* on reading, in Bloy's preface to a book by his godson Pierre Van der Meer, the following definition of a poet: "a vessel of suffering, one of those beings who cannot fall except upwards and who, to their perpetual anguish, are captives of the mud below." This same mentality—but placed in the light of a truth which Baudelaire, "exiled in the imperfect," had to content himself with desiring—illumines the wonderful meditation in *La Femme pauvre* upon the death of a child: "Every affliction of the body or of the soul is a malady of exile." And it prompted the letter of August 25, 1905, to Raïssa Maritain: "There is only one sorrow—to have lost the Garden of Bliss; and there is only one longing and one hope—to find it again."

Thought that has haunted men from the beginning of modern times! And it is the greatness of the poets, from the romantics to our own day, that they avowed it as none, perhaps, had ever done before. Even if, held back by some inner obstacle, they could do no more than confess unhappiness, they endowed poetry with that noble function of proclaiming how grievous is the state of mankind when it loses the path of salvation and the hope of grace. A volume could be filled with the appeals which the modern mind, through its poets, has sent out to the world of lost purity, now no more than the borne of nostalgic dreams. Rimbaud, Lautréamont, Nietzsche, Dostoevsky, down to Proust—there is not one of them who did not perceive that all the sufferings of man lead back to it, and that the effectiveness of art always lies in its power to revive that memory. A passage in Ramuz's *Souvenirs sur Stravinsky*, an all too unfamiliar work which goes to the heart of his personal experience, admirably records what, in these days, a soul, unbelieving, can confess of this torment:

> There are things which we hardly dare to say, yet they are those which most urgently need saying...being undoubtedly the most living things in us. *A certain feeling of completeness and the remembrance that we have of it*, without knowing what it is made of—if only we could tell what it is made of! That completeness which, unbeknown to ourselves, we pass our whole life in trying to attain, and which is so rarely attained. A certain completeness which we have known, which is seeking to come to life again...through an outpouring to others, and which once more, outside ourselves, is straining after that union and

unity which were its existence of old... A vague remembrance in us, it may be, that was sleeping, that awakes and makes us reach out once more, across the gulf of time, to the days before the Tower of Babel, before the confusion of tongues, and lets us glimpse once more in the distance the *great lost Garden of Unity*. For that is what we aspire to, unawares yet continually, and with all our strength; and there is no completeness in life where there is no unity...

When you [Igor Stravinsky] spoke to me of your country...and we were walking along in mine, I felt as if there were no longer two countries...because, beyond the two countries and *beyond all countries, there is perhaps the Country* (lost, then found again, then lost once more, then discovered for a moment) *where we have in common a Father and a Mother, where in a flash of perception the great kinship of mankind is discerned for a moment.*

For to re-perceive it for a moment is what all the arts strain after—that and nothing else... We attain, for one moment, to man as he was before the curse... And there is also that curse under which we know ourselves to be (for nothing around us has really come into flower, really found its mark...and all our work is at first done against ourselves and against Someone, all work is a curse)—until, all at once, by a kind of reversal, blessing comes instead, *that co-operation with Someone, there is that possibility of return, that return, that rediscovery...*

In such searching words Ramuz voices the regret for Paradise Lost which runs like a solemn lament through modern poetry—the cry of a soul which, by an authentic "visitation," hopes to come out of *exile* and regain the completeness that prevailed before the Fall.

But Bloy's experience surpasses this sense of nostalgia, since its hopes rest elsewhere than in the magic of art and, above all, it goes much further in a contemplation of Suffering which is neither resignation nor romanticism.

ALBERT BÉGUIN

Bloy is a man who was initiated into spiritual life through suffering and who, step by step, won through to realization of his own destiny. At first he bore his affliction without understanding it, and one day he reached the stage of radical, unreasoning revolt, which convulsed his heart to its inmost recesses. But this violent phase was the immediate forerunner of his conversion and his acceptance of suffering; true, he did not love it yet, but he recognized it as his, and his eyes could henceforth endure the sight of it. The next step of his inward ascent brought him not only to take up the burden of misery but to ask for it as a favor, without perhaps quite knowing the meaning of this eagerness to suffer, this strange desire in him. It took the accumulation of troubles of every kind to lift him once more from love of suffering to the comprehension of that love, possessed at last in its entirety on the day when he divined that human suffering is identical with the suffering of God crucified.

Such were the stages of a slow initiation which took place between Bloy's childhood and his maturity, and which was long the axial line of his work as of his religious life. It would not be untrue to say that this constant thought was to accompany him to his death; but after a certain time it had become so much a part of himself that with its aid Bloy was able to go beyond the vindication of suffering. In his later years this theme did not disappear from his books but it yielded pride of place to the theme of hope and to impatience for the End of Time.

These stages, however, were not exactly successive or measurable in a single dimension; it is impossible to assign them dates which would divide Bloy's inward biography into clearly marked periods. In a way, like all souls truly in love with God, he knew from the outset all that he was ever to know. On the other hand, between one experience and the next he never ceased to retrace the same road of initiation, so that, at an early stage, he was already able to describe in advance the last of his "conversions" and to announce that, after having long been the advocate of Suffering, he would become the advocate of Promise. In reality, the two great objects

LÉON BLOY: A STUDY IN IMPATIENCE

of his contemplation, Suffering and Promise, were linked together indissolubly, and he never raised himself to the second without crossing once more the whole expanse of the first, as he had just done when, at the time of his greatest tribulation, he wrote to Ernest Hello the important letter dated April 19, 1880:

> ...I have given up that book [*Le Symbolisme de l'Apparition*]. This is the reason. When I undertook it I was worlds away from thinking of the advent of the Holy Spirit. This work of interpretation, as I conceived it, was to be in terms of the *reign of suffering, that is to say of Jesus Christ*. I intended to take my stand on the tradition of the Holy Fathers and to reject with horror all suggestions which tempted me to abandon it. In a word, *I proposed to look at the past*.
>
> You have seen how far out of my way I was carried, and how enormously my framework became enlarged. Today there is no more framework. It has burst in all directions, and *the sudden burning and devouring longing for the third reign has seized me* and absolutely changed my point of view. A fresh start will have to be made now, and I am certainly not in a state to do it at the moment... *I am not at all the same man*.

But let us go back to Bloy's inward biography and the history of his apprenticeship to suffering—with the full knowledge, however, that we are simplifying the facts and introducing a somewhat artificial chronology.

From his childhood Bloy could not recall ever having known any other intense feeling than that of continual suffering without any definite reason, and this is what he refers to whenever he looks back upon the past. The actual circumstances of that lonely youth are, indeed, of little consequence: the indifferent position of his family in the material scale, his rebellion against any kind of discipline, his clashes with his father who uttered that prophetic curse: "You will always be alone!" The beginning of *Le Désespéré*, particularly in the first version, gives a terribly gloomy but obviously symbolic picture of that provincial childhood. It is easy to divine that the sufferings of "Caïn Marchenoir" are not due to circumstances; they are inexplicable, congenital, so firmly rooted in the very texture of his soul that later he recognized in them the evidence of a vocation." On November 21, 1899, Bloy wrote to his future wife:

> *I am sad by nature*, as one is small or fair by nature. I was born sad, profoundly, horribly sad, and, if I am possessed by the most violent longing for joy, it is because of the mysterious law of the attraction of opposites…
>
> I remember that when I was a child, a tiny boy, I often refused, indignantly and rebelliously, to take part in games and pleasures the very thought of which made my heart beat with joy; because I thought it nobler to suffer and to make myself suffer by renunciation… *I had an instinctive love of unhappiness, I wanted to be unhappy.* The very word *unhappiness* thrilled me.

Only the violence of the revolt in which they culminated can bring home to us the dramatic intensity of those youthful troubles, which continued throughout his adolescence. After heated disputes and after repeatedly kicking over the traces, Bloy finished by refusing to submit to any training or apprenticeship and by running away from home, at eighteen, in a state of despair bordering on madness. "My unfortunate father," he wrote later to Dom Guéranger, "was obliged to take me away from school at a very early age because I stuck a knife into my little comrades—sign of a charming nature!…" He himself speaks of "a kind of psychological sleep, at the far end of which lurked the suicide into which I nearly plunged." And, "the wild fury of awakening passions having swept all before them," he had early "lost his faith" and lived for several years on end in the "fiercest Pride, Sensuality, Sloth, Envy, Scorn and Hate," exhausting "all the tortures and all the agonies of spirit and body." Thus he foundered in

LÉON BLOY: A STUDY IN IMPATIENCE

a spiritual night into which he was ever afterwards afraid of relapsing, the horror of which he painted in nearly all the characters of his novels and his "unkind stories," and of which, above all, he angrily sensed the presence in most of his contemporaries. Many of his outbursts are addressed to persons in whom he divined the same despair, cloaked by an attitude of hypocritical assurance. When he came to discover that some of his friends were living like this in a spiritual void, he exhorted them in moving terms to renounce a pride in negation which he knew only too well. Even more than his own reminiscences, the entreaties or abuse which he addressed to Georges Landry, Louis Montchal, Maurice Rollinat, Jehan Rictus, and J. K. Huysmans, and the extraordinary letter dated April 12, 1877, to Paul Bourget, reveal how clearly Bloy recalled his former agonies:

> *Pity for your soul*, which you imprison, which you oppress, which you dishonor, which you *starve to death* and which one day perhaps you will violently slaughter without even knowing what you are doing, without for one moment suspecting the enormity of the disaster, with a blind stupidity that is enough to make all the Angels and the Saints of earth and heaven weep with terror—pity, that most human of all the feelings of our hearts...is waxing in me.

We know well enough that this objurgation had no effect on Bourget. But the man who spoke of despair in such accents had himself experienced it in the extreme form of "paroxysms." In another letter, dated November 21, 1875, he recalled his state of mind round about 1870:

> There was a time—and it was just before the Commune— when *hatred of Jesus and of his Church became the sole thought in my mind and the sole feeling in my heart*. It was the most intense and burning passion in me, one of those *supernaturally* deep passions which seem to be of the very essence of the soul.

It is not for nothing, however, that Bloy uses the epithet "supernatural" for the revolt that took complete possession of him and, in its intensity, resembled that need for Justice which was soon to devour him "like a Dragon famished since the Flood." There is a real continuity between these two forces, these two passions—so much so that Bloy's deepest distress was quickly and inevitably followed by his violent conversion, lock, stock and barrel, and by the sudden birth of Love in the very, place which had been inhabited by Refusal. All Bloy's many testimonies to his return to faith concur in this, despite their diversity of language, while the unfailing vividness of his imagery attests that the revulsion was instantaneous and shattering. The impasse in which he found himself imprisoned is clearly defined in two deliberately "shocking" lines in the original version of *Le Désespéré*: "One day there was absolutely nothing for it but to die or to lay hold of some mechanism of hope, no matter what the cost. I became a Christian..."

Thus everything points to a veritable inward *catastrophe*, ineluctable as an earthquake, and, at the same time, inexorable as a logical conclusion. To Dom Guéranger he describes what happened as follows:

> One day it pleased God to make me a Christian. How did that miracle come to pass? I do not know. But the effect was sudden and marvelous. With joy I received the supernatural infusion of this great faith. I wept, I prayed...

And to Abbé Angers, in 1882, he spoke of Barbey d'Aurevilly (their meeting in 1869 was a crucial one), saying that the Master had fixed him "like a pious barn-owl on the shining door of the Church of Jesus Christ."

Everywhere images of fire, furnace and conflagration serve to express the suddenness of the flame which consumed him; but none of these images is so powerful as the account of Leopold's conversion in *La Femme pauvre*:

LÉON BLOY: A STUDY IN IMPATIENCE

Leopold, blessed by the priest, *juxta ritum sanctae Matris Ecclesiae*, had been visited in all his senses, as with the oil of anointment: upon his cruel eyes, which had not beheld the Face of Pardon; upon his unheeding ears, which had not heard the groans of the Holy Spirit; upon his savage nostrils, which had not inhaled the fragrance of the Divine Will; upon the tomb of his mouth, which had not eaten the Bread of Life; upon his violent hands, which had not helped to carry the Cross of the Lord; upon his impatient feet, which had gone everywhere except towards the Holy Sepulchre.

The word *conversion* so debased in any case, did not adequately express his *catastrophe*. Someone stronger than he had seized him by the throat and carried him into a house of fire. His soul had been torn out of him and his bones crushed; he had been flayed, trepanned, burnt; he had been reduced to putty, a kind of clayey substance, which had been kneaded into shape again by a Workman, gentle as light. Then he had been thrown head first into an old confessional, the boards of which had creaked beneath his weight. And all that had happened in a single instant.

Such an abrupt *volte-face* was not destined to interrupt the suffering which had for so long been consubstantial with the soul of Léon Bloy. Far from finding relief in conversion, he made the discovery that his vocation of pain had taken a definite form and rooted itself still deeper in him. What he had known hitherto he now perceived to have been nothing but a torment of the flesh, mere animal suffering; henceforth he knew, with a sudden and certain knowledge, that this intensity of suffering was bound up with something which he could not yet clearly define but which had mysterious affinities with spiritual ardor. There had been a transition from one to the other. By some strange continuity, his suffering, far from passing away in the fervor of the love of God, had multiplied. The flame of pain which ravaged his darkened soul had, without being less devouring, become the clear, aspiring flame of worship.

A letter to a priest, only a few months after his meeting with Barbey d'Aurevilly, bears witness to that astounding experience and establishes, between his recreated spiritual life and his unabated suffering, one of those striking synonymities which Bloy produces every time he is confronted with a mystery.

> I am now penetrated through and through by the divine truths which you Ministers of God expound. That ought to calm my heart and spirit. And yet, when I look into myself, I find no more tranquility than in the days of hatred and revolt. *My anguish now runs in a straight line. That's all.* With the light of Faith, *I have succeeded in finding out why I suffer.* I have learnt to know myself, I have a better view of my soul's distress; but with it I have been given terror, and *it* is a dreadful gain. A speculative Catholicism cannot satisfy me. My fiery soul demands an ardent practice.

The following years—for which we have detailed evidence in the letters to Georges Landry, Barbey d'Aurevilly and Blanc de Saint-Bonnet—were given up to meditation on this mystery of Suffering. "Terror" is a "gain," because Bloy has the feeling that, thanks to it, God is making him "travel the spiritual road with great strides," without giving him "time to breathe."

Two letters, both of them earlier than Bloy's first writings, contain the whole of his doctrine of Suffering, which he was already able to formulate clearly, although a long trial of patience and many afflictions had still to be undergone before he came to possess this doctrine fully—or rather to let it possess *him*. For a spirit which makes such demands as his is so eager to give itself, to participate without reserve in the truth it has perceived, that it can never content itself with having *understood*. It has been said that it takes time before the truths at which we arrive become flesh of our flesh.

LÉON BLOY: A STUDY IN IMPATIENCE

Applied to a man like Bloy, this saying assumes a vastly more inward significance than could have been in its author's mind. Before each of the mysteries which he discerned, whether love or suffering, Bloy was essentially an *impatient man* for whom joy in his own clear-sightedness was not enough. What he now affirmed had the force of an amazing divination: he was later to strive with all his strength, his attention and his humility to live it, to make every moment of his existence conform to it.

So on April 25 he wrote to Georges Landry the great letter from which a passage has already been quoted, on the efficacy of suffering, which enters the human heart to "bring it to life." He then explains his thought:

> Suffering...is that diamond key with which I entered my own heart; it is that holy veil imprinted with the bleeding Face of our gentle crucified Savior. We know that the stars are always in the same place in the heavens but that, as the state of the atmosphere varies, sometimes they seem much further off, and sometimes they seem much nearer and resemble tears of light ready to fall upon the earth. So it is with God. Joy makes him seem far off, while *affliction brings him near to us and it is as if he took up his abode in us.* When afflictions come, we instinctively feel their connection with the favors that went before them... They come one after the other, knocking repeatedly upon our poor hearts with so modest and yet so celestial a mien, that, beneath their transparent disguise, it is easy to know them for angels. *A heart without affliction is like a world without revelation; it sees God only in the faint gleam of twilight. Our hearts are filled with angels when they are full of afflictions...*
>
> Suffering seals us within the will of God as in a tomb; it shrouds us like the winding-sheet of deep night; it gradually contracts our horizon, and the vast universe dwindles for us. It shrinks still further; first one object disappears, then another;

we become less and less a prey to distractions. Our inward life is more awake. Our soul grows strong. And now we are upon Calvary... The line of darkness has touched Jerusalem itself.... Even the consolations of the Spiritual City have disappeared. The helmets of the soldiers barely cast a last faint reflex upon the dark background. The greenness of the mountain becomes black. For a moment we are blinded... Then, by degrees, the white form of Jesus takes shape in the midst of the profound darkness. His blood flows warm upon our hands when we seize the Cross, for it is not an apparition: it is Life. We are with God, our Creator, our Savior. He is wholly ours. He is what the estrangement of his creatures has made him for us. He was always the same in our souls, only he was eclipsed by the false brightness of his creatures. He appears at last in the night, like the stars. The pale midday moon does not seduce us with her beauty. It is only at night that she charms us. And *it is the darkness of the Calvary of the spirit which sheds upon our souls the soft radiance of our wondrous Savior.*

For all its poetic splendor and truth of expression, this letter nevertheless shows that Bloy was only at the beginning of his initiation into suffering. He had just grasped the fact that affliction, by *concentrating* the soul upon itself, makes it more capable of knowing the suffering God who is always present in it, but veiled by what Pascal called "distraction"; and he expresses it *by* that image of stars assuming the likeness of tears—the image which, with its converse of human tears transfigured into constellations, was to become the most frequent metaphor in his work, because it touched his inward experience at an essential point. This experience, thus entered upon in his youth, is the one which so many of the spiritually great have passed through the apprenticeship of a night of the soul in which, cut off from the created world and earthly "consolations," in the depths of unspeakable gloom, the fullness of suffering *brings God near.* It should be noted that Bloy already goes beyond a mere vague

LÉON BLOY: A STUDY IN IMPATIENCE

feeling of that nearness: even in this early period, when he is manifestly drawing inspiration from the writings of the mystics and making use of a poet's resources, the form assumed by the object of his contemplation is a very distinct picture of the scene on Calvary.

It remained for him to define the link which he perceived between the agony of Jesus Christ and human suffering; to understand, through suffering itself, renewed unceasingly, and through the growth of love, why this link exists. It is—as he soon realized and was *constrained* to establish clearly—because suffering, even when not understood, even when submitted to and not chosen, is always, mysteriously, *imitation* of the crucified Lord. Calvary is "North" for the creature, the point towards which the compass of our deeper life directs us. And, if our torments draw us towards it, this is because they are substantially the actual torments of Jesus Christ "in agony until the end of the world." Bloy had had an intuition of this during the 1870 war; he had discovered then that there is a sort of identity, or at least a necessary correspondence, between ordeal and Joy, and that this bond may be discovered in the destiny of each individual soul, as well as in the destiny of the Church and of Christianity. "It is when the Church suffers that she may truly be said to triumph," he wrote at that time. "*A Christian without suffering is a pilgrim, without a compass. He will never reach Calvary. Must not the Passion of Christ, consummated in the ineffable thorn-crowned head, be fulfilled in his members too?*" These lines go straight to the heart of the mystery of suffering: made like unto Christ by the afflictions through which we share his agony, we thereby become members of his body, and, thus associated with the other members of the Savior, we are ushered into the supreme Joy: the *Communion of the Saints*. Such was to be the culmination of all Bloy's meditations on suffering: the certainty that it creates the most indestructible union between men (who, outside it, remain cruelly alone), because it links them all to Calvary. Once more the eyes of the youthful Bloy were opened, by a sudden intuition, to a truth which from then onwards he never ceased to explore and "conquer."

ALBERT BÉGUIN

A second great letter, written in 1879 to another young friend, Michel Ménard, shows how these few years had already brought Bloy a clearer consciousness of this mystery:

> Suffering is necessary, it is the very essence, the vertebral axis of moral life... Our Savior Jesus has suffered so much for us that, but for an understanding which must surely have been reached between his Father and himself, it would not have been permissible henceforward even to speak of his Passion, the mere mention of this Fact being a blasphemy so enormous that worlds would crumble to dust. *Well, then! What are we? Lord God! The members of Jesus Christ! His very members.* It is our unspeakable misfortune that we continually take the utterances of the Scriptures for figures and symbols. We believe, but we do not believe substantially... We do not understand that we are the members of the MAN OF SORROWS, of the Man who is uttermost Joy, Love, Truth, Beauty and Life only because he is the eternally distraught Lover of Supreme Suffering. The Pilgrim of the ultimate anguish, who has hastened across the Infinite, from the depths of Eternity, to endure it, and upon whom are heaped, in tragic unity of time, place and person, all the elements of torture amassed in every human act accomplished in every second of duration over the whole surface of the world in the space of sixty centuries... From that starting-point we can measure everything. In declaring us members of Jesus Christ, the Holy Spirit has clothed us with the dignity of Redeemers and, when we refuse to suffer, we are nothing but simoniacs and prevaricators. We were made for that and for that alone. *When we shed our blood, it is upon Calvary that it flows, and thence over the whole earth...*
>
> Everything in us is identical with Jesus Christ, on whom we are naturally and supernaturally modelled. Accordingly, when we refuse any suffering, this means that, for as much as he is in us, we adulterate our own essence and bring into

LÉON BLOY: A STUDY IN IMPATIENCE

the very flesh and even into the soul of our Leader an element which profanes its integrity and which he must expel from himself and from all his members by an inconceivable multiplication of tortures... The essence of my thought is that, in this fallen world, *all joy manifests itself in the natural order and all suffering in the divine order*. Pending the judgment in the valley of Jehoshaphat, the wretched man of the Fall can lay claim to nothing but the *happiness of suffering*...

Here the exegesis of Suffering takes on a still more complex richness, for Bloy's scrutiny stops short in surprise at this apparent contradiction: suffering is great, since it makes us resemble the crucified Lord; but at the same time the agony of the Savior is prolonged and multiplied by all men's actions since the Fall. A further effort of thought was required to explain this paradox. Yet Bloy was able to go back to this passage, without making any changes, first in the *Symbolisme de l'Apparition* (the manuscript of which lay on his desk for forty years, until his death) and later as one of the meditations in *Dans les Ténèbres*, in 1917. It is so intimately linked with the center of his "supernatural" life—as he liked to put it—that, when we rediscover it among writings which date from his last summer on earth, there is nothing, either in the style or in the thought, that betrays its early origin. At the present juncture, however, Bloy does not go deeply into the meaning of the communion of the saints and the justification of suffering in that dogma as a coherent whole.

He had still to grasp (and this was to be his second "conversion" and the turning-point from which we may date his impatience for the Final Coming) what was and what remains, in its very substance, the agony of the Lord. The secret of suffering could not be fully revealed to him until he came to understand the anguish of the Son of God, giving his life and his blood for men and seeing, in the eternal *present* of his torture prolonged to the end of temporal history, that men do not return his love but do their best to put it aside, and by this obstinate refusal delay, from age to age, the Descent from the Cross. Bloy had seen from the beginning that human pain enters into divine affliction; but he had not yet seen that that suffering has its substance in the "incomprehensible postponements" of the work of Salvation by creatures bent on eluding the love of Jesus. That, for the time being, was no more than a presentiment in Bloy's mind, and for several years it was to find expression in his famous fits of rage: rage at the sight of the world as it is, humanity bent on inventing the means to flee from the one demand made by the blood offering of God, and giving itself up to all kinds of futile occupations and activities in order to escape from the only thing that counts. Bloy's anger is the first-fruit of his impatience to see an end to the torments of Jesus, and it is in this sense that he could say it was born of his tenderness. "Pity cannot quench anger in me, for my anger is the daughter of an infinite foreboding… *My anger is the effervescence of my pity*," he wrote on September 3, 1889. And again on April 13, 1895, he confessed: "Yes, it is true, *I have been full of hatred since my childhood, and nobody has loved mankind so simple-heartedly as I have done*. But I have abhorred the things, the institutions, the laws of the world. I have had an infinite hatred of the World, and the experiences of my life have served only to exacerbate that feeling."

———

This irascible prophet was really an embodiment of love. His final initiation into the meaning of Suffering was to be accomplished through the claims of charity for poor souls—claims which constrained him to live to the uttermost, even to the point of *wanting to suffer*, the ultimate consequences of that sense of solidarity between all creatures which had been the outcome of his first great effort in solitary thought. So true it is that only by experience, practice and love could he really discover what meditation very imperfectly revealed to him. He had to make his personal way of life conform absolutely to the Communion of the Saints before he could *know* that reality and find what part the positive value of suffering played in it.

LÉON BLOY: A STUDY IN IMPATIENCE

In the years following his first dazzling revelation of Christianity, Bloy, who (his correspondence proves it and it can never be repeated too often) had a heart overflowing with affection, was surrounded by friendships to which he gave himself without stint. His friends of those days were his "neighbor" in the immediate and limited sense of the word—concrete, living, personal presences in which he saw a manifestation of the community of human beings, the tangible reality of the Church, the Body of Christ. Great was his anxiety when he encountered in these cherished beings an obtuseness of the understanding or a refusal of the will which estranged them from the love of God and from Hope. Barbey d'Aurevilly, that great writer who was a Christian only in outward show, grieved him particularly, and Bloy, whose meeting with this older man had been of such decisive importance for his own life, could not bear to see him vegetating in a spiritual ignorance ill-disguised by the brilliance of his work and his personality. "You were the torch by which God kindled me, and it is impossible that the prayers you have lighted in me should not end by warming you too," he wrote to him in 1873. And it was worse still with Georges Landry, whose eyes Bloy tried in vain to open, throughout twenty years of friendship, as he later tried with Bourget, Rollinat, Huysmans, Jehan Rictus and Louis Montchal.

Faithful to his experience as one who had entered spiritual life through suffering, and convinced of the universal reversibility of sorrows and joys, he was to offer his very life for these blind friends, calling down upon himself the utmost torments, in prayers that were "like a storm," in order that these others might be succored and rescued from darkness.

This is a new and important stage: Bloy was no longer content to understand the part played by suffering, nor even to accept it. He "wedded it for love." For he knew now—his friends' distress had taught him—that the second commandment is like unto the first; that the love of created beings, no less than the love of God, takes its bearing from suffering. The communion of the saints was revealed to him in its ultimate, peremptory consequences: "Greater love hath no man than that a man should lay down his life for his friend." For to each, if he wishes, it is granted to suffer *for* others. In a mysterious, divine balance, every grief has its counterpoise in a near or distant joy, as every happiness of one creature must be paid for by the sorrow of another. This mystery of Reversibility, though so readily intelligible, is among those to which most exception is taken: and this, it must be admitted, is probably due to the fact that a shortsighted devoutness often interprets it (in all good faith, but with deplorable narrowness) as a rule of accountancy, which implies a God doing business in miseries and insisting that his creatures should be solvent. Bloy, on the other hand, thanks to the inward logic of his doctrine of Suffering, perceives the true significance of this marvelous link between men and from men to God, which makes it possible to take on afflictions in order that they may benefit others. Once it has been grasped that suffering is nearness to God, it is obvious that a sorrowing heart, and particularly a heart that has learnt to love suffering sufficiently to plead for it, can offer up much more effectual prayers than anyone else, and can prevail upon divine mercy to stoop down to the creature for whom it intercedes.

Here, more than in any other phase of his life, Bloy, not content with fathoming the mysteries of faith *by* means of his understanding, seems to feel the need of another form of possession—an active possession lived in his daily life. With all his heart he asks for suffering because in it he hopes to find both the transparency of a gaze lifted to God and the power to make a gift of himself to the beings who are dearest to him. Thus, as he afterwards wrote in a letter to his future wife, his prayers to be allowed to suffer explain his whole life:

> You know, beloved, that at one time, many years ago, I prayed for months on end to have much to suffer for the glory of the Lord. My almost unceasing supplications were so ardent, so passionate that I can give you no clear idea of them… But, believe me, of all the events of my life this is the only one that

LÉON BLOY: A STUDY IN IMPATIENCE

can explain it. God, who knows us perfectly, listens to our prayers with indulgence, and he *does not give us what we ask for but what we need*. That thought should be the source of all Christian resignation. I asked him to make me suffer for my brothers and for Himself, in my body and in my soul. *But I had in mind very noble and very pure sufferings*, which, I now see clearly, would still have been a joy. I was not thinking of this diabolical-suffering which he sent me, and which consisted in his apparent withdrawal from me, abandoning me without defense in the midst of my most cruel enemies.

The tortures Bloy refers to—so unexpected and so different from what he had imagined when he believed that he already loved suffering as one can only love it after having known it—are those which afflicted him all the rest of his life. But the lowest point in his plunge into misery (which was also, of necessity, the time of his most decisive progress towards the Light) can be situated very exactly in the years 1877 to 1882: it was the time of "Véronique," dramatically recalled in *Le Désespéré*.

The details of this terrible story are well enough known, in the version given in the novel, which is very faithful to the underlying truth of the facts: Anne-Marie Roulé, loved with a violent passion by Bloy; the man who had been "dazzled by the face of God," prey to a "dizziness" by which he was "sucked in towards creatures of clay molded in that Likeness"; the "great tribulation of the flesh," mingled with an impulse of ardent charity, which worked such a transformation in Véronique that in the end she outstripped her guide. Then came the impenetrable secret of these two beings, living with their confidant, Ernest Hello, under the all-powerful impression of the revelations which Véronique received in her ecstasies and which so strangely chimed with the whole inward life of Bloy himself. The visionary foretold the approach of fearful catastrophes, which were to herald the end of the world, and prophesied for Bloy—who never forgot this promise, taken by him as a divine intimation—that he should be a witness, or perhaps even more, in the hour of the final Apocalypse. But while he was waiting, from day to day, for these prophecies to be fulfilled, another gulf opened: Anne-Marie Roulé went mad and had to be shut up for the rest of her life.

Bloy's writings alone can give any idea of his hopes and 'disappointments in that extraordinary period, his transports of worship and rebellion, his impatience and his torment. "*I have so raging a hunger and thirst for the glory of God upon earth,*" he wrote to Hello on Wednesday in Holy Week, in 1880, "*that I count the days like a madman.*" And, when "the vengeance of Divine Justice" did not come upon the date on which he had confidently expected it, his revolt burst forth in the letter dated April 19:

> I am unhappy beyond all expression and understanding. I have been wounded in my faith, my hope, my love. Today, Monday, for the first time for I know not how long, I have not received the sacrament and I have not uttered a prayer. I could find nothing in my heart but *the most bitter and savage resentment against so hard and so thankless a God.* I have long given everything. In nearly all my prayers I have offered my body and my soul to the most horrible, the most diabolical tortures, *on condition that he, for his part, would make himself what he said he would be—my servant.* With the help of his grace, no doubt, but at the cost of sufferings of which you have no conception, and of which the mere recollection lacerates me, I accomplished in two years an unparalleled work of patience—nobody could have believed that a man stripped of everything could even dare to undertake such a task—and it was all for the glory of God. And in return everything is denied me. *I should be ashamed to treat a mangy dog as God treats me.*

It was only after thirty-five years of suffering that Bloy, shortly before his death, found an answer to that cry of impatience and rebellion. That answer is contained in what is perhaps the most beautiful of his letters, written on January 4, 1915, to Jean de La Laurencie, and quoted in full on a later page of this book. As if he recollected the very words of his letter to Hello, he said, looking back over his whole destiny: "I have not done what God wanted of me, that's certain. Instead, I have *mused over what I wanted of God*, and here I am, at sixty-eight, with nothing in my hands but paper."

But already in July 1889, a few days before he first met Jeanne Molbeck, who was to become his wife, he recalled in his diary the terrible collapse which had followed the exaltation of the extraordinary hopes inspired by Véronique's predictions:

> My past, all my wretched past! How I wish I could blot out the remembrance of it. *How can I express from what Orient I fell and by what catastrophe?...* Mysterious period, afflictions which seemed beyond human strength. And those years of dereliction, of faithlessness, of ignominy, coming after the Dazzling Vision!!! At that time—I can still see the place, quite near Paris, in a little house standing by itself—I used to sit up night after night through a bitter winter, and the first chapters of *Le Désespéré* were punctuated with such dismal groans that the neighbors were disturbed by them.... God, who had willed this trial, knew that it would bring me down, and that I should roll to the bottom of the abyss. But it was before his Face, covered with blood, that I fell, and never for a day have I ceased to see it.

Among his writings, however, the one which best conveys the spiritual intensity accompanying these strange alternations of delirious imagination and dejection is the letter addressed to Mme. Charles Hayem in 1883—that is to say, shortly after the events in question. In spite of the underlying lassitude, this confession is striking evidence of the fact that, in Bloy's own eyes, his expectations had been nothing but the transports and importunity of a boundless love and the "raging" desire to see the end of Christ's agony. Almost immediately after the cry of revolt came not mere resignation but an actual passionate acceptance of suffering, of ignominy, of the apparent injustice of fate:

> *It is so good to complain of what one loves, and what I love is God, the Christian God, the Christ with bleeding wounds, the Man of Sorrows.* I reproach him with being so un-triumphant in a world which he has redeemed, and with having abandoned his most faithful friends when he went away suddenly to his Father, nearly two thousand years ago. He himself is called the Father of the poor and, to judge by what is happening in the world, it would seem to be the worst of crimes to be under the law of that frightening paternity, such is your suffering and disgrace if you are the legitimate son of the Father of the poor. Oh! I know very well what they preach to us: that we should be resigned, that we should accept and be glad to have our hearts laid waste; that compensations will be meted out and accounts balanced at the end of ends. But *it is characteristic of love to be impatient, and extreme love is extremely impatient. Every Christian must needs long for the glory of his God and suffer horribly from the endless absence of that glory.* I say every Christian but I mean every man, since we are told that man is *naturally Christian.* Poet, I shall blind you because I am Faith, I shall drive you to despair because I am Hope, I shall devour you because I am Charity, I shall press you down into the mire because I am purity itself, I shall whelm you with darkness because I am light. Those who despise all these things and despise you, those Vile and Stupid Ones, I shall exalt beyond measure, I shall seat them upon thrones, and it is upon your dying face that they will rest their unclean feet. After that, if you cry to me, it shall be as if you did not cry.
>
> The specialists in resignation, who did not want anything very sublime and have never suffered, find it easy to say that

LÉON BLOY: A STUDY IN IMPATIENCE

this injustice is only apparent, that it actually hides a higher justice which is wholly inscrutable. I know all that much better than many of these pedants. But still it is wellnigh twenty centuries since the Redemption, and this sad spectacle is to be seen every day: a poor wretch who had dreamed of beauty and is reduced to seeking his bread upon earth.

One is conscious of something quite different here from the catastrophe of a human passion (tragic though that may seem to the imagination) or even than the exhausting struggle of a soul in love with purity against the temptations of the flesh. True, there were such Battles, and very violent ones, in Bloy's association with Véronique, and during all the years of dereliction which followed. But anyone tempted to give them too important a place, or to forget that they were only episodes and, as it were, outward manifestations of a drama which was that of a soul made for the knowledge of divine mysteries, would find it difficult to explain how this tribulation could be simultaneous with the spiritual progress that Bloy was then making. On more than one occasion he stated that it was precisely at this time that he discovered all he was ever to know and understand, and it is quite certain that, from about 1890, the period of the great "illuminations" having come to an end, he lived upon their substance until his death. Not only has it been possible to ascertain that his first two books, *La Chevalèlre de la Mort* and the wonderful *Révélateur du Globe* (with its amazing mastery of thought) were composed during his association with Véronique, but, more important still, it was then that he began that *Symbolisme de l'Apparition* which contains the whole of his work in embryo. For, during the very years when he was passing through the crucible of his strange adventure, he met Abbé Tardif de Moidrey, who initiated him into the methods of symbolical exegesis as well as into the revelations of La Salette. This double discovery enabled him to renew his long contemplation of the mystery of Suffering and to shape its final course.

ALBERT BÉGUIN

At La Salette, in Léon Bloy's birth-year—and he always paid great attention to these coincidences in time, which were logically of great importance in his conception of History—the Virgin Mary appeared to two children, Mélanie and Maximin, as they were tending sheep, and the "Very Beautiful Lady" began to weep. "Her tears fell one by one, slowly, down to her knees," Mélanie reported. "Then like sparks of light they disappeared. They were shining and full of love." And the Mother of God had pronounced some words, each of which, when he read them, went straight to Bloy's heart, for they seemed to be in the direct line of his own thoughts.

> If my people will not submit, I shall be forced to let go my Son's hand. It is so heavy, so weighty, that I can no longer restrain it…
> The time that I have been suffering for you all!…

In the secret message which Mélanie was not to reveal until later, the announcement of the impending punishment of the men guilty of withstanding God was given more definite form, in terms which seemed to Bloy strangely like the predictions of Véronique:

> …God will strike as never before.
> Woe unto the inhabitants of the earth! God will spend His anger and no one will be able to escape such a host of misfortunes.
> …The most terrible calamities and the most stupendous events are at hand; all must be prepared to be ruled with a rod of iron and to drink the cup of the wrath of God…. Italy will be punished for her ambition in wishing to shake off the yoke of the Lord of Lords; she will be given up to war; blood will flow on all sides, the churches will be closed or profaned, the priests and the monks will be driven out; they will be put to death, to a cruel death. Some will abandon their faith, and great will be the number of priests and monks who will turn from the true

religion; there will even be Bishops among them.... People will be transported from one place to another by evil spirits.... France, Italy, Spain and England will be at war; blood will flow in the streets; Frenchman will fight against Frenchman, Italian against Italian; later there will be a general war, which will be terrible... Paris will be burned and Marseilles engulfed; a number of great cities will be shaken and swallowed up by earthquakes; men will think that all is lost; there will be nothing to be seen but slayers, nothing to be heard but the clash of steel, and blasphemies.... A forerunner of Antichrist, with troops from various nations, will fight against the true Christ, the only Savior of the world; he will shed much blood and will seek to destroy the worship of God in order that men shall look upon him as God. The earth will be visited with all kinds of plagues, besides pestilence and famine, which will be general; there will be wars until the last war...

The time is at hand: the gulf is opening...

If these prophecies of the "Secret" confirmed Bloy in his conviction that the time of the Apocalypse was approaching, the tears of Mary made a still greater impression upon him. He was seized with that stupefaction which he was to voice in 1900 in *Le Fils de Louis XVI* (in a passage later incorporated in *Celle qui pleure*):

"*The time that I have been suffering for you all!*" What extraordinary and disturbing words!

In so enormous a catastrophe, that which is absolutely incapable of suffering nevertheless suffers and weeps. Beatitude sobs and implores. The All-Powerful declares that she can bear it no longer and begs for mercy...

The account of his first arrival at La Salette, told by Bloy in *La Femme pauvre*, perpetuates his first impression in language of unforgettable beauty (and it is not surprising to find in it the image of tears transformed into stars in the night sky, since that, too, is in Mélanie's statement, quoted above):

> What shall I tell you? When I reached the top and saw the Mother sitting on a stone and weeping into her hands, near that little fountain which seems to flow from her eyes, I fell down at the foot of the enclosure and poured forth tears and sobs, asking mercy of Her who was called *Omnipotentia supplex*. How long did that prostration last, that flood of Cocytus? I have no idea. When I came there, twilight was only just gathering; when I rose to my feet, weak as a convalescent centenarian, *it was completely dark and all my tears seemed to be sparkling in the blackness of the skies, for methought my roots had turned upwards.*
>
> Oh, my friends, how divine that impression was! Around me, human silence. No other sound than that of the miraculous fountain, in unison with that music of Paradise made by all the mountain rills and sometimes, in the far distance, the clear bells of some grazing herd. I do not know how to express it. I was like a man without sin who had just died, I was so free, now, from suffering! I burned with the joy of the "violent" who, as our Savior Jesus said, take the kingdom of heaven "by force." Surely an angel, some very patient seraph, had loosened, mesh by mesh, the toils of my despair, and I was drunk with holy madness as I went and knocked at the door of the monastery where travellers are lodged.

This revelation was to color the whole of Bloy's spiritual life: she who is Blessedness knows suffering, then! She who is Eternity speaks of the *time* that her trials endure! What inscrutable mystery is hidden beneath these contradictions? Is man so powerful, in his fallen state (which is not over and done with, something that happened long ago, "of which we should suffer the consequences: *we are falling all the time*, and that is why *Eve weeps*: her tears go with

LÉON BLOY: A STUDY IN IMPATIENCE

us into the pit"), is man so much the master of history that God has resigned his sovereignty into man's hands and can no longer complete the work of Salvation so long as his creatures withhold their consent? Is the suffering of Eve at the same time the suffering of Mary, and, again, the same as the interminable agony of Jesus?

To so many questions, Bloy now perceived, there is no other answer than worship and prayer. And that was how he was to live: imbued with the constant sense of a divine suffering, of a supplication from God, adjuring men to set a term to his torture. Longing for that agony to end that very day. Imbued also with compassion "for the prophetic tears" of the Mater Dolorosa, who wept upon the Mountain, imploring her people to have pity upon themselves." And surely, like Clotilde in *La Femme pauvre,* rising from her knees, after her first communion, with "the very remote, infinitely mysterious impression of *having consoled Someone ineffable.*" Meditating upon the "unutterable groans" of the Holy Spirit exiled upon earth until the looked-for Advent. Perpetually uniting the Three Persons of the Trinity and the Holy Virgin in a single transport of love for their infinite suffering, and longing that something, the suffering offered by human beings and transforming their own hearts, might at last put an end to the terrible procession of imperfect Centuries.

But this transfiguration began to take place in Bloy himself and, after the tempest of private miseries, after the suffering he had lived and the revelation of La Salette which confirmed it, there was to be a long dark period, lasting from about 1880 to 1889; these years were not in vain, for Bloy entered more fully into the experience that suffering brings nearness to God. La Salette by inspiring him with the conviction that God suffers, and with adoration for this God who weeps, filled him with that most profound understanding granted only to the importunity of love. It would not be wrong, I think, to say that not till then did Bloy comprehend to the full what he had written many years before in his great letter to Landry on Suffering. It had taken Véronique and La Salette, to make him realize how much truth lay in the wonderfully clear definition which he had given, at that time, of the relation between human affliction and divine anguish.

He had seen, indeed, that perfect suffering can belong only to Jesus Christ, since he hears the whole of it every minute—outside time, which parcels it out for us. Simultaneously he showed that suffering is not an accident, but the condition proper to us, although our intelligence and our feelings—perceiving things only in the fragments into which time cuts them up—are incapable of grasping in its totality that suffering through which we are made like God. In the 1873 letter, after the passages already emoted, he continued:

> I should never end if I tried to describe the marvelous effects of Suffering on man's faculties and on his heart; it is the *handmaid of creation*. That is the apex of metaphysics..."
>
> It practically never happens that, either in sorrow or in joy, we embrace the whole of the present simultaneously. In everything that happens to us what is implicit always goes beyond what is expressed. That is what we mean when we speak of a growing sorrow. It is not Sorrow which grows; it is our sense of it, and this progress is bound up with the imperfection of our minds. That is why we often seem more heroic than we really are. Of our burden we bear only what we see, and we see only part of it. Our Heavenly Father lowers it gradually, sharing the weight between his own hand and our shoulders until habit makes us able to bear the whole pressure without being crushed by it... Through our understanding or our feelings we can never keep pace with the present. That is why sufferings are generally less painful than they may seem; for we bear them by degrees, almost unawares. *Do you know why Jesus Christ has suffered so much?* I will try to give you a transcendent idea of it in a few words. *It is because in his soul, all his lifetime, the present, the past and the future were absolutely one and the same.* This is strikingly true of the Agony in the Garden. But that thought is an abyss...

LÉON BLOY: A STUDY IN IMPATIENCE

These early letters, however, still show a Bloy groping towards comprehension of sorrow; from then onwards, thanks to suffering prayed for and obtained, thanks to what the revelations of La Salette and the Véronique episode taught him, his former intuitions were steadily deepened. In particular, he substantiated them and shed light upon them by linking them up more and more closely with the whole of his inward life, first of all, and then with the whole of Christian doctrine: In the earlier phase his progress had been intermittent, brought about by a series of sudden visions; now became more and more a matter of patient exploration. But not a peaceful exploration; for, even after his marriage—which marks the close of the period of fiercest torment and the end of certain inward-dangers—Bloy's life remained what he had wished and asked for it to be: a life of suffering. The trials and miseries for which he had prayed were not lacking and they often had that unexpected quality of humiliation which, as he had said to his future wife, made his sufferings so unlike the "noble" afflictions he had had in mind. Bloy had continually occasion to repeat that "God does not give us what we ask for, but *what we need.*"

The death of his two sons in infancy was doubtless the hardest experience of sorrow which it remained for him to undergo—so hard that the allusions to it in his diary, if frequent, show an uncharacteristic restraint. It is in *La Femme pauvre* that the true echo of this grief must be sought; for there, having transposed it to the plane of fiction, Bloy could speak more freely. The terrible scene of the death of the child (compared with which the celebrated parallel in *L'Education sentimentale* is the paltry invention of a novelist) ends with an overwhelming passage, revealing not only Bloy's grief as a father but the enlightenment which came from it to crown his doctrine of suffering:

> In the presence of the death of a little child, Art and Poetry seem veritable paupers... A mother's groans and, still more,

the silent heaving of a father's breast have a very different power from words and colors, so much does human pain belong to the invisible world.

It is not exactly contact with death that causes such suffering, since this punishment has been so greatly sanctified by Him who called Himself the Life. It is all the joy now over that rises and snarls like a tiger, breaks loose like a hurricane. It is, more precisely, the magnificent, heart-rending memory of the *sight of God* for all peoples are idolatrous, thou hast often said, O Lord! Those sorry *likenesses* of Thee can worship only what they think they see, all this long time that they have no longer seen Thee; and their children and them the Paradise of Bliss.

For there is no other sorrow than what is related in Thy Book. *In capite Libri scriptum est de me.* Do what we may, we shall not find any suffering outside the circle of fire and the Sword which turns every way to keep the Lost Garden. All affliction of the body or of the soul is a malady of exile, and that rending pity, that ravaging compassion stooping over tiny coffins, is surely what recalls most forcibly *the famous Banishment for which mankind without innocence has never been able to console itself.*

The whole story, *La Femme pauvre*, with its lavish but coherent use of symbols, is built up on the idea of suffering that saves, because it "belongs to the invisible world" and revives the memory of the lost garden, and also because it "brings to life" in our souls the bonds of universal fellowship which are their very essence. Complex and mysterious relations, long hidden, weave themselves between all the characters, and each of the incidents in this extraordinary novel literally springs from the all-powerful working of the reversibility of sorrows and joys. And this is so up to the stupendous epilogue, in which the death of Leopold in the flames, already secretly linked with the fate of his worst enemy and with the agony of poor Villiers de Aisle-Adam, coincides with the "conflagration of the spiritual holocaust" which, in the same hour, consumes Clotilde and makes her, henceforth, that truly *poor* soul, placed in possession of Life because she embraces total poverty. And once more it is the "malady of exile" that is expressed in her supreme utterance: "There is only one sadness, the sadness of not being saints."

We have now reached the central point of that whole acceptance of Suffering, which, in Bloy's case, bears no relation to wisdom, prudence and resignation but to the extreme violence of love. The center is indeed there, in that paradox: suffering has never any other cause than estrangement from God, but all suffering brings one near to God. Or put it this way: God is both Blessedness, lost and mourned for, and Suffering, since through our fault, because we turn our backs on Blessedness, he is God crucified "until the of the world." Everything, then, is ordained by the fall, which has made man this creature of regret, exile, sorrow, of God himself—of God who can only be Joy!—the "God of tears," the Lord upon the cross, the "groaning" Holy Spirit, and the Virgin Mary in tears upon the Mountain! Within this same synonymy, which unites, in God, Blessedness Suffering, is to be found again in the heart of man, as the reflex of that which, since the birth of sin, has existed in God for human eyes.

Such is the presentiment which we find in Bloy from the outset—that secret identity of misery with the joy which *"bears a frightening resemblance to it."* But now, thanks to long years of trial, thanks above all to La Salette, this presentiment has become a theological certainty. In the amazing evocation of Paradise which forms the third chapter of *Celle qui pleure*, there is this sentence, rich with all Bloy's complex thought: "The essence of Paradise or of the idea of Paradise is *union with God already in this present life, that is to say the infinite Distress of the heart of man,* and *union with God in the future Life, that is to say Blessedness."*

Strange and profound parallel! Wonderful inversion which vindicates itself by an aching awareness of "Exile"! The union of the human soul with God cannot, in itself, be other than perfect

Blessedness—but, since that is impossible in this blighted world, it here assumes the aspect of utter Distress.

According to one of Bloy's definitions (to be abstracted from all his meditations on the Holy Virgin: the *Symbolisme de l'Apparition*, the *Introduction à la Vie de Mélanie, Celle qui pleure*, and *Dans les Ténèbres*), Suffering is the face which the divine Blessedness has turned towards man since the Fall—or rather, *during* the fall, for "we are falling all the time"—the only face of which man can catch a glimpse. Man in exile, and perpetually shutting himself out from Joy, can now approach it only through suffering.

> It is commonly said that joy is the opposite of sorrow and that these two spiritual or corporeal impressions incompatibles... How can people be made to understand that at a certain height *they are the same thing* and that it is, easy for a heroic soul to make them so?... Where are they today, the heroic souls?... Integral heroism, all in one piece, without seam and without stain, heroism bearing the stamp of eternity, where is it to be found? It is that of the complete Christian, who has given all for the love of God. (*Dans les Ténèbres*)

Here again, love alone is capable of understanding and overcoming contradictions. And it is love which, in the last year of Bloy's life, inspired him with this prayer:

> The God of Tears! What do these two words mean and what is this God? None other than the Holy Spirit. It is through him that we are alive, and tears are the sign of his presence. Woe unto him who does not weep. Tears are the oil of those lamps which the virgins of the Gospel must keep alight, lest the Bridegroom come in the middle of the night and say to them "I know you not." *Tears are so much the gift of the Holy Spirit that wherever they flow God must needs draw near*, since he said that he himself would wipe away tears from off all faces.

LÉON BLOY: A STUDY IN IMPATIENCE

They are so precious that we are not permitted to shed them in vain.

Lord God! Grant me to weep when waking and when sleeping, to weep always as did thy prophet. If my tears are not pure, change them into blood, and if that blood is worthless, let it become rivers of fire; but, no matter how, make me weep, since therein lies the means of blessedness, the infallible secret of drawing down the Comforter! Consider the infinite multitude of men who have wept since the beginning of time. I know well that many of their tears were in vain. There were tears of pride and tears of lust; there were tears of hate and of anger. But there were, and there are always, the tears of that Suffering which thou didst wed for love. Their abundance is as the Flood, and thy Spirit moves upon the face of the waters as of old, when thou hadst not yet created the world.

It is through love, too, that all Bloy's meditations center in one figure, who reappears throughout his work: Our Lady of La Salette weeping over men and over the sufferings of her Son. She is for Bloy the real, living image of that identity of suffering with joy which became more and more clearly revealed to him as the pivot of the Christian life. In a passage written in the summer of 1917 he puts into her mouth these words: "My son has said that those who weep are blessed, and it is because I have wept all the tears and suffered all the agonies of the generations that all the generations call me blessed."

This "Mater Dolorosa," who sometimes recalls Péguy's "Eve"—and for Bloy there is nothing far-fetched about such a comparison between the two Mothers of mankind—shows men a face wet with tears because "the Earthly Paradise is Suffering, and there is no other," as Bloy wrote in his introduction to the *Vie de Mélanie*. He added: "She weeps as She alone can weep. She weeps endless tears over all this long list of prevarications, and over each of them. *She is stricken by them in the very midst of her Blessedness. Reason loses its foothold. A Blessedness which 'suffers' and weeps! Is such a thing conceivable?"*

No, it is not conceivable by reason, and that is why, having arrived at this point, Bloy can find nothing but words of adoration, powerless to express more than the *presence* of a mystery. We are reminded of another of his sayings: "When one speaks lovingly of God, human words are all like lions that have gone blind and are looking for a spring in a desert."

This mystery is that of the analogy between human suffering and something which must be in God, which we can only conceive as the suffering of God, but which, in him, doubtless bears a different name. All that we are able to say—because this is part of our most reliable experience, and the tears of La Salette, like the agony of Christ, recall it to us—is that man's suffering bears an inexplicable relation to what we call divine suffering. It is the reflex in the shadow, as Bloy once suggested in *Le Salut par les Juifs*: "Since we are taught from our earliest days that we were created in God's image, is it then so difficult simply to suppose…that there must be in the Impenetrable Essence *something corresponding to ourselves, without sin,* and that the grievous conspectus of human afflictions is but *a dark reflex of the inexpressible conflagrations of Light?"*

Moreover, is not the value of suffering sufficiently attested by the fact that the Son of God desired it for himself, that he wished to be loved under the aspect of a body wounded by nails, a head bleeding beneath thorns, and that his Mother, in her turn, came and showed two children her eyes filled with tears? Here the whole mystery of the Incarnation presents itself for contemplation, with this fact forever incomprehensible, that Eternity chose to come down into time, and Blessedness to experience suffering.

Inextricably bound up with the fall and the exile—for since then the Earthly Paradise is to be approached only through, suffering, and this very suffering alone can convince us that the Lost Garden still exists—human affliction is necessarily bound up with the Redemption also. For it has become the only means of progress

LÉON BLOY: A STUDY IN IMPATIENCE

towards a God who offered himself for torture and who, since then, is mysteriously present in all creatures who are a prey to pain or even to the deepest disgrace. Bloy wrote to Henri de Groux on December 3, 1904:

> Jesus is at the center of everything, he takes upon himself everything, he bears everything, he suffers everything. It is impossible to strike a living being without striking Him, to humiliate anyone without humiliating Him, to curse or kill anyone whatsoever without cursing or killing Him. *The most worthless blackguard is forced to borrow the Face of Christ to receive a buffet from no matter what hand.* Otherwise the blow could never reach him and would remain suspended, in interstellar space, for centuries and centuries, until it had met the Face which pardons.

Again, Suffering is linked with the great hope of the End of Time, which will bring the fulfilment of the Redemption. Once a creature has, by suffering, known Jesus, the Man of Sorrows, it cannot live without setting its whole heart upon this consummation, praying for this with all its fervor, craving a share in the interminable agony, in order to hasten its end. Every pang suffered seems to it like a benediction, making it more intensely a part of the pain-racked body of Christ, and hastening the moment when all souls shall have been so thoroughly "set on fire" that the hour of completeness can strike. That is why suffering, which *makes* us members of Jesus Christ, is also the only source of love between men: "I say that someone loves me," we read in *La Symbolisme de l'Apparition*, "when that someone accepts suffering through me or for me... *A proud and generous soul seeks suffering with eagerness, with ecstasy.* When a thorn wounds it, it leans upon that thorn in order to lose nothing of the bliss of love which the thorn can give it by piercing it more deeply."

Bloy's life organized itself round these convictions as soon as he had attained them; and this inward life became uniform, since it always resolved itself into viewing all things in the light of its impatient hope of the End, of the love of Our Lady of the Seven Sorrows, and of the secret analogy that exists between the torments of Christ on the cross and the pains of men, who *are* his suffering body. From Bloy's books a hundred passages could be quoted, each a flash of intuition summing up the same truth, repeatedly discovered in the most varied episodes of history or of his personal life. A letter written to his future wife on December 7, 1889, will suffice, for it goes to the very heart of this Christian metaphysic of suffering:

> Do you know, my love, what is the hardest thing for the soul? It is to suffer, I will not say *for* others, but in others. That was the most terrible agony of the Savior, Beneath the dreadful outward Passion of Christ, beyond that procession of tortures and ignominies which are already almost more than we can dimly imagine, there was his *Compassion*, which we should need eternity to understand—a harrowing compassion utterly beyond words, which put out the sun and made the stars reel, which made him sweat blood before his crucifixion, which made him groan his thirst and cry to his Father for mercy during his agony. Had it not been for that frightful compassion, the physical Passion might perhaps Have been for Our Lord no more than a long swoon of bliss, although it was so appalling that to see it as it really was would be more than we could endure without dying of fright.
>
> *Think what it means that Jesus suffered in his heart with the omniscience of a God, and that in his heart he had all human hearts, with all their sufferings, from Adam down to the end of time.*

There is something strange about a life and thought so centered upon the experience of suffering, and it is natural to seek an explanation for it. Let us steer clear of those who would call in the

LÉON BLOY: A STUDY IN IMPATIENCE

aid of this or that "psychology" or reduce Bloy's adventure to a few biographical incidents. Interpretations of that kind merely spread a layer of false science over the reality of a spiritual discovery, and their point of departure is always one of the most mistaken ideas to which the aberrant mentality of modern times has given birth: the tendency to imagine that the "psychological" is first in importance and in time and that, once the "facts" which may have prompted a man's meditations have been laid bare, the "reason" for those meditations has been found. No view could be more unsound, and this type of criticism, based on a purely positivist notion of human nature, has wrought great havoc and is still doing so. Admittedly Bloy comes into Léon Bloy's works, and enquiry into his personal life is as tempting as it is legitimate; but there should be some consensus of opinion as to what deserves to be called by this name of "personal life" or "personality." The incidents of a man's career, the particular events unearthed by delving into letters and diaries, are no more "true" and "authentic" in their original form than when they have been transposed into the language of poetry, of symbols, of the coordinating imagination. A man is pursuing his real career at the very moment when, by recreating or grouping its fortuitous incidents under a scrutiny which transforms them, he *invents* a meaning for them. When a "worshipper of the Face of God" has resolved, as Bloy did, henceforward to write only "for the Three Persons of the Trinity," when he has devoted all his efforts and his genius to treating his life as a visible subject for interpretation, as a mere "datum" in which he seeks to trace "the footprint of the Invisible," it would be no less futile than sacrilegious to try and resolve everything into "what really happened." And to apply oneself to such a task would be to confess an inability to distinguish between plain respect for historical objectivity and the search, the approach, the desire for Truth, which is a very different thing. Bloy, singularly immune from this impoverishment and confused thinking, characteristic of his contemporaries, was a man who took no interest in his own life and in his originality (self-conscious though it was, and often arrogantly asserted) except in so far as it seemed to him a valid means of knowing God. In his work as a whole, and *above all* in the autobiographical passages, we should not look for anything that is not the interpretation of a discovery. The one thing of importance here is the object of a desire to know which is identical with a desire to love: and there is no doubt as to this object: it is none other than "the God of Abraham, of Isaac and of Jacob."

"*Personality, individuality is the peculiar vision which each man has of God.*" So runs Léon Bloy's profound definition. Conversely, it may be said that every Christian soul—and not only that of the visionary, the mystic, the saint—is in some measure *singled out* by the vision which God has of it, and which bears the name of vocation. Complete contemplation, full understanding of mysteries, is not of this world, and the most that is ever granted to man is a glimpse of some small part of the divine secret. But it is to this personal favor shown to him that each should conform in his efforts towards perfection and towards knowledge, for it is like the name by which he is called and to which he has to answer. Bloy's works contain other references to this mystery of "identity," it being one which continually engrossed him and prompted some of his most profound utterances. On June 6, 1897, he wrote concerning Rodin's *Balzac*, which shocked him because the sculptor, disregarding the universally familiar features of his subject, had had the "insanity" to suppose that he could "substitute anything he liked" for them: "*The personality, the human individuality written and signed by God on each face, and so formidably, sometimes, on the face of a great man, is an absolutely sacred thing, a thing for the Resurrection, for eternal life, for the beatific Union.* Every human countenance is a strictly private door into Paradise, which cannot be confused with the other doors, and by which only one single soul will ever enter..."

The "identity" of Léon Bloy, the door into Paradise reserved for him, is not impossible to recognize: doubtless he was an enthusiast for the Glory of God and a worshipper of his Mercy; but he was more essentially a prophet of his Justice and a man who, prostrate

LÉON BLOY: A STUDY IN IMPATIENCE

at the foot of the Cross, never "for one day" ceased to see "the Face covered with blood."

From his diaries and his letters and from dated passages in his other works a curious fact is to be noted. Year after year, with almost unbroken regularity, it was at Easter that he sank to the lowest depths of misery: of outward distress, apparently accidental, and of aridity or desolation of spirit. And It was in the summer months that the "furnace" of worship was rekindled within him and that he wrote, in the space of a few weeks, one of the great books which had long been maturing and which, before taking final shape, had always been left on one side and apparently forgotten for several months (thus *Le Salut par les Juifs* came to be written in 1892; *Jeanne d'Arc* in 1914; the *Meditations d'un Solitaire* in 1916; and *Dans les Ténèbres* just before his death). Then, after the festivals of "the two Good Ladies," as country people call them, once the anniversaries of Our Lady of the Seven Sorrows and of La Salette were over, sadness returned in a milder form as Christmas approached. There is sure to be someone, a psychologist or a belated disciple of Taine, who will credit a constitution of this particular strain (Périgord crossed with Spaniard) with an exceptional physical sensibility to the sun and the seasons, and thus account for the inward ardors of June and July. But, for a Christian like Bloy, who from the time of his marriage to the time of his death received the sacrament every morning and let his meditation feed upon the daily sequence of texts appointed by the Church, the days and months of the earth were first and foremost stages in the liturgical calendar. A key to his yearly anguish at Eastertide may be found in the cry, recorded in his diary under the date April 14, 1895:

> Easter. I feel cold to the center of my soul and am as near as possible to despair. That is the effect this great festival has upon me. Easter Sunday is usually painful, sometimes terrible. Impossible to hide my distress, which might be expressed more or less in this way: *I cannot feel any joy in the Resurrection*

because, for me, the Resurrection never happens. I always see Jesus in agony, Jesus on the cross, and I cannot see him otherwise.

How am I to struggle upwards from this abyss?... Over and over again the Ecclesiastical Year begins once more, always the same, and Our Lord never bursts forth! Non venit regnum Dei cum observatione. *I know that very well. But, because no sign is to herald the coming of this Kingdom, does that mean that we have to wait for it forever?*

These words clearly mark the two focal points in Léon Bloy's religious life: the suffering of Christ, whom we shall not cease to crucify anew until the Last Day, and a sorrowful longing for that day which each spring seems to promise but never brings. Perhaps, after the strange inward silence of Easter, Whitsuntide inspires this devotee of the Third Person of the Trinity with a fresh hope which kindles the fire of the following months—although, in his cry for the Coming of the Holy Spirit, Bloy often seems like a Christian for whom the gift of the tongues of fire is as "non-existent" as the joy of Easter. (Not that he does not *believe*, in the most orthodox and submissive manner, in the Resurrection on the Third Day and in the peaceable manifestation of the Spirit to the Apostles; but he does not *see* them as he sees the Cross or the End of Time, which it seems to have been his mission to contemplate.) The truth, I think, would rather seem to be that, from the beginning of the summer, his year revolves round the festivals of the Virgin Mary, because she is for him the Queen of Tears, always present to his love, and because it is this figure of Suffering that revives his annual exaltation...His "human countenance," not to be confused with any other, is thus governed by Suffering, and it was not in his power to alter that nothing in his underlying life was turned towards peace except this constant cry for absolute Peace, the end of time, the moment when everything should cease to form the interminable agony of Jesus and his suffering members, for the final triumph of the beatific vision. But Bloy could only imagine this peace as supervening after

LÉON BLOY: A STUDY IN IMPATIENCE

inconceivable convulsions, in the midst of that amazement which he often tries to suggest by an accumulation of superlatives or of images of fire.

The truth is—and it can never be sufficiently stressed—that for Bloy only one thing counts: to arrive at an ever purer vision, to make himself ever more transparent, more fit to live near the heart of Jesus. To be truly understood, his whole conception of suffering must be placed in this perspective, and its great lesson is that nothing matters but to attain, by every possible means, to the highest degree of spirituality within the reach of man. If he so *loved* Suffering, it was certainly not for the sake of feeling intensely, after the manner of the romantics, nor for the sake of exercising the heroic virtues of resignation, extolled by a moralizing stoicism which still leads many Christians astray. Bloy knew that a certain way of giving precedence to morality and to human effort is one of the most deadly obstacles encountered by the soul in its advance towards true inward transparency. The world of the modem Catholic offered him only too many examples of that obtuseness, of that imperviousness to love which may result from a moralism without spiritual life. He had a justifiable horror of what cautious piety calls resignation, for he knew, by long and trustworthy experience, that suffering should not merely be accepted, as a bracing discipline (which may be a pagan precept), but should be chosen, because it is truly, essentially, a window opening upon the Invisible, a way of approach to Blessedness.

Such are the depths in which the *Joy* of Léon Bloy is to be sought, that joy which so many minds, scared by his violence or disconcerted by his vindication of Suffering, protest they cannot find in him. It exists, nevertheless, but it is synonymous with his misery, because to the end of his life he remained a worshipper of the Cross. His last writings are sad enough to make the heart break with compassion if, in reading them, one thinks of what that old age was like—solitary in spite of wonderful friendships, inconsolable over the state of the world and, above all, of France, tortured by the delay in the great events for which he was waiting and, quite simply, overwhelmed by the recurrence of daily wretchedness and haunted by the wholesale carnage of 1914. And yet, between the lines of this confession of desolation, who can remain insensible to the great tranquility which supervenes at the approach of death, when Bloy is summing up the meagre total of his life and his work? The wonderful books of his last years express neither resignation nor disappointment but peace descending upon a soul certain at last that its hour is at hand and that the sight of the Justice of God—whether indulgent or implacable is of little moment!—will be the gift of long-awaited Joy. Bloy had never wanted anything except to see the Justice of God here in this life, in so far as man can have the means of seeing it; when death was approaching, he understood that the moment was not far off when the vision should be his. It was in this mood that, in January 1915, he wrote the moving letter to La Laurencie, in which he judges his whole life, as if to cast it down at the feet of his Judge:

> The little that I have, God gave it me without any of my doing, and what use have I made of it?
>
> The worst evil is not to commit crimes, but to have failed to do the good one might have done. It is the sin *of omission*, which is nothing else than non-love—a sin of which no one accuses himself. Anyone observing me day by day, at the first Mass, would often see me weep. These tears, which might be holy, are instead very bitter tears. At such times I do not think of my sins, some of which are monstrous. I think of what I might have done and have not done, and, believe me, it is very black. Do not tell me that it is the same for everybody. God had given me the sense, the need, the instinct—I do not know how to put it—of the Absolute, as he gave quills to the porcupine and a trunk to the elephant. An extremely rare gift, of which I have been conscious since my childhood, a faculty more dangerous and torturing than genius itself, since it implies a constant and

LÉON BLOY: A STUDY IN IMPATIENCE

raging hunger for something which does not exist on earth, and it is the way to infinite loneliness. I might have become a saint and a worker of miracles. I became a man of letters!

If people knew that those phrases or passages they are pleased to admire are only the residue of a supernatural gift which I have atrociously bungled and for which I shall be called to dreadful account!

I have not done what God wanted of me, that's certain. Instead, I have mused over *what I wanted of God*, and here I am, at sixty-eight, with nothing in my hands but paper!

Oh! I know very well that you won't believe me, that you will put this down to some odd kink of humility. Alas! when you are *alone*, in the presence of God, at the end of a very dark lane, you see yourself as you are, and you are in a bad position for imposing upon anyone! True goodness, goodwill pure and simple, the simplicity of little children, all that calls for a kiss from the Mouth of Jesus, you know very well that you have not got it and that you have really nothing to offer to poor suffering hearts when they beg for help.

But a still more beautiful passage shows Bloy as an old man already reaching beyond the threshold of the next world. Never, perhaps, has any man's mind carried him so far along the path to death, going to meet Judgment, taking upon himself all the distress of an imperfect creature, all the solitude of a long life suddenly left to its nakedness, but also all the hope of one who has always loved Justice with the same love as Mercy, and Sorrow as much as Joy. This passage, "received in church" on the day of the Transfiguration, August 6, 1916, was later placed at the beginning of the *Méditations d'un Solitaire*:

I am *alone*. Yet I have a wife and two daughters who love me and whom I love. I have god-sons and god-daughters whom the Holy Spirit seems to have chosen. I have tried and trusted friends, far more of them than the ordinary allowance.

But all the same, I am the only one of my kind. I am alone in the antechamber of God. When it is my turn to go in, where will they be, those whom I loved and who loved me? I know that some of them who know how to pray will pray for me with all their hearts; but how far away they will be then, and what dreadful solitude before my Judge!

The nearer one draws to God, the more alone one is. It is solitude raised to infinity.

At that moment all the Sacred Words, read so many times in my dark vault, will be made manifest to me, and the Rule that one must hate father, mother, children, brothers, sisters and even one's own soul, if one would go to Jesus, will weigh upon me like a mountain of burning granite.

Where will they be, the humble churches with their mellow walls where I prayed with so much love, sometimes, for the living and for the dead? Where will they be, the precious tears which were my hope as a sinner, when I was worn out with loving and suffering? And what will have become of my poor books, in which I sought the history of the merciful Trinity?

On what, on what shall I lean? The prayers of the loved ones whom I have given to the Church, will they have time and strength to get there? Nothing assures me that the Angel appointed to guard me will not himself be trembling with compassion and shivering like a half-clad starveling, forgotten outside the door in the depths of winter. I shall be unspeakably alone and I know in advance that I shall not have even a second in which to plunge into the abyss of light or the abyss of darkness.

"I am forced to accuse you," my conscience will say, and my most devoted friends, infinitely remote, will confess their impotence. Defend yourself as best you can, poor wretch!

"It is true that, next to God, we owe you the life of our souls," they will say, sobbing, "and that makes us hope that your soul will be treated gently. But look...there is between us and you the great Chaos of Death. You have become unimaginable to us, and a partaker in unimaginable Solitude. We can but wring our hearts in prayer for you. If you have not been absolutely a *disciple*, if you have not sold all and left all, we know that you are there where a thousand years are as a day and where a single look from the Eyes of your Judge may pass like a flash of lightning or last through untold ages. For we can conjecture nothing, save that you are inconceivably alone and that, if one of us were able to go to you, he would not be able to recognize you. But that again is impossible for us to understand. God be with you then, until the unknown hour of the universal Judgment, which is another mystery, more impenetrable."

Adjuro te per Deum vivum, said the High Priest, to force Jesus to speak. This stupendous summons, which dimmed the stars, still endures, and this will be the last cry of humanity, when it sees itself alone, at the end of ends, in the incomprehensible Valley of Jehoshaphat.

CHAPTER II

Poverty, Money, and the People of Israel

―――◆◆▸―――

> Would it not be enough if all the miseries, all the afflictions of the poor and all their sufferings were collected and gathered up into a bundle, a sheaf? We should then have the History of God.
>
> – August 3, 1899

> Anti-Semitism, a thing peculiar to modern times, is the most horrible injury Our Lord has received in his Passion, which is still going on; it is the most outrageous and unforgivable buffet, for he receives it *on the Face of his Mother* and from Christian hands.
>
> – January 2, 1910

I.

After he had entered upon the "supernatural life" through Suffering, it Became Bloy's aim to make his mind as transparent as possible to light of grace and to penetrate further and further into the mysteries hidden beneath the surface of history and of the state of mankind. His efforts towards this progress in spirituality, which was all-important to him, took the form of a manifold and continual work of exegesis, in which Bloy, in very precise and methodical fashion, concentrated his attention upon one aspect after another of the real, always charting his course towards the Absolute by the same objects of contemplation: the suffering of Christ crucified, the hope of the final Advent of the Holy Spirit, and the lamentations and threats uttered by the Virgin Mary on the mountain of La Salette.

Both in reading the Scriptures and in showing the exact points in the course of temporal history where they had been confirmed, Bloy strictly adhered to the rules of thought which he had adopted from Abbé Tardif de Moidrey. The precepts of this "symbolical exegesis" may best be summed up by quoting a few passages in which Bloy formulates them with admirable clarity:

> Like the Eucharist, the Words of the Sacred Book feed the soul, and even the mind, without its being necessary to understand them. (November 4, 1910)

> The only profitable way of reading the Psalms or the Book of Job, for instance, is to put yourself in the place of the speaker, since He who speaks is always, necessarily, the Christ whose members we are. (August 26, 1894)

> The Word of God is infinite, absolute, irrevocable in every way and, above all, it is in the highest degree repetitive; for God can only speak of Himself. (*Le Salut par les Juifs*, 1892).

The wonderful explanation which Bloy gives of human history follows these precepts, as we shall see, and he treats it exactly as if it were revealed utterance. His starting-point is this conviction that intellectual knowledge is as nothing beside the light of Faith, since the true object of spiritual craving is not explanation but mystery.

LÉON BLOY: A STUDY IN IMPATIENCE

That is why revelation—the revelation which, if we are really attentive, can be read in the facts of the created world, as well as the revelation of the Scriptures—cannot be completely *understood*, in the ordinary sense of the word: it must be *received*, as "one receives the Bread of Life. It always bears several superimposed meanings, none of them exclusively valid, and each no more than a fitful flash across our feeble intelligence: "Revelation is a wan sky obscured by mountains of dark cloud from which the shaft of lightning sometimes darts its tip, but straightway plunges back into the gloom."

And these meanings are repeated endlessly, every Word of God having ultimately only one and the same sense, since each of them denotes God—that is to say, to our minds, *the Mystery* whose presence we can mark, record and worship without being able to say what it is. If our sudden soundings nevertheless enable us to fathom the coherent text of the Book or of the Universe, it is thanks to the Redemption, which has brought us into the great fellowship of the mystical Body. Because we remain members of Jesus Christ, the mind of man, totally blind in itself, is capable of "putting itself in the place" of Him who wrote the vast text. But this requires an attention which is the reverse of intellectual curiosity; that self-surrender which is accomplished by a soul ready to silence its superficial faculties.

> I actually know very little, and I have never understood anything except what God has enabled me to understand when I made myself like a little child. (October 31, 1889)

Like the great mystics, Bloy also knew, early in life, that nothing can be grasped except by inward scrutiny. The human soul, through the *Redemption*, has become greater than the whole universe and is thus capable of containing and finding that universe within itself. No reality will be truly intelligible—that is to say, contemplated so profoundly that its aspect of mystery is revealed—unless it is considered in the light of the first of all mysteries: the love of God, conferring upon his creature the faculty of discovering in itself the true meaning and life of everything. Bloy notes in his diary on June 6, 1894:

> The dreadful immensity of the abyss of heaven is an illusion, an outward reflex of our own abyss, perceived "through a glass." *Our eyes should be turned inwards* and should busy themselves with a sublime astronomy in the Infinitude of our hearts, for which God chose to die.
>
> No man can *see* anything but what is in himself. If we see the Milky Way, it is because it *really* exists in our souls."

In a letter to Elisabeth Joly which is like a confession of faith, Bloy, in 1912, expressed himself more clearly still:

> You have been told that you have an immortal soul which had to be saved etc., but no one has told you that *this soul is an abyss in which all the worlds there are could be swallowed up, in which the Son of God himself, Creator of all worlds, has been engulfed*; that this soul is in truth the tomb of Christ, for the deliverance of which, in the olden days, multitudes gave their lives…

With the attention he accorded to the secret meaning of every human fact, Bloy bent his gaze upon Poverty. He loved it, not with a gentle Franciscan love, but in his own way, with a sort of violent passion, and with the hope of finding in it, as in all suffering, the hidden presence of God.

One of Bloy's claims to greatness, among the most evident even to those who do not understand his Christian message, is the *"fellowship of impatience"* which he acknowledged with *"all the rebellious, all the disappointed, all the thwarted, all the damned of this world."* These lines from Le Désespéré proclaim a profound solidarity with the poor wretches who have been crushed by social injustice and are in revolt against it. But we must be clear in our minds as to what it is that, while allying Bloy with the rebellious, the "damned of the earth," distinguishes him from them. True, he surpassed Proudhon and Marx in denouncing not so much the scandal of social inequality as the scandal of all resignation to that inequality. Those who consider wealth as conferring privilege, who claim that happiness depends upon *it* and set up Money as an idol, come in for his most virulent and magnificent invective. But, if he identifies himself with the threats which rise from the downtrodden multitude, if he is surprised that their patience still endures, his own rebellion is unaccompanied by any hope of social progress, by any desire, even, to establish a world from which poverty has been driven out.

He was the passionate and sometimes strangely biased admirer of Napoleon, but no word uttered by this great man shocked him more deeply than that saying to which so many worthy people find no difficulty in subscribing: "I consider it a very important and glorious aim to put an end to beggary." A code which "presupposes the non-existence of the poor" was to him an intolerable monstrosity: "Such a thing had never been seen in any Christian legislation. The poor always had their place in it, sometimes even the place of honor which is their due… *'Begging is prohibited.'* Napoleon had erased the Poor Man and that was his outrage perpetuated."

That is why, in Bloy's view, the Emperor who was able to get the better of wealthy England and all the princes of his time was to be defeated by "ragged Spain," whose beggars belong to God…

To cure misery by rooting out poverty; to make the poor rich: this eternal illusion of social reformers could not win support from Bloy, who saw in it the worst of crimes, since it was tantamount to providing all men with that false "happiness" of possession, those burdensome "goods" which darken the soul and make it opaque, impermeable to Light. Wealth, for him, was an evil, not so much because it spelt unfairness as because it dimmed the transparency of one's being and impeded that vision of the Truth which could be obtained only by renunciation of earthly possessions and by love of Suffering.

This, it should at once be noted, does not mean that Bloy acquiesces in earthly injustice and shuts his eyes to the material inequality which gives all the power to a few and debars the rest from participation. He is entirely free from that meanness of the "right-thinking" conformists who, on the pretext that Justice is not of this world, obstinately refuse to change anything in a social order which, Jacques Maritain has said, secretes misery as its natural product. There is nothing obscure in the paradoxical co-existence in Bloy of a most vehement indignation at the selfishness of the privileged few and an idea of Poverty which makes him write that he has "wedded" her "for love."

All that he had to say on this subject—he who lived the whole of his life in very real want—is a commentary on a few words of the Gospel, words which are often quoted with circumspection and the, reserves customary among theologians and preachers, but which Bloy himself accepted in their intangible meaning. He had too personal an experience of misery to gloss over its horrors; but he also knew the cost of Poverty too well not to love it.

———•••———

Blessed are the poor. Poverty is a gift from God, for nothing intervenes between God and the eyes of him who is stripped of all earthly possessions. If he has been deprived of satisfactions in this world, he has in exchange the promise of some day receiving all the real joys. Prepared for contemplation by his very destitution, his sight purified of all that might have dulled it, he will enjoy, more immediately and entirely, the vision of uncreated Light.

Nay, more: it is his already, and he receives everything without having to wait. That is the conclusion of *La Femme pauvre*: "You do not enter Paradise tomorrow, nor the day after, nor in ten years; you enter *today*, when you are poor and crucified." That is to say—for

LÉON BLOY: A STUDY IN IMPATIENCE

here again we have the mystery of the imitation of Jesus Christ through suffering—when one is brought near to God by misery.

———•••———

The poor ye have always with you. Poverty is eternal in history and cannot be expelled from the world *by* decree of men or by legal safeguards. Eternal, because it is one of the names for eternal and prolific Suffering, and because in it is realized "what is lacking in the sufferings of Jesus Christ."

But there is more in it than that, and the mystery of Poverty goes deeper. Or, rather, the very profound mystery of participation in the poverty of the Lord manifests itself and becomes perceptible to the senses through the mystery of the participation of the poor in the visible community of men. The union of the creature with the crucified Redeemer (accomplished in the union of creatures one with another through common membership in the mystical body of Christ) is nowhere more clearly symbolized than in the effects of Poverty.

The human reason, with its own means and standards of judgment, finds no suffering and no misery comprehensible or admissible in this world. But there is none that is unnecessary as soon as we try to make out its place in the divine plan. For everything remains dark and unintelligible, everything is seemingly unacceptable because seemingly unjust, so long as we consider the individual in the isolation of his particular destiny and endeavor to explain him as a separate self-contained being. On the other hand, while perhaps not "explaining" this destiny, we can penetrate to its secret depths if in the fellowship of all men—living, dead and yet unborn—we recognize the mystical body of Christ. All suffering then becomes part of the agony of Jesus and, being the price of redemption, it is necessarily a form of grace. Hence the incomprehensible and universal interdependence of sorrows and joys, the wonderful relation through which an affliction is always "in its right place," since it balances a happiness, since it "pays" for the happiness of a known or unknown being by reason of the indefinable links between every creature and his fellow. "*Christianity means suffering through one another.*"

This constant miracle of an unerring balance is probed by Bloy even more deeply in regard to Poverty than in regard to Suffering. Needless to say, he rejects any interpretation which would seem to justify not poverty but wealth: nobody has more harshly denounced the monstrous attitude of the "right-thinking" who accept the misery of others and the easiness of their own lot on the pretext that the one balances the other. What better proof is there of this than the chapters in *Le Sang du Pauvre* on "worldly priests" or on "the murderous mockery" of the so-called "charity" entertainments, and the many indignant references to the practice, in churches, of relegating the poor to a humble place far from the altar, while the "notables" monopolize the velvet of the front pews....

If poverty is a form of grace, this is because it is an *appeal* to charity—in other words, to the element of divine love that is in each of us. If our Christianity were the real thing and souls had not become hardened, the appearance of a single poor men or woman would wake the spark of love in every sleeping heart, and thus the beggar would serve for his neighbor's salvation. As was still the practice not only in Christian Russia (known to us through its great novelists or from such testimonies as the *Récits d'un Pèlerin* recently translated into French by Jean Gauvain) but also, not so very long ago, in country districts of France, hospitality was shown to beggars because one of them might always turn out to be the Lord himself, the Poorest of the Poor, come down to earth again. Poverty is divine because it plays this part for others, because in appealing to charity—not good works, or almsgiving, but *charity*, which is the love of God in his creatures—it *bestows* charity. It is the poor who give, by receiving, by asking, and who thus *bring God to life*, for a moment, in hearts which listen to them.

Thus from man to man a network of endless exchanges is woven, outside which they are not "alive." For this is indeed the point, and

LÉON BLOY: A STUDY IN IMPATIENCE

here we touch upon one of Bloy's deepest intuitions, which calls for some explanation: an intuition that casts a very strong light upon the nature of human personality, or, as Bloy preferred to call it, our *identity*. He was literally haunted *by* our ignorance of our true nature, our real vocation, and by our inability to define ourselves—a state of affairs caused partly by the inexhaustible diversity of souls and partly by the unconscious but essential links between them. Without knowing these links it is impossible to say anything of the identity of a creature; for, defined by his vocation—the part which it has to play in the plan of universal fellowship—it has no other real existence than its place among the congregation of souls, and that will be revealed to it only after death. This mystery of "identity," which merges into the mystery of the Communion of Saints, is examined in one of the most beautiful *Meditations d'un Solitaire en 1916* with a clear-sightedness unrivalled except perhaps in Péguy's magnificent passage on the "silence of the race" (in the *Note conjointe*).

> *What every man is exactly, none can say.* The most favored can, at best, cite ancestors discovered, several centuries back, in the dark corners of history, whose names, inscribed in ancient muniments, can still be read on a few tombstones spared by time.
>
> Bumpkins like myself know nothing, or next to nothing, beyond their paternal or maternal grandparents; but each and all have an invincible ignorance of their *supernatural kindred* and the drops of more or less illustrious blood on which the proud base their claims do not constitute anyone's IDENTITY...
>
> Every generation is supernatural. The entries in the parish records, of which you are sometimes so proud, know absolutely nothing about your soul, and that register of nullity can only deal with your body, catalogued in advance for the cemetery. If there is a genealogical tree of souls, the Angels alone have access to it. The other trees called by that name are deceptive and uncertain. The genealogy of souls! Who can understand that?

ALBERT BÉGUIN

Each of us has a soul infinitely different from other souls and mysterious in origin. It may come from above or from below, from far away or from near at hand, but it goes where it has to go, infallibly... I know quite well that I was born on a certain date, in a particular place, and that I bear a name among men. I have had a father and a mother, I have had brothers, friends and enemies. All that is incontestable, but I do not know the *name* of my soul, I do not know whence it came, and consequently *I have absolutely no Idea who I am.* When my soul leaves it, my body will crumble into dust, and the beloved creatures who survive me, weeping, heirs of my ignorance, will be able to refer to me in their prayers only by the *borrowed name* which served to separate me a little from other mortals.

I have often thought of this strange affliction, which seems to trouble nobody...

By reason of the spiritual kinship which is inexorably hidden from me, there is perhaps, in some desert, a horrible savage whose soul is twin to mine, and our two souls may, at the same time, be first cousins to that of the odious William of Hohenzollern, or of some other unforgivable profaner of the Face of the living God, who made him in his own Image. All that is certainly possible and I venture to say, from the depths of my darkness, that the more frightening such associations, the more probable they are. This should make one feel profoundly humble.

To this agonized question regarding the impenetrable secrecy which shrouds our true personality, Bloy finds the answer in another secret, faintly glimpsed but dazzling—that of the Communion of Saints. We shall not understand it until after death, but it is possible, even now, to divine at least that, thanks to universal fellowship, the soul of each is denoted and defined by its hidden affinities with other souls:

LÉON BLOY: A STUDY IN IMPATIENCE

It is the choir of all the souls since the creation of the world, and in this choir the parts are arranged with such marvelous precision that it is impossible to play truant. The inconceivable exclusion of one single soul would endanger the eternal Harmony. The word "reversibility" had to be invented to give an idea, for what it is worth, of this vast Mystery.

Men have played with the idea that the heavenly spheres, which calculation places at an awe-inspiring distance from one another, are in reality, to seraphic eyes, a compact mass of immense bodies as close to one another as the grains of a block of granite. Applied to the infinite world of souls, this paradox is a truth. But each is ignorant of its neighbor, as the luminaries of the Milky Way are ignorant of their nearest fellows, with which they blend in the incomprehensible harmony of all these Titans of splendor...

The one thing that we can dimly perceive, with trembling and adoration, is the *constant miracle of an unerring balance between human merits and demerits,* so that the spiritually destitute are helped by the wealthy, and the bold do duty for the timid. And this happens quite without our knowledge, according to the wondrous unknown law of the affinity of souls.

A movement of Grace that saves me from dire peril may have been brought about by an act of love performed this morning or five hundred years ago by some obscure person whose soul was in very mysterious correspondence with mine and who thus receives his reward...

Such thoughts are in keeping with our apocalyptic age. Millions of men are flying at each other's throats in Europe and Asia through the will of one lunatic. What does it mean, the conflict of this stream of souls? Where do they come from? Who are their kith and kin and where are they going to, after having shed their pitiful vesture of flesh?

Oh, the stupendous and supernatural silence which suddenly replaces the monstrous din of battle! *Infinite silence in the darkness or in the light, one knows not which. But then, what ineffable encounters and surprises there must be. Inaudible voices, the faces of souls recognize each other once for all through the diaphanous partitions of race and the translucent walls of the centuries...*

"There it is, your *identity*!" the Judge will announce, addressing the consciousness of each one. And this is really all that it is given to us to imagine of that dread moment.

The miracle of Poverty lies in the fact that through it those links with other souls, by which each of us becomes what he is in the eyes of God, are made necessary and living. That is what Bloy meant when, in a difficult chapter of *Le Sang du Pauvre*, he distinguished between Misery and Poverty. Misery, he explained, is privation of what is necessary, that is to say of Love; he is miserable who does not receive the one thing that is indispensable, namely charity. Poverty is privation of the superfluous, that is to say of earthly possessions; the poor man lacks those advantages which others enjoy, but he is rich in all the charity which he arouses in his neighbor and which at the same time awakes in himself. For he bestows upon a soul love and even salvation, and that is a gift no one possesses until he gives it. (And once more we find Bloy's path converging with Péguy's and bringing us very close to the marvelous verses in *Eve*:

> ...Et par la vous savez que tout homme dépense,
> Et que le plus avare est le plus dépensier.
> Et que le charitable est le seul bon boursier,
> Le seul qui sache un peu gouverner sa finance.
>
> ...Celui-là seul qui met son front sur mes genoux
> Est seul maitre du temps et seul martre du lieu.
> Et seul il sait garder ses misérables sous,
> Celui qui donne au pauvre et redemande à Dieu."

LÉON BLOY: A STUDY IN IMPATIENCE

[...And by this you may know that all men spend,
And the meanest miser is the greatest spender.
And the charitable man is the only shrewd investor,
And his accounts alone will balance in the end.

... And only he who comes and lays his forehead on my knees
Is master of the place and master of the day.
And, alone, he can save his miserable sous
Who gives to the poor and bids the Lord repay.])

It is in this sense that Bloy can say that "Poverty unites" while "Misery isolates": the one brings the soul into the fellowship of souls, and that means that the soul is assigned its place and made to exist according to its vocation and its identity, in bonds of love with its neighbor which make it a member of Jesus Christ. But the horror of misery is that it deprives a man of these bonds and that it literally kills a soul by thrusting it out of its vocation, out of the communion.

> Poverty brings men together, Misery isolates them, because poverty is of Jesus, misery of the Holy Spirit.
> Poverty is relative—privation of what is superfluous. Misery is Absolute—privation of what is needful.
> Poverty is crucified, Misery is the cross itself. Jesus bearing the Cross is Poverty bearing History. Jesus on the Cross is Poverty bleeding upon Misery.

The strange likening of Misery to the Holy Spirit and to the Cross can only be explained by the whole exegesis of the Trinity, which is one of the most abstruse chapters of Bloy's thought. One or two points of this exegesis will be discussed on a later page; here it may suffice to note that the misery of the Holy Spirit, vagrant through the length and breadth of history, is the image by which Bloy repeatedly strives to typify the sufferings of God in the face of man's disobedience after the Redemption, as he waits interminably for the kindling of his creatures by love, which will merge into the coming of the promised Kingdom. It is the Creator vainly begging for charity, and deprived, even He, of what is needful.

Hence Bloy's anger against the rich: not against those who have possessions, but against those who kill themselves by acquiescing in the misery of others and even the misery of God. In condemning themselves to *non-existence*—since they refuse love—they also kill the poor; for they deprive the poor of the charity which would "bring them to life."

Woe unto the rich! Such is, in effect, the third Gospel saying which Bloy discusses, taking it in its fullest sense and rejecting the subtle distinctions through which it is watered down by a Christianity that comes to terms with the world. Woe unto *the rich*, and not to the *bad rich*, which, says Bloy, would be pleonastic.

> A bad rich man, if these two words *have to be* brought into association, is like a bad official or a bad workman, that is to say a person who does not know his job or does not do it properly. The *bad rich man is one who gives* and who, by dint of giving, becomes a poor man, "a man of longing," like the prophet Daniel, who foreshadowed Jesus Christ.

The exact words of the Gospel are: *Vae vobis divitibus, quia habetis consolationem vestram.* What is the "consolation" thus referred to? We know now: the consolation which the rich man can find in the possession of earthly property is the complacency which wards off Suffering and throws it back upon others. It is refusal to Endure and to Love, in other words rejection of God, who can be approached only through endurance and charity, by entering into the communion of the suffering members of Jesus Christ. "*Consolationem vestram!* What inverted desolation is implied by that ineffaceable saying, and, on the other side, what longing!"

LÉON BLOY: A STUDY IN IMPATIENCE

The Poor Man for his part has no "consolation," but he has something else which is much more valuable; he has *Longing*, and that is what gives him dignity, what makes his being more transparent, more capable of receiving God than the opaque being of the rich man. In him poverty, the absence of consolation, hollows out the cavity which is Longing, a gap, a void, an empty space asking to be filled, and one which can only be offered to God and filled by God. Alms are an insufficient answer to the appeal of this Longing, for alms are the gift of what is superfluous, of that which none has a right to possess. Charity alone is sufficient, being the gift of what is needful: the gift of oneself, of love, the giving of God by the soul to another soul. And it takes that gift, and nothing less, to quench the Longing of the Poor Man, that thirst which "is the man himself."

> What must one day bring so terrible an indictment against the rich is the *Longing of the Poor*. Here is a millionaire who keeps for himself without using it, or spends in a moment on some idle whim, what for fifty or sixty years the poor man has desperately craved... Every man who owns more than is indispensable for his material and spiritual life is a millionaire, and accordingly the debtor, of those who have nothing ...
>
> When one is not exactly a wicked man, one gives alms, which means giving a very small part of one's superfluity, for the voluptuous pleasure of stirring up longing without satisfying it. The almsgiver gives other people, that is to say what belongs to other people—his superfluity. *The charitable man gives himself by giving what is needful to himself and thus the longing of the poor man is appeased.* That is the Gospel and there is no other...
>
> To mock the Longing of the poor is the unforgivable sin, since it is an outrage against the supreme spark of the torch which is still smoking and which we are so strongly enjoined not to quench."

A word of caution, however! This condemnation of the rich—which must not be abated of any of its violence and which is pronounced "in fellowship of impatience with all the rebellious"—is uttered from the only standpoint at which Bloy ever consents to place himself: the standpoint of the Absolute, the Supernatural. His anger against the rich and the "landlord" (one of the prominent characters in his "human comedy") does not spring from a need for material equality, and still less from a hope of inaugurating a better state of society by means of new institutions. Nothing matters for him but to know whether souls are dead or alive, whether they are mounting towards love and the knowledge of God through participation in Suffering, or whether they are estranging themselves by refusal to suffer: in other words, whether they are helping to shorten or to prolong the agony of Jesus Christ, renewed in his members and never to end until all souls shall be consumed in the conflagration of the divine flame.

Nor should Bloy's invective against the rich and his infinite tenderness for the poor be confused with any form of humanitarianism. He shows this clearly in a letter to Jehan Rictus, written in 1901, in which he distinguishes his "supernatural" point of view from the social "evangelism" of the *Soliloques du Pauvre*:

> You call yourself a Christian. Very good. Perhaps, indeed, you are more of a Christian than you think. But you seem to see only a Christianity devoid of any *supernatural* element—which is unintelligible and a contradiction in terms.
>
> "Jesus came for the poor," you say. Well, of course! But he *came for the rich too*, in order that they should make themselves poor through love, and you must be aware that hundreds of thousands of saints have obeyed. *Jesus came for* SOULS; *that's the proper thing to say.*

Again, in *Le Sang du Pauvre,* in another passage of the same tenor and showing the same preoccupation with the attainment of

LÉON BLOY: A STUDY IN IMPATIENCE

a more or less effectual transparence to God, he wrote those simple words which bring out the profound affinity, instinctively recognized in common parlance, between Poverty and Charity (or as much of charity as survives in modern souls): "Man's place is so near to God that the word *poor* is a term of affection. When the heart is bursting with compassion or love, when one can hardly restrain one's tears, that is the word which springs to one's lips."

The *parable of Lazarus* gave Bloy the opportunity of going still deeper into the mystery of poverty. Lazarus, "laid at the gate of the world, full of sores," prototype of the "Beggar whom God cherishes in contrast to the gluttonous and voluptuous Rich Man whom he cursed," Lazarus can only stand for Jesus Christ. While he lives in the depths of want, the perfect type of Poverty, the rich man feasts and refuses him the crumbs from the banquet. The unjust man no doubt imagines, for his own reassurance, that the distance thus placed between the two men through the rich man's hardness of heart inevitably exists by the law of this world. He is far from suspecting that it will subsist in eternity, but that *he* will then be the one vainly imploring an act of love to bridge the gulf. "Woe unto the rich man," once more, for, having in this life repelled love, which is Life itself, he has separated himself *forever* from love. So true it is that our "time" involves and determines *our* eternity. He who, having rejected charity, has killed himself, will one day find himself separated from all "consolation," because the distance that he had placed between himself and his neighbor will have become the immense inspissation of impassable Death.

> It might be thought that the separation between this rich man and this poor man could not well be greater. But to both of them death comes and separates them in a very different way, *as body from soul*, and the great "Chaos" intervenes, mysterious and unbridgable abyss beyond any man's conceiving—Death itself forever incomprehensible. The rich man then, from the midst of horrible torments inversely foreshadowed

by the pleasures of his table, cries out to the beggar in his glory, not even daring to ask for as much cold water as is contained in the "cup" of the Gospel, but only one drop of that water, on the tip of the beggar's finger, to cool his tongue; and it is on Abraham's intercession that he counts to obtain it. He could not have fared worse. Abraham pleads the impassable gulf. It is your refusal that makes this gulf. Lazarus asked no more of you when you took delight in his tortures. Your inexorable *consolation* has become his and there is nothing to be done.

Bloy, when he wrote this striking comment, perceived one of the profoundest truths of the Gospel: the peculiar purpose of earthly existence is to give souls the chance to accept love and through love to make themselves such that, after this life, they will escape from the "great Chaos" of death and enter into the beatific vision. But those who have refused this chance can never have it again. Such is the value of temporal life. Placed in the mouth of the Elder Zossima, in *The Brothers Karamazov*, there is an interpretation of the parable of Lazarus which goes as deep as Bloy's, since Dostoevsky, too, knew that Charity is the means of knowing God, and that it is necessary to have approached Jesus Christ *hic et nunc* if one is to escape the hellish torture of being no longer able to draw near to him through all eternity. "What is hell?" asks Father Zossima. "I define it as the suffering of no longer being able to love." And he goes on:

> Once, in the infinitude of space and time, a spiritual being, by appearing on earth, had the opportunity of saying "I am and I love." Once only, a moment of active and *living* love was granted to him; to this end he was given earthly life, limited in time. And that fortunate being rejected this inestimable gift, did not prize or love it, spurned it with irony and indifference. Such a being, having left the earth, looks into Abraham's bosom, converses with him, as we are told in the parable of Lazarus and the bad rich man; he beholds Paradise, can raise himself

LÉON BLOY: A STUDY IN IMPATIENCE

up to the Lord; but what torments him is precisely this, that he is there without having loved, that he comes into contact with those who have loved and whose love he has disdained. For he sees things clearly and says to himself: "Now I know; and, despite my thirst for love, that love will be worthless, will represent no sacrifice, *for earthly life is over*. And Abraham will not come to assuage—were it with but one drop of living water—my raging thirst for spiritual love, with which I burn now after having scorned it on earth. Life and time have run their course. I would gladly give my life for others, but *it is impossible, for the life which might have been sacrificed to love is over, a gulf separates it from my present existence.*"[1]

Whatever the subject of his meditation, Bloy never expresses himself completely in any other way than by the exegesis of a biblical

---

1. TRANSLATOR'S NOTE *on the quotations from Dostoevsky.*

    My own translation of these passages was made from the French version quoted by M. Béguin. I have since been able to procure Constance Garnett's translation of *The Brothers Karamazov* from the original Russian, and reproduce below her version:

    "Once in infinite existence, immeasurable in time and space, a spiritual creature was given, on his coming to earth, the power of saying, 'I am and I love'. Once, only once, there was given him a moment of active *living* love, and for that was earthly life given him, and with it times and seasons. And that happy creature rejected the priceless gift, prized it and loved it not, scorned it and remained callous. Such a one, having left the earth, sees Abraham's bosom and talks with Abraham as we are told in the parable of the rich man and Lazarus, and beholds heaven and can go up to the Lord. But that is just his torment, to rise up to the Lord without ever having loved, to be brought close to those who have loved when he has despised their love. For he sees clearly and says to himself, 'Now I have understanding, and, though I now thirst to love, there will be nothing great, no sacrifice in my love for my earthly life is over, and Abraham will not come even with a drop of living water (that is the gift of earthly active life) to cool the fiery thirst of spiritual love which burns in me now, though I despised it on earth; there is no more life for me and will be no more time! Even though I would gladly give my life for others, *it can never be, for that life is passed which can be sacrificed for love, and now there is a gulf fixed between that life and this existence.*"

symbol. What he had to say about Poverty he illustrated by bringing out the meaning which the words "Poor" and "Money" assume in the Scriptures.

Nobody—unless it be, once again, Péguy—has equaled Bloy in denouncing the modern scandal of Money and its lordship. Nobody has done more to show the baneful influence of the all-powerful metal, and he would have subscribed to these recent lines by Georges Bernanos:

> What shocks people in our social system is not—as they are reported to say and as they perhaps believe—the material power of Money; it is that Money has the air, not of a tyrant, but of a Master, and of a legitimate. Master, honored and blessed... It is the sight of Money, after all its sly or barefaced usurpations, gradually assuming the aspect of a moral and spiritual force...

And I think he would also have subscribed to the conclusion reached by Bernanos, who, for the same spiritual reasons as Bloy and impelled by the same urgent demands and the same hopes—as a Christian, in fact—likewise feels himself "in fellowship of impatience with the damned of this world."

> I have put my hopes in the hands of the rebels. I appeal to the spirit of Revolt, not through a blind, reckless hatred of Conformism but because *I would rather see the world risk its soul than deny it*. I do not expect the men of whom I speak to organize the future City, the New Christianity, but I hope that they will make it possible, by forcing the masters of consciences to answer, once for all, yes or no. *Our only chance lies in the kindling of spiritual forces*, no matter what hand applies the firebrand.

But Bloy was eager to press on beyond these indignations and impatiences to the secret source of hope from which the Christian feeds them. He went to the Scriptures for an explanation of the present power of Money.

He points out first of all that, in the Book, Silver currently means God, or "the pale face of Jesus"; that, more precisely, every word of revelation being a metaphor which stands for the Lord, this word is the symbol of the Blood of Christ shed upon the cross.

This parallel, not easy to grasp at first, becomes clear as soon as one remembers that Christ also identifies himself with the Poor Man. *Ego sum pauper.*

From this to understanding the earthly role of Money is but one step for a mind trained to discover on the plane of temporal history an exact analogy with the history of the Redemption, in all its episodes and all its meanings. Money is the blood of the sacrifice, poured out by the Poor Man, Jesus Christ, to redeem all, to pay for all. On earth it is likewise the substance of the poor, their life, their labor and their ruin, at the price of which the "consolation" of the others is purchased. The blood of the poor thus pays for this consolation—which, making the soul opaque to light, impenetrable to love, is the sin against the Holy Spirit—just as the Blood of the Cross redeems the sins of men. How is it, then, that Money, signifying in the Scriptures Christ and his blood, has become in time the cursed instrument of injustice?

Such is the series of symbols implied by the title of Bloy's book *Le Sang du Pauvre,* the immediate meaning of which is "money" and the hidden meaning "the blood of Christ." And such is the question he strives to answer in commentaries which, at first sight, may seem rather alarming. This, for instance, is the opening passage of the book:

> The Blood of the Poor Man is money. Men have lived by it and died of it for centuries. It expressively sums up the whole of suffering. It is Glory, it is Power. It is Justice and Injustice. It is Torture and Bliss. It is execrable and adorable, the flaring and flowing symbol of Christ the Savior, *in quo omnia constant.*

Revelation teaches us that God alone is poor and that his Only Son is the only beggar. *Solus tantummodo Christus est qui in omnium pauperum universitate mendicat,* said Salvian. His Blood is that of the Poor Man by whom men are 'bought with a great price'. His *precious* blood, infinitely red and pure, which can pay for everything!

It must perforce be represented by money, then; money that one gives or lends or sells or earns or steals; money that kills and brings to life like the Word, money that one worships, the eucharistic money that one *drinks* and that one *eats*. Viaticum of vagrant curiosity and viaticum of death. All aspects of money ate aspects of the Son of God sweating the Blood that takes everything upon itself.

Where is the way out of this series of paradoxes, which are not the dialectic of argument but the essential contradiction inherent in reality itself, the mere statement of which reveals the presence of a profound mystery? Can the mind of man ever be clear enough to do more than note the existence of this incomprehensibility? Is it forbidden to venture (as Bloy thought possible) a hypothesis which would resolve the contradiction?

For Bloy everything is explained by the fact that humanity has not accepted Salvation, and that the work of Redemption, completed in the *Consummatum*, nevertheless awaits its fulfilment in the course of the ages. In this world in which we live, from the time of the Cross and until man, in the Final Kindling, opens his mind to the absolute truth of the divine words, it would seem that "Christianity is in vain, the Word of God is in vain." We know Bloy's lament over this refusal which prolongs the sufferings of Christ in "the postponements of the Redemption," and his impatience for a catastrophe that will bring them to an end. But, with regard to Money, not content with renewing his lamentation and repeating the threats uttered at La Salette in the name of "heavy-handed" Justice, he has tried to understand how the stubborn mind of man had come to change the meaning of the sacred words to such an extent that Money, for instance, could, in the Scriptures, continue to stand for the Savior while assuming, in the life of the nations, the weight of a curse.

The reason is—according to one of Bloy's most cherished ideas, which recurs in connection with the People of Israel and throughout his exegesis of History—that to depart from Faith, the sole source of true understanding, means straightway to lose possession of the symbols. But, for a mind like his, which takes every assertion in its complete reality—as it were, in the absoluteness of its power to produce effects—this does not merely mean that the modern mentality has lost its ability to decode a symbolic language. Such an act of rejection, of incomprehension, is something more serious, affecting the very being of creation and of creatures more profoundly than a mere change of psychological attitude or a new orientation of thought would seem to do. Failure to understand the Symbol, that is to say the Word of God, cannot be an act without repercussions; for, by sealing the soul against light, and thus depriving it of Faith, which alone gives life to the spirit, this act *effectually*—and not just mentally—dissociates the symbol from what it symbolizes. A *real* cleavage takes place, a fatal separation of the one from the other. From the moment when Faith has been left behind, the symbol becomes impenetrable; in other words, it begins to exist on its own account and there is no possibility of passing through it to the reality to which it corresponds; then it is that the whole visible world ceases to show "the footprint of the Invisible" and begins an autonomous existence—a life without life—instead of deriving the fullness of its being from the fullness of its meaning.

That is what happens to money, as to all other symbols of God which have ceased not only to be understood figuratively but really to *be* symbols. Such is the power left to man's freedom. But man without faith, henceforth incapable of finding the reality hidden in the symbol—incapable of discovering God in his Word as well as in his Creation, nature or history—runs to what is now only a simulacrum and begins to worship it. Thus deadly idolatry is born.

ALBERT BÉGUIN

It is—the Gospel itself describes it—the act of Judas, who, losing the sense of the link which unites Christ to his symbol, money, leaves the One for the other and makes the tragic exchange of the Savior for the pieces of silver. He thus foreshadows what humanity will perpetrate when, forgetful of the symbolic relation, it has dissociated Money from Christ, seen in it no longer the symbol but the equivalent of God, and worshipped Money in itself, instead of beholding in it the mysterious "translation" of the Lord.

And since the time of Judas his sacrilegious act has been continually renewed. All the worship which the faithful devote to their God is now bestowed upon Money. It is revered, it is exalted and the colloquial expression "eating money" betrays the celebration of a satanic Eucharist. How is money eaten? Here it is necessary to revert to the transposition of all revealed truth to the human plane, and to remember then that, because it was the Blood of Christ, money is the blood of the poor. To "eat money" is tantamount to eating the substance of the poor, to devouring the poor themselves and feeding upon their sufferings in an anthropophagy beyond all bestiality.

This would make it easier to grasp Bloy's idea of the *deadly* part played by money and the reasons for his lifelong anger against a world which, by idolizing the pale simulacrum, confesses to what pitch it is carrying its denial of God. Here again what Péguy expressed in simpler language receives confirmation from Bloy in an exegesis which, by more abstruse means, arrives at the same conclusions. For Péguy money practices its black magic by tampering with the flexibility of the living life, opposing it as an agent of death, of "rigor mortis"; and a society which distributes savings-bank books to school children has chosen a fitting emblem, siding with death against life. In his *Note conjointe*, Péguy writes: "Just as the Gospels contain the whole of Christian thought, so the savings-bank book is the book which contains the whole of modern thought. It alone is strong enough to stand up against the Gospels, for it is the book of money, which is Antichrist."

LÉON BLOY: A STUDY IN IMPATIENCE

To this discovery of Péguy's, Bloy's thought serves as an extension inwards; for he defines the *life* which money kills. If Péguy's use of the word retains a suggestion of Bergson, for Bloy it means the life of the soul open to divine light and, at a deeper level, Him who said that he was "the Way, the Truth, and the Life." And this is clearly what Péguy had in mind when he gave the name of "Antichrist" to money, an influence of death reigning over this "modern world," its property, as he saw it, being to "debase everything."

―――・・―――

Nevertheless, Bloy's thought was destined to take a final turn thanks to which the dreadful logical development that had led him to condemn the whole contemporary world could end on a note of hope. This world may, indeed, yet be saved, for in it, side by side with those who "eat money" and devour the poor, there is still a "people of God." These chosen people of modern history are the poor, those who suffer as the crucified Lord suffered and who are near to Him through pain: those whose blood is consumed in a sacrilegious eucharist, those whose life is an involuntary but acceptable imitation of the Passion of Christ. Amid the horror of a world of denial, the poor have the advantage—even if they cannot *know* it—of being victims. In them, in their wretched daily lives and in their hearts, money has not become a simulacrum to which they burn incense. It has remained the living blood of these creatures of suffering and, despite their ignorance of symbols, it has thus kept its analogy with the Blood of Christ. Blessed are the poor, once more, for they escape death.

Under the date December 10, 1903, Bloy's diary contains the wonderful peroration to a lecture which he gave at a Christian workmen's club, a "little modern catacomb, *without a landlord*," as he calls it. In order to express what a living soul is, he has recourse to two of his favorite images, the furnace and the stars, which always mark the places where his thought runs deepest. And what he conjures up in this language of fire is precisely the fellowship established by intensity of *life* between all those who, thanks to poverty, happily escape that deadly hardening which overtakes men of money.

> ...In the olden days, more than three thousand years ago, the People of God were the Hebrew people... Since Jesus Christ, *we are the people of God, you and I, every one of us*; *you, the joiner; you, the locksmith; you, the clerk, the scavenger or the poet. It is everyone who is poor, everyone who suffers, everyone who is humbled to the dust.* They form a huge flock in the wilderness, an infinite multitude of sad hearts in search of Paradise. There are some who just manage to earn their bread, who never have an hour to cultivate their souls, and give it up in the end.
>
> Anyway, who is there to instruct them, guide them, encourage them? The clergy, of whom there are not enough, are mostly hopeless nonentities. As to the Léon Bloys, when there are any they are strangled and smothered, so that it is impossible to discover them and there is no means of hearing them. That leaves only the employers and the landlords. Frankly, it is not enough.
>
> Yet souls *do* exist! "You have been bought and paid for with a great price," said St. Paul. I should think so! It took no less than the blood of God! Those are things that we cannot understand. But what we very well understand is that nothing in the world or in hell would be capable of paying for our souls...
>
> Saints have declared that, if by God's permission a soul could be seen as it really is, this would mean instant death for us, as if we had been cast into a furnace or a volcano. Yes, *anybody's soul*, the soul of a bailiff, the soul of a concierge, would burn us up.
>
> Ah! Lord, what a sorry people of God! A strange and inconceivable people of God! A continual, universal procession, a stream of torches which outglow the stars and do not know themselves! Sirius, Aldebaran, Altair or that terrifying star of the constellation of Hercules, upon which our sun is rushing at

LÉON BLOY: A STUDY IN IMPATIENCE

a speed increased by several million leagues per second—stars like that, I say, absolutely shrouded in darkness, undetectable yet sure, since they all cost the blood of Jesus Christ: of such is the People of God. *Furnaces as big as worlds, but invisible, and unaware that they are furnaces...*

I have come to tell you that we are all of us extremely important underdogs, since together we are the People of God, not being landlords. But such language, of course, applies only to souls, and I naturally had yours in mind. Your souls! oh, my mind is always dwelling on those invisible furnaces! Ask the first bourgeois you come across. He will tell you that the serious thing in life is to fill your bellies. At that rate there is nothing serious about me and, I tell you frankly, I don't know how to talk to meat. You have just had proof of that.

All the difficult symbolism of money reappears, with a touch of satirical paradox which hides a very earnest purpose, in *L'Exégèse des Lieux communs*. The originality of this book has led to much misunderstanding, and some have given it their approval when it was better calculated to make them bristle. Bloy has chosen a peculiar method of casting in the teeth of the modern world its extreme spiritual penury. This world, as we know, is one whose vision is reduced to a single plane, one which neither perceives nor admits what lies beneath the surface, and which uses symbols without suspecting the depths of significance hidden in them. Men no longer realize how everything is linked together in the divine creation and linked a second time by the Incarnation, which has given all things visible their value. They have become incapable of discerning the chain of identities through which the least word spoken, however "meaningless" it may seem, is related to something far beyond its apparent purport. Thus the commonplaces uttered daily by the Bourgeois, for the expression of his pedestrian "wisdom," are vile in the sense in which he uses them and betray the utmost degradation of soul; but these hackneyed phrases bear another meaning, of which even those who employ them are profoundly ignorant; and, like all words, they remain charged with divine truth. The Bourgeois, without in the least suspecting it, continues to speak figuratively. All that he says about money, for instance, (and these particular maxims, which form the backbone of the "morality of the respectable," are naturally the most numerous in Bloy's *Exegesis*) is repulsive when taken, as the Bourgeois takes it, in its literal sense; but it becomes luminous and full of windows upon Mystery as soon as one recalls that money stands for God. "To eat money," "Money has no smell," "You can't live without money," "You don't throw money out of the window," "I don't spit on money" are so many disgusting phrases which Bloy interprets in their symbolical acceptation for the confounding of those who utter them.

Two of these commentaries, taken from the first series of "Commonplaces," may be emoted here. They will serve to illustrate that spirited and robust side of Bloy's character to which this survey hardly does justice. First of all, "*You can't live without money*":

> In-con-tes-ta-bly. It is so true that, if you have no money, you are forced to take other people's. That can, moreover, be done in a very fair and honest way.
>
> "I don't force anybody," a money-lender at one hundred and fifty percent remarks affably, "but I run risks and *money has got to work.*" To live without money is as inconceivable for this just man as to live without God for a hermit of the Thebaid. And both of them are right, since their object is *identical*, inexpressibly IDENTICAL.
>
> Having already abundantly proved that it is impossible to live without eating, it is almost superfluous to demonstrate the vital necessity of money. "Eating money!" the fathers of families howl in chorus. What a flash of light that metonymical phrase is!
>
> Well, what could one eat, just tell me that, if one didn't eat money? Is there anything else that is edible in the world? Isn't it as clear as day that Money is that very God who wants to

be devoured and who alone keeps us alive, the Bread of Life, the Bread that saves, the Wheat of the Elect, the Food of the Angels, but, at the same time, the hidden Manna which the poor seek in vain?

It is true that the Bourgeois, who knows nearly everything, does not penetrate this mystery. It is also true that the meaning of the words 'to live' is not clear to him, since the money without which he magnanimously maintains that one cannot live is, nevertheless, for him," a question of *life or death…* Never mind. He has it, and that is the main thing. If he does not himself eat it, others will eat it after him, that's certain. But when he utters these formidable words, I defy him not to resemble a true prophet and not to proclaim God with infinite force. *Trahitur sapientia de occultis.*

And here is another passage in which Bloy is still more successful in making everyday words give up all their hidden meaning: "*Money does not make men happy, but…*":

This is a first-class commonplace, which calls for one of the confidants of ancient tragedy. Someone should add immediately: "But it contributes to it." Then it would be perfect.

That humble contribution, so happily tempering the melancholy harshness of a confession which might be considered blasphemous, should be singularly efficacious. It is like sugar to the conscience or balm to the heart.

"Yes, it's true," the Bourgeois muses profoundly, "money does not make men happy, especially when it is not there. It almost does so, undoubtedly, but not quite." Something is lacking, everyone has to admit, and it is infinitely sad to witness this impotence of money, which ought to ensure the felicity of those who worship it, since it is truly a God.

I have more than once pointed out that silver, significantly depreciated in our day, is, in the Bible a, clearly identified symbol for the suffering Word, which is the Second Person of the Holy Trinity, the Redeemer. Thus, to say that it does not make men happy is, for a Christian, an assertion which is bold to the point of impiety; and, indeed, this commonplace is of Christian origin—I find proof of this when so grand a style is watered down to make God *contributory* to the mirth of fools.

A pagan would say straight out: "It is money that makes men happy," and he would be dreadfully right. But you, vile Bourgeois professing yourself a Christian, you upon whom all the symbols of divine Life die like pearls on a leper, you who undoubtedly think that a five-franc piece is blessed, why lie about it? What can you be frightened of? Your incomprehension of prophetic Likenesses is unfathomable and you are not the one to be afraid that, by dint of calling upon Money, you will conjure up the bleeding Face.

Bloy's Diary and other works contain many passages in which his denunciation of the scandal of money is simpler, more direct. First of all, there are those in which he depicts his own misery, and, less well known but extraordinarily powerful, those in which, describing contemporary society, he voices his indignation less against the inequalities of fortune than against a certain refusal to *see* and to love, to which "good works" usually serve as a hypocritical screen.

Among these avenging passages few are so legitimately violent as that chapter in *Le Sang du Pauvre* called "Le Système de la Sueur" (*The Sweating System*). Bloy recalls the labor of children in industry during the last century, and this time the strength of his tenderness is not to be denied He had meditated long upon this deepest abyss of social injustice; yet even in this martyrdom of childhood he still found a confirmation of blessedness through poverty and suffering:

The evangelist St. Luke heard the Sweat of Jesus Christ as it were great drops of blood falling down upon the ground. This

LÉON BLOY: A STUDY IN IMPATIENCE

faint sound, incapable of waking the sleeping disciples, was to be heard by the most distant stars and was to have a strange effect upon their wanderings. What are we to think of the sound, fainter still and much less heeded, of the numberless feet of these poor little children going to the task of misery and suffering exacted from them by accursed scoundrels, yet, without their knowing it and without our knowing it, going in this way to their elder brother of the Garden of the Agony, who calls them and waits to take them in his bloodstained arms? *Sinite pueros venire ad me. Talium est enim regnum Dei.*

Is this resignation? It would be a great mistake to think so. Bloy may marvel that so much pain suffered unjustly brings the victims nearer to the Crucified and opens for them, in advance, the kingdom of God. But on the human plane he cannot contemplate without fury the idea that there are people who justify such atrocities, and learned theorists who codify them into *systems*. Thus, it is in this same chapter that he becomes most threatening and that his impatience is ready to sanction mutiny:

> *The most incomprehensible thing in the world is the patience of the poor*, dark and "miraculous" verso of the Patience of God in his mansions of light. When suffering has gone too far, *it seems as if it should be a simple matter to fell the savage beast or disembowel it.* There are precedents. They are even numerous in History. But these revolts were always convulsive, short-lived movements. Immediately after the paroxysm, the Bloody Sweat of Jesus began again silently in the night, under the quiet olive trees of the Garden, the disciples still sleeping. This Agony of his has to be continued for so many unfortunates, for such a number of defenseless beings, men, women, and especially children!

Bloy, moreover, had had an opportunity of observing a society which had tried to remedy these social ulcers. This was in Denmark during his visit there in 1899–1900. He came back appalled, and his diary of that period preserves the memory of his quivering indignation. The social conditions of that "advanced" country made him shudder with apprehension, for it had not taken his prophetic eye long to divine that the Denmark of 1900 foreshadowed the future towards which materialist civilization was necessarily tending, with its inhuman "order," its disguised injustice and all the shams of its moralism. How can we, in our turn, help being *frightened* by Bloy's prescience, when we read the description he gave, forty years ago, of Danish institutions and ways? How can we fail to recognize in it our own portrait or that of one or other of the "Europes" of tomorrow of which we are offered blueprints, the idea being that we should pay for them with streams of blood?

How big with terrible warnings is this picture of a society which seems organized for the sole purpose of replacing all relations of neighbor to neighbor by the administrative operation of "social welfare" and mechanized "good works." At one end of the social chain, he who possesses—and for whom this fact of possession already represents the dangerous "consolation" that obscures his vision—is a man whose conscience is easy. He prides himself on not being unaware that life is a struggle for many of his fellow men, though he is reluctant to admit that "want" still exists "in our times," after all that has been done to get rid of its awkward presence. He gives part of his income to relieve the afflictions of distant, somewhat mythical beings who are said to be suffering from that suspicious lack of money which is generally due to failure, laziness, insubordination to established laws, or wanton waywardness. Having been to school, he emotes the grasshopper of the fable... But he is not without benevolence. He gives, then, at the beginning of each month (working out his budget "to the last farthing") he makes out a dozen postal orders for the benefit of "recognized charities," which, by way of reminder and to give him the illusion of having "got something for his money," send him a booklet, a calendar or a packet of postcards. Two or three times a week his doorbell rings and a lady in a dowdy hat hands him

LÉON BLOY: A STUDY IN IMPATIENCE

a collecting book, in which, conscientiously, he inscribes his name and the amount of his mite, before going back to his business, rubbing his hands with satisfaction at having done a good deed. Sometimes he puts on his best clothes to attend a "charity entertainment" (an expression which makes only a few rebels like Léon Bloy stamp with rage); on Saturdays he walks about displaying in his buttonhole some new gewgaw the school children have sold him, so that the passersby can see how open-handed he is. The horrible thing about this organized "charity "—but a thing which no longer seems to strike anybody—is that this man never sees the "predestined victims of disinheritance" whom he is "helping." Actually, he does not *give* anything, for the whole affair is confined to a series of money transactions. He does not know what the recipients of his almsgiving look like and thus forgoes the bond which true charity would create between him and them. He declines the present which the poor man could make to him: shielded from the spectacle of the "longing of the poor," he takes care that boundless distance and the precautions of a shocking hygiene separate him from his neighbor. For he is anxious to preserve himself from a contagion which he dreads more than anything—the contagion of suffering.

But at the other end of the chain, he who receives assistance is equally cheated of his privilege, which is to receive from others real charity, the personal gift, the love alone capable of appeasing his hunger, of satisfying his longing. Were he to receive their help, he would then have the joy of *giving* to others that love of which both have need and which would link them together in the closest fellowship. But he is not allowed anything save *money*, which is anonymous and lacks humanity; a thing with a purely material value, abstract and impersonal. And, since no money is given without something in return—for that would be "throwing it out of the window"—he is required to give in exchange all that he has left. They demand an increasing part of his *liberty*, laying down the law as to how he should live, making out his budget, blaming him for all "unnecessary" expenditure, keeping an eye on his behavior.

They open his cupboards in order to count his shirts and make up the correct number; they organize his leisure, his holidays and his children's upbringing; while their mania for teaching, their pride in imparting instruction, is the crown of this interference with individual initiative. And the worst of it is not that a fussy society thus encroaches upon the freedom of the poor, but that the poor take it lying down and let themselves be treated like minors.

Between these two men, the one who "gives" and the one who "receives" (it being impossible to say which suffers the greater frustration of all the best in him) nothing passes but miserable money in infinite isolation from all living creatures. And all this happens in the midst of a strange euphoria, made up of satisfaction on the part of officials whose administration "works well" and vanity on the part of countries which have "got rid of poverty."

The indictment which, following in Bloy's wake, the reader is led to bring against this dreadful travesty of charity does not, of course, mean that society, as a body, should cease to take an interest in distress or that it should not do all it can in the way of alleviation. But nothing is more deadly than those palliatives which aim, not at saving the poor from want, but at maintaining the social order—that is to say the "established disorder "—by suppressing the poor man, because he is a ferment of revolt. Such cold beneficence is the result of an exact calculation; it is not *for* the poor man but *against* him, against the danger he represents.

In truth—and here we come back to Bloy's profoundest idea—this flight from one's neighbor is nothing else than a flight from God: when we avert our eyes from the poor man and seek to get rid of him, we are in reality excluding by a double and triple cordon Him who was the only absolute Pauper. More than anything else the man in comfortable circumstances dreads having to *love* his neighbor and to love God in his creatures; he thrusts far from him the mystery of the existence of the poor; he refuses to face it because he is still aware that it is the mystery of life itself, the unique mystery of the Fall, of the Redemption, of Penitence and Hope.

LÉON BLOY: A STUDY IN IMPATIENCE

Once again Dostoevsky offers a confirmation of Bloy's whole train of thought. He too saw that the modern world may be summed up by its refusal to love. He too understood that, at the bottom of this refusal, there was first of all the unintelligence of the. "intelligent": their inability to see the concrete reality of persons who thus became an object of horror to them in the end. Bloy teaches that this incapacity, which condemns the whole of modern life to the growing tyranny of the abstract, has come from the separation between visible symbols and their invisible significance. Man no longer loves men and no longer loves God because he no longer *sees* them. And, conversely, he refuses to see them because he no longer wishes to love them. So it is Ivan Karamazov, the "rebel," the intellectual, who makes the plainest confession of a fear of charity, and who presents the exact programme of contemporary society when he sneeringly observes:

> I have never understood how one could love one's neighbor. To my mind, one's neighbor is just the one person whom one cannot love; at any rate one can only love him at a distance... A man must be hidden for one to love him; as soon as he shows his face, love disappears... In my opinion the love of Christ for mankind is a sort of miracle impossible on earth. To be sure, he was God: but we are not gods... *Beggars, particularly those with any fine feeling, should never show themselves* but should ask for alms through the advertisement columns of the newspapers. In theory one can still love one's neighbor; at close quarters it is practically impossible.

II.

For Bloy the exegesis of the destiny of Israel was closely connected, with the doctrine of Poverty. To Bernard Lazare, who had just been reading *Le Salut par les Juifs*, he wrote in 1892: "You had the power to see that the Poor Man was the nucleus of my thought, the adored captive in my lonely tower. That, indeed, is all I have to say."

Le Salut par les Juifs is the most difficult of Bloy's works because, as he himself observed in a letter dated November 9, 1907, it is "less a book than the outline of a book," or, as he said to Raïssa Maritain on September 25, 1905, the *Salut* represents, "in surprisingly small compass, years of work, prayer, and suffering out of all proportion."

It should therefore be borne in mind by the reader that Bloy does not set out to give a complete explanation of the mystery of Israel and of Christian doctrine on this point, but, "in small compass," in miniature, a necessarily groping translation of his own inward experience in regard to that mystery. The book is not a theological dissertation, careful and precise in all its terms, but a cry of love, which, being the human expression of very recondite truths, must often content itself with approximations or with hyperboles substituted for things that cannot be known.

Thus all kinds of precautions are necessary if we are not to lose sight of Bloy's real intentions, for even the least prejudiced mind might be led astray by his methods. Of none of his books was he so proud as of this, "the only one," he said, "that I should dare to present to God without fear." And in a number of letters, addressed to Rabbi Zadok Kahn, to Bernard Lazare, to Moses Ballin, and to Raïssa Maritain, he repeats that the book is "assuredly and incontestably the strongest and most magnanimous thing that has been written *for* the Jews, in the Christian world, since the eleventh chapter of the Epistle to the Romans." Thus the anti-Semites have scarcely ventured to avail themselves of those passages in Bloy's works which might be made to serve their own ends; he had shown too clearly how far he was from sharing their standpoint.

The circumstances in which Bloy made up his mind to write *Le Salut par les Juifs* are themselves rather illuminating. The infamous campaign of a man like Drumont had shocked him, not so much in itself as because of the appalling ease with which it won the approval of the pious.

LÉON BLOY: A STUDY IN IMPATIENCE

Don't run away with the idea that my new book, which I shall soon have finished, is a polemic, a counter-blast to Drumont... It has nothing to do with that gentleman. But *I was enraged to see this vast question of Israel dragged down to the level of the most sordid financial investigations* and I wanted to speak, too, and say what nobody else seems able or bold enough to say...

Those who look for me on the side of the Jews will be making a mistake; those who look for me on the other side will be making a mistake; and those who look for me between the two will be making the biggest mistake of all.

As might be expected, Bloy does not stop at a humanitarian protest against Drumont's coarse accusations. As soon as he begins to handle such a subject, he comes into his own, that is to say he gives his mind solely to revealing, by exegesis of the Scriptures and by meditation, the fact that, where there seems to be a "problem" to be solved, there is *a mystery* to be detected. Thus he adopted a method which consisted in going to the extremes of antithesis, in first of all bringing the contradictory aspects of reality face to face, in order to lay bare the truth that is not in either of these aspects but in their irreconcilability. On January 28, 1906, he wrote:

In '92 in consequence of a resounding scandal engineered by Monsieur Drumont, I wrote *Le Salut par les Juifs*, from completely disinterested motives, although I was harassed by want, my sole object being to serve justice and glorify God, whose promises to Israel are *in aeternum* and cannot be expunged. This book, conceived in the spirit of the oracles of the Scriptures, had to go to the heart of things, or fail completely. Thus I was constrained to adopt the method recommended by St. Thomas Aquinas, which consists in *exhausting all possible objections before summing up*. An excellent method, of great philosophic fairness, but one which put me out of court with the very people whom I set out to honor as, I think, no Christian had done for nineteen centuries. They would not look beyond my premises, *failing to observe that the violence of those premises was calculated to give the utmost* force to my conclusions.

The "premises" were the present state of the Jewish people; the other side of the antithesis consisted in the irrevocable promises with which that people had been favored; the conclusion was to be a demonstration of the fact that the same nation could remain "chosen," the bringer of Hope, while falling to the lowest depths of degradation. More than that: Bloy set out to prove that this degradation is, in some sort, the confirmation of the ancient promises, the sign that they have not *been* withdrawn. At the time when he was writing his book, in June 1892, Bloy made this quite plain:

> *To express my contempt* for the horrible traffickers in money, for the sordid, poisonous Sheenies who sicken the universe, *but at the same time to express my profound veneration for the Race* from which Redemption came forth (*Salus ex Judaeis*), which, like Jesus himself, visibly bears the sins of the World, *which is right in awaiting* its *Messiah*, and which has been preserved in the most complete ignominy only because it is invincibly the race of *Israel*, that is to say of the Holy Spirit, whose exodus will be the triumph of Degradation. What a subject!

There is a masterly summing-up of the whole book in the 1905 preface, written for that second edition which was a present to Bloy from his young friends Jacques and Raïssa Maritain. These lines do not affect the text of the book, which Bloy left as it stood; but they bring out the central idea more clearly and dispel the uneasiness which some of the existing chapters might legitimately arouse:

> Leaving on one side the question of supernatural inspiration, it may be said, without any doubt, that *Le Salut par les Juifs* is the most forcible and urgent testimony by a Christian in favor

LÉON BLOY: A STUDY IN IMPATIENCE

of the Eldest Race since the eleventh chapter of *Saint Paul to the Romans*.

"If the fall of them," says the apostle, "be the riches of the world, and the diminishing of them the riches of the Gentiles, how much more their fullness? If the casting away of them be the reconciling of the world, what shall the receiving of them be but life from the dead?"

From its first line, *Le Salut par les Juifs*, which might be taken for a paraphrase of this chapter of St. Paul, points out that the Blood which was shed upon the Cross for the redemption of humanity, like that which is poured out invisibly, every day, in the Chalice of the Holy Sacrament, is naturally and supernaturally *Jewish Blood*—the immense river of Hebrew Blood which has its source in Abraham and its mouth in the Five Wounds of Christ.

And that is all. There is nothing more to know.

Without ever losing sight of that passage from St. Paul, apart from which there is no valid interpretation of the destiny of Israel, Bloy thus proceeded by way of a double exegesis: exegesis of Scripture and exegesis of the facts of History, which confirmed each other as the two languages of one revelation. The greatness positively promised to the Jewish people in both the Old and the New Testament and the ignominy into which that people has fallen in the course of modern times—both these mean precisely the same thing, in a strange correspondence of the "abyss above" with the "abyss below." In order to see this, all that is needed is to take the standpoint of the Absolute, the only one of which Bloy's thought is cognizant.

Thus from the outset he dissociates himself from those advocates of the Jewish cause who have nothing with which to confront persecution but an ideal of earthly equality and human justice, and a horror (perfectly legitimate, praiseworthy and even indispensable) of all discriminative laws applied by men to men. Those who put their trust in that humanitarian ideal necessarily begin by denying any difference between nations; while Bloy, as may be seen from a later chapter, considers that each nation in history has received a vocation peculiar to itself, and that the differences between them, far from being inauspicious human inventions, are *facts* which have their meaning in the book of revelation by Time. Incidentally, it happens only too often that the champions of this justice of non-discrimination, not very sure of their initial assertions, make hypocritical concessions to modern anti-Semitism; there is, they say, a Jewish question, a problem posed by the existence of this wandering ethnical minority; in the life of the nations the scattered Jews are an embarrassment which should be neutralized by judicious legal measures; perhaps it would not be wrong to admit, for this one nation, that there is such a thing as a "national spirit," which is a spirit of negation fraught with dangers…

To which Bloy, to which any Christian, could reply: the Jews in their present state, with the particular spirit that many of them hawk about in the midst of the nations, cannot be harmful except in a dechristianized or falsely "Christian" world, which confronts them, not with robust faith, but with the feeble barrier of legislative and police precautions. They are "destroyers"? True, but only in so far as they resemble us, only in so far as they symbolize—the more patently *because* they remain the Chosen People—our own despiritualization, vociferating more violently a refusal which is that of the whole of mankind, in its common disobedience. And here, as with regard to money, Bloy's ideas closely correspond with the finest words that have ever been written about the Jews—Péguy's lines in *Notre Jeunesse*:

> In normal times the people of Israel are *like any other people*: all they ask is that the times should not become *abnormal*. They know too well the cost of being the carnal voice and the temporal body… They have so often *paid for everybody, for us*… Do not let us exult over them. How many Christians have been driven with whips along the path of salvation!…

LÉON BLOY: A STUDY IN IMPATIENCE

Israel's unmindfulness of the prophets is equaled only by sinners' unmindfulness of the saints. It may even be said that the unmindfulness of Israel *stands* for the unmindfulness of sinners.

Bloy's "premises" are thus taken from his observations on the present misery of the people of Israel. But in reading his account of this decline and fall, in which he does not mince matters, it should not for one moment be forgotten that he is working towards a conclusion which he looks to the Scriptures to furnish. Without reproducing the violent language of the terrible opening chapters of *Le Salut par les Juifs*, one might sum them up as bringing out three facts.

The first is the *separation* of Israel. This people has a destiny apart, and the most objective historian is forced to recognize it. Dispersed among the settled nations, it is the only people that has never found assimilation possible, that keeps its own way of life; and no economic, ethnical or rational explanation has ever succeeded in throwing light on the very obscure causes of this separation. It must be accepted as a "datum" against which no effort of human justice, no universalism avails. But let there be no mistake: that can never justify anyone in rejecting or condemning the Jews "as such." This paradox finds its expression in a striking passage from Bloy's pen:

> Meanwhile I maintain, with every fiber of my being, that a synthesis of the Jewish question is the height of absurdity, failing acceptance of the so-called "Prejudice" which sees in Jacob *essentially a branch broken off*, relegated to the most abject decrepitude, without hope of compromise or return so long as his "Messiah" has not come down to earth in a blaze of glory… I know quite well that, strictly speaking, the Israelites can be called our "brothers"—on the same score, I fear, as the plants and animals so designated by the seraphic Saint Francis, who never made a mistake. But to love them as *such* is a proposition

from which nature recoils. *It is the miraculous super-display of the most transcendent sainthood or the illusion of an imbecile religiosity.*

The last sentence of this quotation deserves to be underlined, for it is of the utmost importance: to love the Jews on the natural plane, without motives of charity which are explicitly Christian, is a deficient action and, therefore, from Bloy's absolute standpoint, abhorrent, like any other act uninspired by faith—so much for the humanitarian conception, which remains extraneous to the mystery of Israel. But mark what follows: love for the Jewish people may be "the miraculous super-display of the most transcendent sainthood," which surely means that such love is difficult, heroic, a triumph over all kinds of deep-seated repugnances. But it means, above all, that here we have the charity necessarily instilled into one whose understanding has gone beyond appearances and penetrated to the discovery of the secret to which the Scriptures so plainly point: a secret revealed, in particular, by Saint, Paul, but, like every saying in the Sacred Book, accessible only to eyes made clear by Faith.

The second fact is the extraordinary *vitality* of this dispersed people. Not only is it a race apart, but there is in it a staying power, an internal resistance, thanks to which, through century after century of persecutions, massacres and exoduses, at the lowest ebb of material wellbeing, *it* has still been able to keep alive. Any other people condemned to such a precarious existence would go under; this people does not fall to pieces. Thus it is something unique in the whole course of history: a people whose destiny seems to flout the laws governing the life of nations. Here again, the human standpoint is confronted with an entirely inexplicable phenomenon, and once more there is nothing for it but to assume the presence of a mystery.

This conclusion is corroborated by Bloy's third fact—the strangest of all if taken in conjunction with the election of Israel: it is the present *degradation* of the Jewish people. Vitality and ignominy, Bloy describes them both with an amazing vigor:

LÉON BLOY: A STUDY IN IMPATIENCE

The history of the Jews obstructs the history of the human race as an embankment obstructs a river, to raise its level. There is no moving them and the only thing one can do is to jump over them, which will cause a certain amount of commotion without any hope of demolishing them.

It has been tried often enough, hasn't it? And the experience of some sixty generations is unimpeachable. Irresistible conquerors undertook to wipe them out. Multitudes, outraged by the Affront to the Living God, threw themselves into the slaughter. The symbolic Vine of the Testament of Redemption was tirelessly stripped of these noxious parasites; and this people, dispersed among twenty peoples, under the merciless tutelage of several millions of Christian princes, fulfilled throughout the ages its iron destiny, which simply consisted in not dying, in always and everywhere preserving, through squalls or through cyclones, the marvelous handful of "heavy water" which it believes to be the Fire of God (2 Maccabees 1).

That nape of the disobedient and the perfidious, which Moses found so hard, has wearied men's fury like an anvil of stubborn metal, wearing out all hammers. The sword of Chivalry was notched by it and it shivered the finely tempered blade of the Moslem chief, to say nothing of the cudgels of the mob.

Thus it has been abundantly proved that nothing can be done and, considering what God puts up with, it is surely fitting that religious souls should ask themselves, once and for all, without presumption or foolish rage, and face to face with the Darkness, *whether some mystery, calling for boundless worship, is not, after all, hidden beneath the unparalleled ignominy of the Orphan People, which, though condemned at all the assizes of Hope, will yet perhaps have the right of appeal, on the appointed day.*

Of this degradation Bloy has given us a highly colored picture: that of three old Jews he saw one day in Hamburg, bending over a sack filled with refuse, their sordid faces betokening the lowest depths of vileness and cupidity. And the gulf which opens before the mind that seeks to compass both the divine promises and the actual course of Jewish history is suggested here by an astounding hypothesis: may not these disgusting ancients be the great patriarchs of the Bible, Abraham, Isaac, and Jacob, living on into the modern world and taking on *its* most repulsive aspect? But who is responsible for their abasement? The patriarchs reduced to this appalling misery, or the world which, refusing salvation through nineteen centuries, has brought them to this pass (which does not alter the fact that it was the Jews who were guilty of the first refusal)?

Thus for the third time Bloy's meditation ends on the dizzy brink of an unfathomable question. What, then, is the meaning of this unparalleled, infinitely tragic destiny and this unprecedented fall? Bloy tries to find an answer, not by investigating the material "causes" of these incomprehensible facts, not by carrying on the arraignment of Jewish disobedience, but by listening to the revealed Word. He does not stop at quotations and paraphrases, however; after his usual manner, he selects—as every Christian actuated by love has the right to do, provided he does not claim to be propounding a theological explanation, which by its nature would need to be a complete one—he selects from this particular mystery of Israel what corresponds to his own inward experience, what is illumined by his personal orientation as a seeker of the absolute and a lover of God, and what, in return, throws some light upon the cardinal convictions of his religious life.

The segregation and the survival of Israel actually remain incomprehensible only for those who keep within the purview of human deductions; for anyone willing to take his stand on the perfect logic of a Christian interpretation of history, they become luminous facts.

The "breaking-off" of the Jewish branches, the subsistence of that people in a state which has no resemblance to that of any other nation is preposterous until the truth dawns that this people can only have been set apart *with a view* to some role which it is one day destined to play, at a particular point in the scroll of time. Saint Paul is perfectly explicit on this subject: the Jews are being kept in reserve for the hour of their final conversion, which will be the last and will not long precede the glorious advent of the Holy Spirit; thus, *mirabile dictu*, the history of Christianity is literally subservient to that conversion and is taking place solely *in order that* the Jews may "lay down their arms" to the Messiah whom they disowned. Their separation is thus the normal extension of their election, and by their mysterious survival they are ordained once more, for those with the eyes to see, as the abiding beneficiaries of the most extravagant promise.

At this point it should be noted that Bloy does not take the whole text of Saint Paul's epistle. He contents himself with stating briefly, in a solemn reminder at the beginning of his book, that "salvation comes from the Jews" because the Prophets of the Old Testament spoke from out of their midst, because Christ chose to put on their flesh and sent into the world apostles of that nationality, so that, for the first time, "thanks to their fall, salvation came to the Gentiles." Their obstinacy in not recognizing the Messiah was necessary to enable the Christian gospel, escaping from the closed circle of Israel, to come to the ears of all mankind. With his eyes steadfastly fixed on the future, Bloy merely takes note of these "past" facts; he is well aware that the downfall of Israel has been the "riches of the nations," but he hastens on to what concerns the future, to the "fullness" promised to the Jews, to the receiving of them, which, according to the Apostle, is to be "life from the dead." And, while it is possible to take these words in the sense of a renewal of souls in the course of history, which would not necessarily be the final sign heralding the End of Time, Bloy can and will accept only one interpretation: that according to which the conversion of the Jews is to take place on the eve of the Catastrophe which will set a term to temporal history. That it could not be otherwise is clear when we recall what living love gave direction to his thoughts, turning them immediately towards everything that seemed to portend the time when, after so many postponements, the Messiah would "come down to earth in a blaze of glory." Admittedly, in the impatience of his desire, he throws circumspection to the winds; but is he not profoundly right to seize upon every possible image suggested by his reading of the gospels, that others may be kindled with this same desire, which he feels a special "mission" to proclaim? A mission, moreover, on which he never prided himself, but which he felt had been forced upon him by the progressive stages of his inward life and by the very peculiar course that the "conquest of his identity" had taken. One thing, at any rate, is certain: he never speaks in any other spirit than that of obedience and with the sole purpose of expressing his love and the way in which he had been "dazzled" by the glimpse vouchsafed to him of the Mysteries of the faith. It should also be borne in mind that, in relation to Israel as to every other subject, all that he cares about is to throw as much as he can on the unique mystery of the Salvation brought to sinful mankind by Christ crucified.

The infinite suffering of the Jews, since the worst of treatments has failed to destroy them, inspires Bloy with as great a compassion as Péguy's, whose profound pity speaks, for instance, in the assertion that this people "has not a place on its body that is not bruised." Bloy goes much further in his amazement at this suffering; but because he is trying to look beyond it for such spiritual light as it conceals, he may at times seem more impassive. Moreover, he sees the whole Jewish destiny, with its long train of miseries, moving in the van of an immense Hope. If the Jews have resisted for centuries, bowing their backs beneath the brutality of their enemies, submitting to the worst with a disarming stubbornness for which some have the heart to reproach them, it is because this interminable chastisement is preparing them to resume, at long last, their

LÉON BLOY: A STUDY IN IMPATIENCE

place as the chosen people. For God's undertakings towards them are so explicit that he *is now unable* to accomplish the work of Salvation without the assent of this Race of races. In an unforgettable passage of *Le Sang du Pauvre,* Bloy resorts once more to his favorite image—that of human tears transformed into heavenly constellations—in order to express the depth of Jewish affliction and what it means:

> The Jews are the eldest of all and, when things are in their right place, their proudest masters will feel honored to lick the feet of these vagabonds. For everything is promised to them and, meanwhile, they are doing penance for the world. The right of primogeniture cannot be cancelled by a punishment, however harsh it may be, and God's word of honor is unchangeable, because "the gifts and calling of God are without repentance." It was the greatest of converted Jews who said that, and those implacable Christians who propose to perpetuate to all eternity their reprisals for the *Crucifigatur* should remember this. "Their crime" (it is again Saint Paul speaking) "has been the salvation of the nations." *What extraordinary people are these, of whom God asks permission to save the human race, after having borrowed their flesh, the better to suffer? Does it mean that his Passion would not satisfy him if it had not been inflicted upon him by his well-beloved, and that any other blood than Abraham's would not be capable of washing away the sins of the world?...*
>
> The Jew is essentially proletarian. But the proletariat—like tears—is something common to all people and to all times. *Only, Jewish tears are the heaviest. Theirs is the weight of many centuries... And now these precious tears are in the scales of the Judge of human sorrows, who is no more a respecter of peoples than of persons.*
>
> When the Father wishes the Eldest Son to take his proper place again, I picture *the most splendid night illumining the*

banquet, the tender crescent moon marking the-place of the Holy Sepulchre and the tears of all the poor shining intermingled, unimaginable, in the vault of heaven!

At this point, however, we should be on our guard against a possible confusion of thought. Not that there is anything in Bloy to provoke it; but in these days no interpretation is too fantastic to be entertained... If Bloy recognizes that persecution has a kind of "justification" in the divine plan, because it constrains the Jewish people to keep alive in abnormal circumstances, to survive with difficulty until the time comes for the promises to be fulfilled, this is no excuse for the persecutors. The inherent greatness of Poverty will not serve to whitewash those who are resigned to the misery of others, nor will the hidden meaning of the Jewish martyrdom exculpate the men who are bent on aggravating it. Their action, in the modern world, is so utterly vile that they can urge nothing by way of justification but "questions of brass." And the horror of our times is precisely this: that the one real question, the question of the salvation of souls and of the final consummation, has become that wretched thing—the "Jewish problem." What makes this state of affairs so frightful, so unbearable to think of and so incessantly productive of crying injustice, is the very fact that all, *persecutors and persecuted alike,* are equally blind to the true reasons; equally obtuse, equally incapable of any symbolic understanding of what is happening and any insight into the Revelation. In a world which has lost the power of grasping any but the most material explanations, and of obeying any other commands than those of brutish instinct, the enemies of Israel hunt it down as a foreign body which is a constraint upon their appetites and a rival in their avidities. But what is even worse is that the victims, forgetful of their great destiny and of the Promises made for the day of "their fullness," are now fighting for nothing but their physical existence or for the things they have acquired—their power, their wealth. Under the lash of the tyrant an outcry rises from their ranks; but it is the clamor of a herd whose animal life is threatened. What a falling-off, when one thinks of the purposes for which this people was endowed with such a vigorous instinct of self-preservation! Ignorant of those purposes, ignorant of its sacred difference, all it now thinks of claiming is *the same* right to existence as anybody else, wholly oblivious of the mysterious reasons which would enable it to understand and shoulder (not merely endure) its strange destiny.

Even more distressing than the intolerable injustice of arbitrary violence, this opacity of soul on both sides makes the present pogrom the truly vile thing it is. But who would dare to adopt Bloy's standpoint, when his clear-sighted judgment of the victims runs the risk of presenting the persecutors with the windfall of fresh arguments? One jibs at the improper use which might be made of these mortifying truths, so easy to distort for the purpose of adding still more crimes to the sum total...

Yet, if Jewish degradation is all too glaring, there is at least this to be said for it: that it is a consequence of the Promise which it cannot destroy, and that it is continually being "paid for" by great suffering. Never for one moment should the fact be overlooked that, though conspicuously shameful as the infidelity of the Eldest Race, it still remains a *type* of the general disgrace. The infidelity of the "Christians" must necessarily be still worse. The Jews are reproached with the inauguration and practice of trade in its present form. Why bear them a grudge for what is calmly tolerated on the part of business men calling themselves Christians? Bloy deals with this question in *Le Sang du Pauvre*, and his virulent answer chimes with a celebrated passage in which Péguy recommends an ingenious way of countering the temptation to anti-Semitism. The very simple treatment he prescribes can be carried out in a single day during which the patient has to ask himself, of every act he sees done by a Christian, "What would people say if a Jew did that?" And Péguy declares that by the evening of this well-spent day the patient would be completely cured. Bloy is still more categorical:

Looked at from above, trade is a veritable sacrilege. The Jews, the Eldest Race, beside which all other peoples are as children, and which have consequently had the opportunity of going much further in the direction of evil than other men in the direction of good—out-and-out Jews must feel that this is so. They are the fathers of trade as they were the fathers of that Son of Man, their own purest Blood, whom, by divine decree, they had to buy and sell upon a certain day. Their racial neighbors, the Carthaginians of Carthage, lost ancestors of the Carthaginians of England, must have been good pupils of the Jews. This is no disparagement of them. *When the time comes for their conversion, as has been foretold, their commercial capacity will likewise be converted. Instead of selling dear what has cost them little, they will give freely what has cost them everything. Their thirty pieces of silver, imbued with the Blood of the Savior, will become as thirty centuries of humility and hope, and this will be beautiful beyond all imagining.*

To fall from that into modern trade is a frightening thing, enough to disgust one with life and with death: Much has been said of the vileness of the Jews. This refers, of course, to the trafficking Jews, the dregs of Jewry, leaving out of account the very noble individuals who have been able to keep a proud heart, a "truly Israelite" heart under the terrible *Velamen* of Saint Paul. In what does this famous vileness exceed the servility with which the most supercilious shopkeeper treats a customer presumed to be well off, and, his caddish insolence towards another customer thought to be poor? If it be granted that outwardly their despicable attitude makes them equals, *there will always be, even at this level, the infinite seniority of the Chosen Race and the immense pre-eminence of twenty centuries of very carefully recorded humiliations. Jewish vileness may call down the thunderbolts; the commercial vileness of the Christian can only attract showers of spittle and excrement.*

LÉON BLOY: A STUDY IN IMPATIENCE

But the argument of *Le Salut par les Juifs* relies on a more complex exegesis, of which only the less abstruse points will be dealt with here, namely Bloy's exposition of his views on the symbolism of money and the mystery of Poverty. Some of the other ideas set forth in this book of his call for examination in the light of an exact theological knowledge which the present commentator does not presume to claim.

Bloy finds that the Jews, by refusing to recognize the Messiah, were the first to separate Money from the Poor Man, to isolate the symbol from what it stands for (from *the One* it stands for) and to worship the simulacrum because they had become dead to the Reality. They have thus made themselves the lawful heirs of Judas and re-enacted the apostate's appalling exchange of his Lord for pieces of silver.

They had crucified Christ, but that was only the first act of their crime. For since then, through the ages, they seem to have been obsessed by their own desire to exterminate the Savior. Ignorant of the reality, however, all that they now know of him is the simulacrum—Money, which has become their idol. So they relentlessly persist in crucifying it "in order to fulfil their destiny and not to wander about the world without a calling," and "because it is the Jewish habit to exterminate what is divine." But, Bloy returns, what can possibly be meant by that phrase "to crucify money"? "Why, it means to *raise* it on a gibbet like a thief; to set it up, *to place it on high, to remove it from the Poor Man*, whose very substance it is!" In other and more commonplace words, the Jews put temporal possessions in the place of spiritual and give the simulacrum the honors reserved for Our Lord.

Henceforth the scission is complete: Money and the Poor Man go their separate ways through history.

> The death of Jesus essentially separates Money from the Poor Man, the symbol from the symbolized, in the same way as the body is separated from the soul in ordinary death.

ALBERT BÉGUIN

> *The universal Church born of the Divine Blood had the Poor Man for its portion, and the Jews, segregated in the impregnable fortress of a stubborn despair, kept Money*, the pallid silver scratched by their sacrilegious thorns and dishonored by their spittle, as they would have kept the corruptible corpse of God unburied, that it might poison the universe!

This apportionment was the beginning of a disastrous breach; if the Jews had the misfortune to keep only the symbol emptied of its substance—Money without the Messiah, without the Poor Man whom it represents—and thus fell into idolatry of matter, Christendom has not got its due, either. For, though it may have kept the Poor Man, it is only too obvious, from the actual treatment inflicted on the poor by Christians of modern times, that they too have fallen. Nothing will be re-established until the day when the symbol and what it stands for are reconciled and reunited: that means, on the one hand, that the reunion of the Synagogue and the Church, the receiving of the Synagogue into the Church, will be the only valid sign of the fulfilment of the Redemption, delayed by the treachery of Judas, Jewish idolatry and "Christian" disobedience, so that the conversion of the Jews really *is* the consummation towards which the whole history of Christendom should be directed, as was announced by Saint Paul. But this, again, means, in a more concrete way, that the end of time will not come until everything is ready for the Advent of the Holy Spirit and the Holy Spirit will not be able to come down into men's souls until the new identity of the symbol and its meaning shall have become a reality in each of them, without exception. Or, if that mode of expression is still too obscure: when souls, through love, regain the ability to understand symbols, this new clear-sightedness will be paramount, just as the breach created by human incomprehension was fatally effective. Let our eyes once be opened and Money, as well as the rest of the symbols, will again coincide with the Christ they all represent; the fall will be retrieved and the work of Salvation, now fully effectual, will put an end to temporal history. Such will be the consequences of the conversion for which a seemingly relentless fate is preserving the Jewish people, in its separation and its misery.

Whatever emendations may be called for in these apocalyptic pages of Bloy's, especially as regards that perfect coincidence which he forecasts between the time of the conversion of the Jews and the Parousia, it should be noted that his interpretation is, first and foremost, an expression of the feelings which governed his inward life. Because it gives him pain to think of Christ's Passion continuing from moment to moment, he tries to understand what sin of mankind's is delaying the "descent from the Cross," and everywhere he looks for allusions or signs giving hope of a Reconciliation. But, while stressing this impatience and this very manifest orientation of Bloy's thoughts towards the End of the Passion, it should not be forgotten that he is at the same time a man who unreservedly accepts suffering, a worshipper of Calvary who "always sees Jesus on the Cross and cannot see him otherwise." If the desire of his heart invokes (with what fervor!) a triumph in Glory and perfect light, his way of explaining History and his personal life both show quite plainly that he was not unconscious of Christ's Kingship established in the world *here and now*: the reign of the Crucified in suffering hearts, through suffering itself. It would not be going too far to say that, from the beginning to the end of his work, with the help of exegeses "in miniature" and of extraordinarily arresting images—whatever may be the ostensible theme of his meditation—he has, by his own confession, never done anything but "repeat the same thing." This one and only thing is that feeling which was stronger in him than in anyone else, and which he ascribes to the men of the Middle Ages: the feeling of being "continually present at the death of Christ," the feeling that the Passion is always "happening now."

⁂

Towards the end of *Le Salut par les Juifs* the exegesis delves into very mysterious depths, in a succession of chapters which can only be described as *blinding,* since it would be impossible to analyze their strange analogies without venturing into regions still shrouded with an impenetrable veil. It should be recalled once more that, from the time of Véronique's predictions, Bloy lived in the conviction that human history was literally the history of Christ upon the Cross, and that this agony would end with the advent of the Holy Spirit. He had Saint Paul's word for it that, if the crime of the Jewish people was, and remained, the delaying of this consummation by its disobedience and by its refusal to understand, only the conversion of the Jews would un-nail Christ from the Cross. Thus the final establishment of the Kingdom depends upon their goodwill. Meanwhile their inaction is *immobilizing* all the incidents of the Passion, which continue to take place *now* Peter's denial, the kiss of Judas, the suffering, the humiliation, the agony, the whole drama in its smallest details repeats itself indefinitely, "paralyzed by their will."

The Jews have become "the gaolers of the Redemption." But that does not make them strangers to the Cross; on the contrary, its mark is upon them just as much as upon Christians and the whole of mankind. As Bloy says, in a striking metaphor, "they bear its image *scooped out* in their ravaged souls." This mark, indelibly set upon them, is comparable with the cavity hollowed out in the hearts of the poor by their very poverty. It is a "gaping impress" which, like the longing of the Poor Man, they foolishly try to fill up and assuage with Money, but to which some day, when their eyes have been opened, they will bring the true resource of Love.

That is why Bloy says, so strangely, that the Jews *are right to wait for* THEIR *Messiah.* Not, indeed, that they deserve approval, for having failed to recognize the incarnate Christ; but, convinced that he is still to come, they do not see that it is towards the Holy Spirit that their hope is really turned. It is not the coming of the Messiah that is expected and announced, as, in their blindness, they persist in believing. It is the final fulfilment of the Redemption by the triumph of the Holy Spirit, which, since Pentecost, has been wandering about the earth, an eternal mendicant, brought so low that it must needs

LÉON BLOY: A STUDY IN IMPATIENCE

groan, turned into a suppliant by man's refusal and in particular by the infidelity of the Jews.

This interpretation—this image—brings us to one of the knottiest points in Bloy's message. Despite his repeated protests, some people have persisted in seeing in it the announcement of a new divine incarnation, of a "third age" on earth, to be inaugurated by the act in which the Third Person of the Trinity will become flesh. And it must be admitted that certain of Bloy's expressions, by their boldness and their difficult symbolism, might suggest something of that kind. In reality, he had recourse to these terms—which became ambiguous only if isolated from the rest of his work—in an attempt to express more vividly the stupefaction that besets the mind when it tries to imagine the unimaginable End of Time. No word in any earthly language is adequate, and once again the deepest mystery can be suggested only by images which do not denote the thing itself but arouse something of the Astonishment it will create when it bursts forth before all eyes. Bloy gives it to be understood that the Redemption will fulfil itself by an operation *in men's souls*, which will all be set on fire at the same time by the love of God. When he speaks of the coming of the Holy Spirit, he tries, as far as possible, to suggest this inward operation, this "conflagration," which at long last will offer the world to its Savior. And, although the center of Bloy's thought is obviously elsewhere, projected, as it were, into the future, I do not think that his constant prophecy of a final state in which men's hearts will be completely possessed by the Holy Spirit is incompatible with a full consciousness of what Pentecost implied. He is not unaware that, since the first "Whit-Sunday (of which we only know that he was unable to imagine it, to *see* it, with the same intensity of concrete vision as he saw the Glory to come) the Holy Spirit has been present in men's souls and in history—but with a presence so often, so sadly unrecognized. The spectacle afforded by the mentality of today, and especially the "Christian" mentality, would not have caused Bloy such intense pain, bordering on anger, had he not found it particularly shocking that things should be thus *after* the Comforter had come down from Heaven.

But, narrowed down in this way (and, so far as can be judged by the aid of a certain familiarity with Bloy's metaphorical language, I do not think that any of his writings contradict such a view), that great impatience of his which, in an aberrant but ardent form, he thinks he has rediscovered in the Jews, is nothing else than eager Hope, turned towards the future. The Jews thus appear not only as the people of the Promise, whose past, bound up with the history of God, commands respect—this greatness of Israel is known, or should be, to all Christians—but they are also the vessels of Expectation. And it is here that Bloy discovers one of the reasons why, in spite of themselves, they continue to be associated with the fate of Christendom. It is repeatedly said of this dispersed and derided people that they are unquiet, the people of disquietude, and no more just reproach is brought against them. Jewish disquietude disturbs the quietude of the other nations, who only want to be left in peace and earthly security. But Péguy knows that it is also a ferment, tiresome no doubt, no doubt assuming detestable forms arid modes of expression, and yet creative when it "grafts itself" on the Christian soul. The restlessness of the Jew—indifferent to his present destiny, incapable of taking root, incurably nomad, and turning every house into a tent in the desert—is it not, without his knowing it, the impatience of an eternal traveler, ignorant of his true destination, but at least conscious of being "on the way"? People of disquietude and longing, they live in a state of expectation without seeing clearly what they are waiting for; but this does not prevent them from keeping alive that single-minded orientation of their whole being towards the fulfilment of promises—that attitude which Christians call hope. They long for the end of time, as we should all long for it if we were not so easily contented with this imperfect world. And, apart from the role which, according to the Scriptures, they will then be called upon to play, they have this immediate function of carrying disquietude with them, importunate and even hateful though

LÉON BLOY: A STUDY IN IMPATIENCE

they often make it (for with it they corrode the most sacred things of this world), and upholding it through the ages, whereas too many Christians let this great Longing perish within them.

I shall make no attempt to sum up the final pages of *Le Salut par les Juifs* where Bloy ventures very far into the contemplation of the mystery of Israel and tries to communicate a sense of its uttermost depths by a series of parallels between wandering Israel, "absent from everywhere," and the Holy Spirit, which has itself become "the Stranger in all habitable places," and then between Israel and "the Cross on which is nailed the Salvation of the world." These sumptuous pages should be read in full, and any paraphrase would, I fear, inevitably sacrifice some of the meaning which Bloy's own words alone can convey.

From these pages, however, it may be seen that the destiny of Israel, like all the other outward subjects of Bloy's books, merely provided him with a means of approaching certain spiritual profundities which it is difficult to make intelligible in any other way than by images, themselves mysterious. As we know, his sole aim was to produce *the sensation of mystery*, of its ineffable presence; and it would be rash to set about the divestment of such a *text*. At all events, only attainments as dazzling as Bloy's own would warrant such an undertaking.

It is surely wiser, since Bloy has shown us the true nature of the Jewish problem (which he, more than anyone else, has brought back to its proper plane), to see what lessons we can draw from it.

The first and most obvious is that this problem is absolutely insoluble so long as men try to propound it without reference to what the Scriptures reveal on this subject. This means that it is, in the strict sense of the term, a *mystery*.

A mystery does not call for solution but for contemplation and for a capacity to feel astonishment. Bloy's whole book aims at arousing this in the reader. But then it is not his concern to propose measures for assigning the Jews their rights in human society and determining the extent, or even the legal existence, of those rights. To anyone questioning him on that subject he could make only one reply: that the destiny of Israel, its adversity, its tears, its embarrassing presence amongst us and the cruelty of our conduct towards it cannot be remedied by any legislation, since this people's vocation of misery is the consequence of its disobedience and the terrifying aspect of its election. A distress which has such origins cannot have any other end than that announced by Saint Paul. If that is no excuse for persecution and does not absolve anyone from seeking to relieve the misfortunes of the poor Jews who have been shamefully treated; if compassion for them remains an imprescriptible duty; if we should exert ourselves to combat injustice because *"we are always on the right side when we are with those who suffer persecution"*—all this does not alter the fact that it is hopeless to try to solve the "Jewish problem" by earthly justice and by mere goodwill between men.

But—I think the foregoing analyses show this—the Christian has no call to judge the Jew for his disobedience, or to be indifferent to his fate. There is a close connection between the Jew's destiny and the Christian's; it is the *same* history, proceeding from the same fall, through the same consequences, to the same conclusion. It is not merely that Israel has a place at the beginning of the Christian era—since God chose Jewish blood to redeem sin—and at the end of that era, since the "fullness" of Israel will consummate the Redemption. But, in addition, the destiny of the chosen people, because it is conspicuous, serves as a striking *image* of the destiny of all of us, the one in which the secret of that destiny is most legible, both in its overwhelming adversity and in the dazzling promise of the End. The Jews should be dear to us in their abasement as in their impatience, for both are, as it were, an infinitely magnified representation of our own spiritual misery and our hope.

Bloy accepts this solidarity and this resemblance in all its implications; hence he cannot escape the conclusion that the disobedience

LÉON BLOY: A STUDY IN IMPATIENCE

of the Christians will, in its turn, provoke a catastrophe which, even if of short duration, will stand comparison with the long and lamentable errancy of Israel.

> Do you not see that, *here and now*, we are fellow-guests at the same banquet of turpitude, and that the day of reckoning has the same whip for both of us?
>
> All the time that they have been teaching you, have not your learned doctors understood that the two whoring sisters of whom Ezekiel speaks have outlived Jerusalem and Samaria, that they still flourish in the perpetuity of the symbol, and that their names today are Synagogue and Church?

"*Here and now*": no phrase of Bloy's throws more light upon the sense in which he continually speaks of apocalyptic events, whether it be the great Apostasy predicted by Saint John or the Coming of the Holy Spirit. True, he places them at the end of time; but, with his keen sense that all moments of history are simultaneous and that all Symbols have a possible application to the various ages which we believe to be successive, he is not unconscious that the Holy Spirit which was to come has already come, and that the great apostasy of the Christians and its terrible punishment, announced for a future time, have already begun. We know, indeed, that this was the cause of his constant distress and his worst rages. Thus too literal a meaning should not be attached to the succession of the ages, to which such and such a passage seems to refer; nor is there reason to be shocked when he speaks of the present unworthiness of the "Church." It is abundantly clear that, when, in profound consciousness of the common infidelity of Jew and Christian, Bloy places the Church on the same footing as the Synagogue, he is once more expressing his grief and pain at the state of the *Christian world*, but in no way doubting that, in the midst of the worst apostasy, the Church remains intact, despite all appearances and despite the blindness of the very ones who are authorized to speak in her name.

ALBERT BÉGUIN

The greatness of Bloy lies in his impatience, and his most abstruse prophecies have no other meaning than this: *here and now*, on equal terms with the Jews, whom we have no warrant for accusing, we are in the phase of disavowal; but, *here and now*, we are saved—that is to say, we have entered into the Kingdom of Glory which is promised to us.

Léon Bloy's thoughts on Israel are summed up in a wonderful letter which shows how far he is from any kind of anti-Semitism. This letter—written on January 2, 1910, to an unknown lady who seems to have been an assiduous reader of the "orthodox press" and to have let herself be carried away by the disciples of Drumont—is illuminating on all these points. It seems to me that anyone who, having read the sentence to which I have given special prominence, can still find excuses for anti-Semitism, must confess that he is actuated by the basest motives:

> ...I tell you and I tell the whole world that there is now no way of escaping the *punishment*, and it is quite conceivable that it will begin this year. I have long been preparing myself for martyrdom. I am preparing my daughters for it, and I am absolutely convinced that there is nothing else to be done. No more is forgiveness possible, nor, it may be, any respite to be hoped for. Two crimes, two outrages have filled up the measure, irreparably. These two heinous crimes are something quite modern; they are peculiar to our age and have never been seen before.
>
> The first is known to you. It is the crime of formal, complete disobedience to Our Lady of La Salette—disobedience which has turned into hatred, and what hatred on the part of most of the members of the Clergy.
>
> Of *the second of these crimes*, contemporary with and mysterious consequence of the first, you are unfortunately only too ignorant. It is called anti-Semitism, *propagated* first by Drumont and then by the Fathers of the Assumption. Since this idea is new to you, I shall try to make myself intelligible.

LÉON BLOY: A STUDY IN IMPATIENCE

How would you feel if the persons around you continually spoke of your *father* and your *mother* with the greatest contempt and had nothing but insults for them, and outrageous sarcasm? Well, that is exactly what is happening to Our Lord Jesus Christ. People forget, or rather they do not wish to know, that Our Lord, made man, is a Jew, the Jew *par excellence*, the Lion of Judah; that his mother is a Jewess, the flower of the Jewish race; that all his ancestors were Jews; that the apostles were Jews, and so were all the prophets; and that the whole of our sacred liturgy is taken from Jewish books. Then how is one to express the enormity of the outrage and blasphemy that consists in vilifying the Jewish race?

Formerly the Jews were detested, they were massacred on the slightest provocation, but they were not despised *as a race*. On the contrary, they were feared, and the Church prayed for them, remembering that Saint Paul, speaking in the name of the Holy Spirit, had promised them everything, and that one day they were to become the stars of the world. *Anti-Semitism, a quite modern development, is the most horrible buffet that Our Lord has received in his Passion, which is still going on; it is the most outrageous and the most unpardonable because he receives it* ON THE FACE OF HIS MOTHER *and from Christian hands...*

The *Advocate of the Holy Sepulchre* in Le Sang du Pauvre seems to you "disconcerting"; you are surprised to see a Christian book "end with the apotheosis of a Jew." Well, how do you want it to end? It was the inevitable ending since the God that we worship is a Jew. What I have just written to you, my dear friend, is not a sophistry; it is the essence, the true essence of Christianity.

Moreover, in writing a book about the Poor Man, how could I fail to speak of the Jews? What people is so poor as the Jewish people? Oh, I know very well there are the bankers and the speculators. Legend and tradition would have it that all Jews are usurers. People refuse to believe anything else.

And that legend is a lie. It applies only to the dregs of the Jewish community. Those who are familiar with them and look at them without prejudice know that these people have another side and that, bearing the misery of all the ages, their suffering is infinite. Some of the noblest souls that I have ever met were Jewish souls.

The conception of the Church at all times has been that *holiness is inherent in this people*—exceptional, unique and imperishable, guarded by God, preserved as the apple of his eye, amid the destruction of so many peoples, for the accomplishment of his ulterior purpose. The very abasement of this Race is a divine Sign, the clear sign that the Holy Spirit is brooding over these men, who, so despised now, are destined to appear in the Glory of the Comforter, at the end of ends.

CHAPTER III

The Symbolism of History, and the Soul of Napoleon

———◆◆———

"The visible is the footprint of the Invisible."

I.

Léon Bloy was a born historian. His first book, a meditation on Marie Antoinette (*La Chevalière de la Mort*, written in 1877 and published in 1891), affords a vast synthetic view of the eighteenth century; the second, *Le Révélateur du Globe* (written in 1879 and published in 1884), took up the story of Christopher Columbus, as treated by Roselly de Lorgues. Then came *Le Fils de Louis XVI* in 1900, *L'Épopée byzantine* in 1906, *L'Ame de Napoléon* in 1912, and *Jeanne d'Arc* in 1915, not to mention the important chapters on the Middle Ages in *Le Désespéré* and *La Femme pauvre* and on contemporary history in *Sueur de Sang*, *Celle qui pleure*, *Le Sang du Pauvre*, and Bloy's diary. None of these works is based on personal research, Bloy being content, as a rule, to take his facts from some professional historian, on whose findings he built up his commentary. Roselly de Lorgues, Gustave Schlumberger, and Henri Houssaye supplied him with material which he did not subject to any criticism, merely taking leave to understand it after his own fashion. His personal sources were much the same as those which Péguy turned to for his *Jeanne d'Arc*: "the catechism, the sacraments, Mass, vespers, the benediction, the breviary, the liturgy, the Gospels…" It will doubtless be objected that recourse to such sources is admissible only for the medieval period—on analogy with Michelet, understanding Joan of Arc thanks to having studied the "Imitation." But Napoleon? And the French Revolution?

To this objection Bloy would have made exactly the same reply as Péguy: "All temporal ages are ages of Jesus… Since Jesus, all temporal ages have been the same, have been one and the same age, of the same infinitely profound nature, literally of the same eternity." That is what Péguy wrote to Monsieur Laudet.

And now Bloy: "Time is an imposture of the Enemy of the human race, driven to despair by the perenniality of souls. We are always in the fifteenth century, as in the tenth century, as at the central hour of the Immolation on Calvary, as before the coming of Christ. We are actually in each fold of the multicolored apron of Ancient History."

Péguy again: "Christendom is one in time, Christianity is one, the Church is one, the Communion is one. That is why the Christian has no need, no need at all, to go in for an archaism of soul…"

And Bloy again: "Events are not successive but contemporaneous in an absolute way: contemporaneous and simultaneous, and that is why prophets are possible. Events unfold themselves before our eyes like an immense canvas. Only our power of vision is successive."

Péguy: "For us Christians, sainthood and the supernatural are the things that make history, the only history that interests us, perhaps the only profound and profoundly real history, and it is all the rest that we should be more inclined to regard as legendary."

Bloy: "History is the unfolding of a web of eternity before eyes that are temporal and transitory."

LÉON BLOY: A STUDY IN IMPATIENCE

The dialogue between Bloy and Péguy on this point, as on so many others, reveals a fundamental agreement, and yet the paths which lead to these parallel assertions, and the ways in which they are applied, differ by the whole distance that lies between two human styles, between two "identities" (to use Bloy's word) and two personal vocations.

What they have in common is, above all, the absolute point of view, which, in Bloy as in Péguy, opposes the modern notion that there is a radical difference between the ages, and substitutes for it an idea that had long been lost: that of successive ages considered as mere *versions*, different but concordant, of one single, eternal and perpetually present fact. For the cardinal point for both writers is the certainty that there has never been more than one Fact worth knowing: the fact of the Incarnation, already *present* before the coming of Christ, and present since then at every moment of human history. "*All ages are ages of Jesus*" and there is nothing else to be known.

But if Péguy, a "Bergsonian" philosopher, analyses with matchless penetration the subtle and paradoxical relations of eternity and the temporal, if Péguy, the poet of Eve and her descendants, discovers that the temporal fidelities of men are "a first attempt and training" for eternal fidelity, and genuine acts of imitation of Jesus Christ—Bloy, applying to history the exact exegetical methods which serve to decipher the written Revelation, attempts to *read* events as a text of divine inspiration.

For Bloy was no commonplace historian! The knowledge to which "objective" and "scientific" historical learning attains came in for a criticism at his hands which is no less just and no less violent than Péguy's celebrated pamphlets, and which, though based on quite different references, often coincides with the latter.

Like Péguy, Bloy had a very keen sense of human ignorance, and of the narrow limits of the "knowable" in the midst of the inexhaustible shifting complexity of the "living." Confronted with history, imagined in its unthinkable totality, we are condemned to the same unknowingness as in face of the Word of God. The historian, like the exegetist, is obliged to confess straightway that he has only rare glimpses of an immense impenetrable reality. Bloy writes ironically: "It is shattering to think how much you have to learn in order to be able to state with authority that you know nothing or next to nothing of the events you have set out to relate!"

We grasp a few isolated facts, and that in itself is something of a miracle; but others, perhaps more important and fraught with more lasting consequences, elude us. They remain profoundly *hidden*; not merely lost, forgotten, extinguished in human memory through the destruction of such records as might have perpetuated them, but actually *imperceptible* to us from the time of their happening, and not to be revealed until, endowed with "our real eyes," we behold the beatific vision. The true hierarchy of facts in the plan of Providence is not more known to us than our personal "identity," and it is of the same order; for what is important in both cases is the multiplicity of relations which, across time and space, weave from soul to soul the "web of eternity." As Bloy expresses it in *L'Épopée byzantine*:

> There is no doubt that prodigious events have been completely, I will not say lost, but *hidden*. How much or how little that distresses us depends on what God has put in our hearts and on our conception of history. We are not entirely ignorant, however. There is no longish period about which at least a few facts are not known—and that may count as something of a miracle where the waves have swallowed up so much. Supposing there was a whole century of which we knew absolutely nothing? What should we think, for instance, if the history of France broke off suddenly, inexorably, at Malplaquet and began again with the return of Napoleon's ashes, without even the possibility of a hypothesis to shed light upon the gulf between? Well, that would not affect the Divine Life which is the one and only history; nor would it affect the intangible conviction that, being made in God's "image," we are destined to know

LÉON BLOY: A STUDY IN IMPATIENCE

everything. *All* that has taken place on earth will come before our eyes at the proper time, before our real invisible and imperishable eyes, and it will be a dazzling effulgence of Paradise to know at last why certain things were not shown to us. It is probable that every day we pass by the Tree of Knowledge of Good and Evil without evening seeing it; and that is assuredly an inestimable boon.

Since the number of facts is infinite, and infinite to the ramifications by which they are linked to one another in an unrecognized coherence, the historian of any period can never embark upon anything but an incomplete work, cut out in arbitrary fashion from the untearable fabric of history as a whole. This is tantamount to saying that he undertakes work which is false from the outset, since the threads attaching one event to all the rest have been slashed at random and replaced by a simple, linear causality which is a pure creation of the historian's mind. Taking no account of true causality, which is unknowable, divine, non-temporal, this kind of fragmentary history can only suppose that pseudo-freedom or senseless chance directs the affairs of this world in place of Providence. Such history is "a mirror for stupid pride in that freedom which perpetually plumes itself on having done as it pleased—never anything else." Thus Bloy gives a superbly ironic description of the historian's task in that chapter of *Le Désespéré* in which his double, Caïn Marchenoir, outlines the symbolic interpretation of it:

> Hypothesis said to Conjecture: "Let's have some fun!" So they got a stark naked old lie to caress them on the yielding couch of Criticism. The amazing highway of history was all crossroads, with weathercocks for signposts, on which unreliable dates pointed the way towards a few carriage-road events along the tiniest non-existent paths leading to impossible verifications. Erudition loaded the shelves of Alexandrine libraries for the sustenance of innumerable rodents in spectacles, whose job it

was to pilfer wisps of straw from the enormous heap of documentary dung excreted by larger animals, while religiously denying themselves even the velleity of arriving at a conclusion.

But what is the cause of this impotence? In order to remedy it, need we do more than improve on methods hitherto inexact and accumulate verifiable details until in the end they add up to impeccable knowledge? Is the dimness of historical learning simply due to the fact that the recording machinery is not yet all it should be?

Bloy is very far from the optimism which supposes that knowledge of details will one day culminate in knowledge of the whole. He knows too well that there is no hope of really grasping any detail unless one has *first* pierced to the Centre of all things. The obscurity of history is a natural obscurity, Having its origin in the very essence of time, and in the present state of humanity. Each minute, as soon as it has been lived, falls into an abyss, and time is made up of the swarming of these minutes, flashes of lightning in a vast night, too swift and too numerous for our "tortoise" pupils to catch their coherence:

> As history unrolls, it immediately becomes God's secret, and authenticity, even at its most convincing to the thinker, is no more than a *probable* opinion. However well documented he may be, a historian, having painfully fished up the fact before him like a bit of wreckage from the dark depths, knows quite well that *he does not see it.* For a large number of historical events, at clearly determined points of time, there are sure and incontestable proofs; but these proofs are, at bottom, based on nothing more substantial than the absolute necessity of such events and such dates. IT HAD TO BE SO and not otherwise. That is the sole criterion.

Things have been thus since the Fall, forever since then mankind has been fast asleep. What has been lost is the clear vision of

LÉON BLOY: A STUDY IN IMPATIENCE

God, which alone would have enabled man to keep "awake"; in other words, still able to *see* his own "identity" (his place in the divine plan, the name by which he is really called) and at the same time to see the whole of creation, which must be grasped in its entirety before there can be any real perception of particular things. One of the finest passages written at the end of Bloy's life (1917) magnificently expresses the sense of that illusion which human life is and remains, and our ignorance of what is really happening:

> We are sleepers haunted by faint pictures of our lost Eden; blind beggars on the steps of a sublime palace, whose doors are closed. Not only are we unable to see one another, but we cannot identify our nearest neighbor by the sound of his voice.
>
> "Behold thy brother," comes the injunction. Nay, Lord, how am I to recognize him in this indistinguishable throng? And how can I know if he resembles me, since he is made in thine image, as I am, and I do not know my own face? Until it shall please thee to wake me, I have only my dreams, and they are sometimes dreadful. How could it be more difficult for me to get things clear! I believe in material, concrete, palpable realities, tangible as iron, incontestable as the water of a river, and *an inward voice from the depths assures me that these are only symbols*, that my body itself is only a semblance and that all that surrounds me is an enigmatic semblance too.

Such is the depth of human night, in which none knows either his own face or the meaning of visible realities that seem to him self-existent and self-sufficing, whereas they are semblances and symbols of another unknown reality. But, over against this illusion, which has the "incoherence and measureless distortion of all dreams," Bloy evokes the perfect clarity of these same appearances in the sight of God: "While men toss and turn in the visions of sleep, God, alone capable of action, really does something. *He writes his own Revelation in the appearance of the events of this world*, and that is why what is called history is so utterly incomprehensible."

The word has been uttered: *Revelation*. History, in its obscurity, is a discourse pronounced by God, perfectly transparent in itself but beyond our power to unriddle save very imperfectly. Yet what seems to us inextricable chaos is the work of divine hands; this thing whose baffling temporal nature dismays us is a work of eternity as well. Every detail of this revelation, albeit so incomprehensible to our intelligence, is a *figure*, and one in which superhuman attention would discover a very precise meaning. But how are we to become capable of even a first weak step in that direction?

In each of his "historical" books Bloy tried to make out something of the hidden meaning of earthly events, considered as symbols by which God is addressing his creatures and making use of their destiny to reveal himself to them. On more than one occasion he set forth the principles on which he thought that such a bold venture might be based. The clearest passages written by him on this subject are to be found in *Le Désespéré*, in which he makes his hero, Caïn Marchenoir, conceive the idea of "enfolding the history of the world in a single embrace," and discovering a key that would unlock the secret of this "Revelation by means of symbols, which corroborates the other Revelation." Like Bloy himself, Marchenoir was initiated into the exegesis of the Scriptures by a priest, in whom it is not difficult to recognize Abbé Tardif de Moidrey. And it is this cleric's precepts that inspire him to go beyond the usual paltriness of human reflections upon history:

> The first idea came to him in the course of those exegetical studies which, with a singularity perhaps unparalleled, were the starting-point of his intellectual life, immediately after his conversion. Relying upon Saint Paul's sovereign assertion that we see everything "through a glass darkly," *this absolute mind had been led by the symbolism of the Scriptures to the firm conclusion of a universal symbolism*, and he had become con-

vinced that all human actions, of whatever nature, contribute to the infinite syntax of an unsuspected and mysterious book which might be called the *Paralipomena* of the Gospel. From this point of view—very different from that of Bossuet, for example, who, disregarding Saint Paul, thought that everything is made clear—universal history seemed to him a homogeneous text, very close-knit and vertebrate, with well-defined bone structure and highly dialecticized, but completely enveloped and shrouded. And what had to be done was to transcribe it in a grammar that could be grasped...

It is not surprising to find that the same image of the *book*, composed of the disorder of human history and ultimately composing the perfect order of a holy scripture, occurs in Claudel, whose *Soulier de Satin* had the very object of raising the confused web of earthly destinies to its true meaning as a discourse of God. And, he adds (faithful in this to the teaching of the Revelation of Saint John), this discourse will not be fully understood until it has been completed:

> What do the disorder and suffering of today matter, since they are the beginning of something else, since
> Tomorrow exists, since life goes on, using up with us the great reserves of creation,
> Since the hand of God has not ceased its movement, which writes with us upon eternity, in short lines or long,
> Down to the commas, down to the most imperceptible dot,
> *The book that will make sense only when it is finished.*

Thus history is considered as a Revelation which confirms the Revelation of the Scriptures. I know what difficulties such a thought must hold, not only for the modern mind unpracticed in reading symbols and mistrustful of any appeal to mystery, but also for a believer disposed to regard the Revelation as unique. For the idea which Bloy adumbrates here is much more complex and much bolder than Bossuet's "Providential" explanation, to which he alludes. He is not content with asserting that the Divine Will is present in Time and directs the course of the ages according to a pre-established plan. That sort of intervention by Providence, so easy to discover, seems to Bloy too one-dimensional, and too manifestly acceptable to the unaided human reason, to account for the mysterious depth of things. It is a notion that does not sufficiently blind the mind and is, for that reason, deceptive. Bloy tries to go deeper, to a conviction calculated to cause alarm, especially among those who cling to the uniqueness of the Revelation by the Scriptures as the only communication from God to men which has ever crossed the abyss, cleft by the Fall, between Grace and degenerate Nature. Let us make an effort, then, to come to grips with Bloy's thought. It is at the heart of his spiritual life.

It may be said, I think, that in his view the history of mankind is not merely a confirmation of God's designs and a language used by Him for speaking of Himself in terms which, while differing from those of the Sacred Books, repeat their exact meaning. Bloy goes so far as to suggest that this history is strictly *the same* as that which is narrated in the two Testaments—foreshadowed in the Old, explicitly described in the New, and taken up again in the course of earthly events; it is the only history, the sole Event that has ever really happened. All the rest can be nothing more than a figurative representation of the history of God, made man and shedding his blood upon the Cross to redeem the sins of his creatures. It is history which a few lines of the Creed, suffice to record: *Qui propter nos homines et propter nostram salutem descendit de coelis. Et incarnatus est de Spiritu Sancto ex Maria Virgine: et homo foetus est. Crucifixus etiam pro nobis: sub Pontio Pilato passus, et sepultus est. Et resurrexit tenia die, secundum Scripturas, et ascendit in coelum: sedet ad dexteram Patris. Et iterum venturus est cum gloria judicare vivos et mortuos. Cujus regni non erit finis.*

This sole Event—comprising, it would seem, a past, a present, a future and an eternal consummation—took place only once, on one

LÉON BLOY: A STUDY IN IMPATIENCE

irreplaceable occasion, preceded, however, by its announcement by the Prophets. Temporal history is, as it were, another form of prophecy, which, according to the changing aspects of time, is at once prior to, simultaneous with, and subsequent to the Event that it records. Thus the same Drama was first lived in the thirty-three years of the Life of Christ—then coming to an end on the evening of his crucifixion—and was *elaborated*, all its implications made explicit a second time, and relived throughout the centuries. But, if the birth and death of the Savior are simultaneous with the vast duration of the terrestrial ages, how can this be reconciled with their apparent succession? How can a brief episode which seemingly happened at an exact date, at a definite point in historical chronology, be the same thing as the whole of that chronology? Moreover, if the Incarnation and the Passion are self-sufficient, do not the Gospels which narrate them likewise suffice to reveal as much of them as *can* be revealed before the beatific vision? What room is there for a second revelation confirming this, which is itself the unique confirmation of all that created beings can know of truth?

Following the train of Bloy's meditation, let us try to approach this mystery, which is the mystery of time, of the surprising necessity for any history at all after the Redemption. Let us try to imagine what connections link the Event narrated by the sacred writings to the innumerable events of history.

From the standpoint of time, which is the only standpoint open to the habitual infirmity of our minds, the Cross is situated at a fixed moment in the progression of the ages, and it cuts that progression in two. There is a "before" and an "after," an ascending history, which is the period of waiting for the Messiah, and a descending history, which is the era of the Christianization of the world. Nothing is finished on the first Easter Day, and the first Pentecost inaugurates the slow and irregular penetration of the consciousness of men by the Holy Spirit, offered for their free acceptance. There we have the usual view of the Incarnation, as a bygone event in relation to which the succession of the centuries can but mark a growing distance along the one and only line of irreversible chronology. And this is so even if the succession of Christian epochs is fundamentally, through all its ups and downs, a steady approach to the light and, despite relapses into infidelity, a progressive radiation which will culminate in a triumph. Seen in this way, history has its justification, since it is the battlefield for the difficult but certain victory of Christ in humanity, which has been given *time* for conversion.

But there is another standpoint—that "of the absolute"—which at first sight seems to contradict this current notion. Viewed from this new angle—in so far as we can detach ourselves from the illusion of time—everything was really and completely terminated in the *Consummatum*. Thus the only Happening which has any reality has come to an end. The work of salvation is accomplished, perfected; nothing more is needed. And it seems impossible to imagine that anything further could happen. Yet history unfolds itself! Yet centuries have followed that moment called final. Is time, then, something more than an illusion for human use? Is it conceivably *necessary*—and necessary to God? Bloy's thought often halts on the brink of this abyss: "Time is all that is needed by the Master of Eternity, who is quite solvent; and time is made of man's desolation."

No light dawns, and the paradox remains complete, impenetrable, exasperating, so long as we rely on speculation to resolve that astounding contradiction which has just led us to suppose that God, in his eternity, has *need* of time: that essential Being cannot do without illusion… There is no way out of such an impasse, unless the doctrine of the Church is asked to supply it. When the best efforts of the understanding come up against a blank wall, it means that we are faced with one of the great Christian mysteries. At this moment, Bloy has recourse to the notion of the *mystical body*. We know how much this idea appealed to him and how his meditations continually reverted to it. Mankind is truly for him the body of Christ and this must not be taken as a metaphor or an analogy, but in its most literal sense. As Bloy says, it must be believed in *substantially*.

LÉON BLOY: A STUDY IN IMPATIENCE

From all of us, dead, living or yet to be born, preceding the advent of Jesus or contemporary with it or subsequent to it, the Incarnation forms the body of the Savior, his members. The history of mankind is not only an imitation of the drama of the Redemption, it *is* that drama itself, extended in time, so to speak—in what, for us, goes under the name of time. But, from the standpoint of eternity, this extension, this dimension of duration, can have no existence. There is no before or after, but the most intangible simultaneity.

Thus the same unique event—the Incarnation of Christ and his life up to the sacrifice on the Cross—unfolds itself, not once in Judea and a second time in the immensity of the ages and of the planet, but on *one single occasion*, which *we* see under two aspects: first as the history of the body that Christ assumed in order to live a man's life (this being history within time and situated at one of time's points); and, secondly, as the history of the mystical body of Christ, made up of the sum of his members (a history identical with time as a whole). But in reality, and for eyes which we cannot possess, neither of these two histories is completed before the other, since they are *one and the same*. Perhaps the simile of the two hands of a watch, though not an exact parallel, comes nearest to giving us at least some idea of the possibility of this synchronism, which is beyond man's understanding. Setting out from noon, the small hand and the large do not take the same course in order to arrive, both together, at one and the same midnight, which ends the day. Yet it is only one point of time that is marked. Thus the life of Jesus, like the small hand, seems to have travelled quite a short distance, only once round the dial, while the history of mankind has made the circuit twelve times. Nevertheless, the hour of the *Consummatum*, which ends the short journey, is identical with the hour of the End of Time, which closes the long progression of history.

"All is finished" on the evening of the Cross, and a second time (but essentially the same) all will be finished when God shall take his creation back to Himself. If our minds cannot conceive the fullness of this mystery, that is because they are unable to escape from the illusive vision of time. History is indeed *the unfolding of a web of eternity before temporal and transitory eyes*. And *events are not successive but contemporaneous in an absolute way*. They are like an immense canvas, all parts of which coexist. *Our vision alone is successive*. Or, as Bloy, continually returning to this mystery, notes in another place, eyes freed from earthly weakness and truly comparable to those of God, such as may be hoped for in the next world, would take in, without any sense of time sequence, the multitude of events.

> If, like the angels, we were capable of encompassing with a single glance all the aspects of an event and the concordances and coincidences (nearly always unobserved) of a multitude of facts, if we could, by dint of attention and love, gather up and interweave all these scattered threads, we should doubtless arrive at a faint perception of God's plan. It is thus that evil spirits, who are angels, sometimes have the power to prophesy through the mouths of their servants.
>
> If, when an event took place, we could encompass with a single glance the infinite multitude of the accompanying gestures of Providence and if, as in a flash of lightning, we could see with what intelligence, what marvelous docility, all facts correspond and rush together, *we should understand everything*, and the dazzling of our minds would not be very different from beatific ecstasy."

As Bloy says, in *L'Ame de Napoléon*, "duration is an illusion due to the infirmity of our nature." In themselves events are linked like the letters or syllables of a word, which is uttered as a single unit, so that none of them is intelligible without the help of the rest. "And that is why prophets are possible."

Prophecy (that of the Old Testament and all prophecy at the same level, that is to say every really intelligent view of universal coherence, every perception of God's discourse in its indissociable

LÉON BLOY: A STUDY IN IMPATIENCE

simultaneity) is thus one and the same thing, be it word of the written Revelation or event taking place as announced by that Word. Furthermore, neither can be understood until, as Claudel puts it, "the Book is finished"—indicating a point beyond the confines of Time. A remarkable passage in *Celle qui pleure* expresses all that an earthly mind can conceive in its contemplation of this matter:

> Because the Divine Word is invariably metaphorical or figurative, prophecies are not verifiable on this side of life, *since their very fulfilment is but another symbol.* In this sense, as in all senses, a prophet goes on speaking. "Defunctus adhuc loquitur."
>
> Certain threats from the Secret of La Salette, such as the fall of Napoleon III, having been very plainly fulfilled, we may be sure that this catastrophe is *itself a presage* of some other great punishment which none, can divine. I would even go so far as to say that this threat is not unconnected with the colossal fall of the first Napoleon; for prophecies are not subject to duration, or to space, and *it is a holiday for the mind to feel them palpitating at the center of time, whence they send forth their rays over* ALL *epochs and* ALL *worlds.*

Between the written Revelation and revelation by the facts of history there is thus a *kind* of identity. But do not let us attribute to Bloy more than he actually says. We shall find that, in this absolute concordance, he re-establishes a definite hierarchy—or "different degrees of highness" as the medieval romance-writer put it, after having drawn this same parallel, which is the great subject of the *Quest of the Grail*. The same story can be told in two different ways, one of them being more pure and transparent, while the other has an admixture of dross; one being absolutely indispensable and the other merely a corroboration. But, before marking down what it is that, in spite of all, places the written Revelation above its repetition in the form of events, and the life of Jesus much higher than the long adventure of the mystical body, let us first impress upon our minds what they have in common, and what conclusions Bloy draws from this for the historian, as he conceives that role.

The first feature which the two "revelations" have in common is the presence of vast hidden elements, shrouded in darkness, from which only fitful flashes emerge. To both are applicable the words which Bloy wrote in *Le Salut par les Juifs*, and which have already been quoted here: "Revelation is a wan sky obscured by mountains of dark cloud from which the shaft of lightning sometimes darts its tip, but straightway plunges back into the gloom."

But another point of resemblance imposes humility and respect as an imperative duty upon anyone setting out to unriddle human history. Revelation forms an intangible whole, made up of indissociable details, none of which are unimportant, since, whatever the variety of words and symbols used, *it is always God who is speaking* and *God cannot speak of anything except Himself*. Exactly the same claim can be made for history: "History is like a vast liturgical Text, in which jots and tittles matter just as much as verses or whole chapters; but, whether it be jots or chapters, their importance is indeterminable and profoundly hidden."

In this liturgical text it is impossible to change anything. Here again Bloy comes very close to the medieval way of thinking, which, when faced with a fact (no matter whether its source was a chronicle, a legend or a poem) was always less concerned to ascertain if it was "confirmed" by "documents" than to understand what non-temporal truth lay behind it. Thus nothing could be more stupid than the practice, dear alike to historians and to "popular wisdom," of substituting a hypothetical event for the one that actually happened. "If they had acted differently… If it could have been foreseen that…" Such language is presumptuous and betrays an absurd faith in the multiplicity of alternatives. The truth is that *facts are absolute in themselves and in all their peripeteias. Historical events are the Style of the Word of God, and that word cannot be conditional.*

LÉON BLOY: A STUDY IN IMPATIENCE

At this point, however, an uneasy question presents itself: Does not all this amount to something more than an assertion that Providence is at work in human history? Are we not on the brink of an uncompromising determinism, in which all-powerful Necessity, destroying man's freedom, will remove his responsibility?

Bloy saw the problem, and he had an answer for that formidable objection which thought will always raise when confronted with Christian interpretations of history. None of them can be satisfactory if it fails to resolve this difficulty of the relation between an unalterable divine plan and the liberty of the creature. Bloy's answer, which is inherent in the logic of his reading of symbols, is to be found everywhere in his historical writings. But the hinge between freedom and necessity is brought out most plainly of all in the passages dealing with history in *Le Désespéré*. We find neither the clear line taken by Bossuet (whom Bloy reproaches with having studied the history of the world "to so little purpose"), nor a blind fatalism. For history can be looked at from two points of view, from one of which it appears to be under the infallible guidance of Providence, while from the other it seems the work of human liberty (and perversity). Are these two points of view irreconcilable, or is their apparent opposition, once more, a symptom of the presence of Mystery?

History is the work of God, and the multiplicity of things in process of becoming reflects a single act, which has sufficed and forever suffices to produce each smallest circumstance. Such is the first aspect, and on this point *Le Désespéré* confirms what we have already found elsewhere in Bloy's writings. For Caïn Marchenoir:

> It was a matter of reducing the multitude of testimonies to such a concise collective formula as could be contained in one shaft of thought. Since it is always God who works, *ad nutum*, throughout the earth, the necessary postulate was a single act, endlessly refracted in all God's creatures. Whether the term used was Fatherhood, or Love, or any other suggestive word,

meditation always led back to that simple view of a *single* infinite DEED done by an absolute Being and reflected in the illimitable apparent diversity of symbols.

Hence, all things are so closely interconnected (since each "reflects" the same divine Deed) that it is immaterial what moment of history is chosen as a subject for meditation; if its symbolic import be read aright, it will lead to an understanding of that Source from which, as starting-point, history as a whole will be revealed in its indissoluble texture:

> At whatever point of time the compass-point was inserted, whether at the taking of Jerusalem or the Defenestration of Prague, in vain the angle widened its gyratory quest: that random point became the center of the universe. The past and the future streamed out in rays of light from that focus, and, quivering, converged towards that umbilicus. A supernatural identity shone forth everywhere at the same time. Man stood denounced as having always done the same thing, moving round in a circle of perpetually similar circumstances.

But, though an operation of God, history is nevertheless, in the fallen world, the work of man; so that its dark events simultaneously body forth the Divine Light and the unfathomable night of sin. Such is the second aspect, which gives Bloy's view its complexity and differentiates it from a too univocal "providentialism." Marchenoir's meditation pursues its course. He finds that, if history is to "mean something," a sacrifice must be made—"the preliminary holocaust of the Free Will, at any rate as modern reason is able to conceive it." Once everything has been given to Providence, once the field has been abandoned to "invasion by the *absolute*," Free Will is "stranded without resources in the dried-up pasture of the *conditional*." Nothing is left but the "irreprehensible solidarity of all that has happened at all times and in all places" and the supremacy of an "infallible plan."

LÉON BLOY: A STUDY IN IMPATIENCE

And yet—so simple is the mystery! and that is why "philosophical and theological quibbles" can make nothing of it—constant co-operation by man and by men's freedom is *allowed for* as one of the necessary factors in this divine plan. The lines which follow deserve the closest attention:

> Since he would have it that history was a cryptogram, the thing to be done was to read the signs and fathom their conjunctions. But for six thousand years now, since the appearance of the first man, the signs had been coming into sight down the stupendously spreading pyramid of the human race. They mingled in combinations innumerable as the sands, of infinite complexity, interwoven, entwined, overlapping, coiled one within the oilier, enlaced and entangled at all levels.
>
> All the hands of night had helped to weave this chaos. The three Lusts, like tireless spinners, had furnished the skein, and the seven Sins, posting hot-foot, had wound it off in all directions, around all the generations, crisscrossing the inextricable vortex of episodes. Love, Death, Suffering and Oblivion had pooled their parables for an endless chaffering in *errata*, in which each of them tried to rake in all the darkness.

Thus the antinomy is not to be resolved by a logical synthesis; for a true understanding of what Bloy's imagery suggests, it is necessary to bear in mind the two dominant characteristics of his personal approach. An intelligence exclusively interested in the *symbolical* significance of everything which presents itself for consideration has no difficulty in perceiving that the same act can be at once a crime on the part of human freedom, given over to lusts, and one of the words of the divine discourse by which God makes known to his creatures what it pleases him to tell them about Himself. An act born of our opacity, child of "the hands of night," emerging from the shades of Death and Suffering, may very well *signify* Light itself, without severing its connection with its dark origins.

For the potency of the symbol lies in the fact that it remains what it is while expressing something else.

Nor must it be forgotten that Bloy was always concerned with detecting and unveiling *the presence of Mystery*, and that this presence is marked by a kind of *negation*. When it is no longer possible to invent an explanation, when knowledge seems nonplussed, when impenetrable night looms ahead, a kind of *blinding* clarity supervenes. For Bloy, as for the mystics, the most unyielding darkness is dazzling. One can go no further—a sign that the point has been reached where nothings more is possible except worship.

> You are anxious to understand how God's foreknowledge can be reconciled with human freedom. Oh! I find it quite simple. It's as if you were to tell me that you don't understand how the idea of the number thirty can be *reconciled* with the idea of five times six—which I don't understand either. I know, *without being able to understand it*, that divine foreknowledge and human liberty don't need any reconciling, because they are exactly, absolutely, essentially and substantially the SAME THING.

So Marchenoir's meditation, in the concentrated dialectic of its interpretation of Providence and its consciousness of the freedom left to sinful man, reaches one of these thresholds of nocturnal light. In a passage in *L'Ame de Napoléon*, written twenty-six years after *Le Désespéré*, in the chastened style of Bloy's old age, a still more precise formula is found for that moment of dazzled perception:

> For Napoleon and for the infinite multitude of lesser men the fact remains that *we are, all of us, symbols of the Invisible* and that we cannot lift a finger or massacre two million men without meaning something which is inscrutable until made manifest by the Beatific Vision. *From all eternity, God has known that at a certain moment, hidden from all but Him, such and such a man will* freely *perform a* necessary *act*. Incomprehensible concur-

LÉON BLOY: A STUDY IN IMPATIENCE

rence of Free Will and Foreknowledge. The most enlightened minds have never been able to pass beyond that boundary.

Special stress must be laid on the beginning of this passage, which would not be so crystal-clear were it not that universal fellowship is made the basis for the full play of the freedom granted to man within the divine plan." We are, *all of us*, symbols of the Invisible..." It is for this reason, because of this bond of the communion of the saints, that no human gesture is without endless repercussions; but it is for this reason too that liberty of action is so absolutely indispensable. In *Le Désespéré* Bloy had already begun to realize that liberty has its source and justification in the "profound mystery of Reversibility," which demands that human actions, in order to have their proper weight in the scale of sorrows and joys, must be *free* actions. The whole passage, moreover, is full of substance and is one that brings home to us the extent to which Bloy's great speculations are based upon love:

> *Our freedom is bound up with the balance of the world*, and unless this is grasped we must needs marvel at the profound mystery of Reversibility, which is the philosophical name for the great dogma of the Communion of Saints. *Everyone who performs a free act projects his personality into the infinite.* If with a bad grace he gives a penny to a poor man, that penny pierces the hand of the poor man, falls, pierces the earth, pierces the suns, crosses the firmament and *imperils the universe*. If he performs an unclean act, he darkens perhaps thousands of hearts that he does not know, hearts in mysterious correspondence with his own and needing him to be pure as a traveler dying of thirst needs the cup of water of the Gospel.

Thus every act is *necessary*, since it is an indispensable part of the pattern of the divine revelation and its absence would leave a hole in the web of universal fellowship; but no act counts—such is the magnanimous will of God and the chance offered to man by His love—unless it is accomplished *freely.*

It can now be seen what "degree of highness" separates, in Bloy's mind, the two languages: revelation by the Scriptures and revelation by events. The first, even if, especially in the Old Testament, it recounts the deeds of men in history, is the work of God alone, and he is always "the One who speaks." In the second, he is certainly Master of the Game, but his love wished men to have a free hand in it too. Thus the work is less pure and more difficult to reduce to its real meaning of revelation.

But, of that meaning whose full import is reserved for our beholding in the hereafter, can we at least grasp some fragment, some glimpse, here and now? Or must we resign ourselves to complete blankness? Can the historian "insert the point of his compasses" in a point of time with any chance of divining the universal connections?

He can (this would be more or less Bloy's answer) provided that, in the first place, he knows that human history is both the history of God and the story of earthly misery since the fall. Provided, above all, that he approaches this knowledge in the only spirit which will discover its secret, the spirit of childlike simplicity and love. For "God, who has pity on our curious souls, allows some fruits [of the Tree of Knowledge], three-parts eaten by grubs, to be picked up beneath it by *those impatient ones who have not the strength to wait for the beatific vision.*"

The impatient ones! That is to say, men of Bloy's stamp, whose love is so great that they cannot wait to know the divine truth, if only in flashes. We already find Marchenoir concluding his meditation on Free Will with significant words, when he answers the objections of those who fear that, by granting too much to the will of God, man may be defrauded of his autonomy: "When Providence takes all, it is in order to give itself. *Consult love, if you do not understand, and go to the devil!*"

LÉON BLOY: A STUDY IN IMPATIENCE

In a different form, the same precept occurs in Bloy's letter to his future wife:

> In reality I know very little, and I have never understood anything except what God has made me understand when I made myself like a little child.
>
> I *am first and foremost, a worshipper* and I have always considered myself lower than the beasts whenever I have set out to act otherwise than from love and through the promptings of love."

He who considers history in this spirit, without any rag of the pride that claims to explain everything, will see the great secret disclose itself. For in itself this secret is extremely simple, once it is looked at from the place where Léon Bloy's soul had its dwelling. It smooths out, once and for all, the difficulty which checked our progress; for Bloy was to discover the reason why history, in which we read the revelation of God, seems a succession of crimes, horrors and nameless cataclysms. The reason, stated briefly, is that this is history after the fall, and that, as we have seen, the sufferings of Jesus in agony are prolonged throughout the ages and repeated from day to day. Through the refusal of his creatures, the history of God has become the history of the interminable sufferings of God. As long as this is so—here the whole exegesis of Suffering comes in again, transposed from the personal plane to the dimensions of history—it is by his own sufferings that man approaches God. Thus there is an inexorable logic in this aspect of revelation by events as a lamentable trail of blood and torture.

Throughout the ages, Suffering never ceases. For in the mystical body it is the fulfilment of the Passion. Needful here, as it was needful in the earthly life of Jesus, it leads to the end of time as it once led to the *Consummatum*, the two dramas being mysteriously simultaneous.

ALBERT BÉGUIN

In reading the history of no matter what people, the Christian imagination is appalled by the wellnigh infinite sufferings—that universal deluge of suffering which hundreds of thousands of men have been called upon to endure throughout the ages, in order to make up "what was lacking in the Passion of Jesus Christ," according to the fearful and wonderful message of Saint Paul to the Colossians!

Down the ages there has been nothing to interrupt the triumph of wickedness and the failure of great enterprises, save the appearance of infrequent saints. But—such is the ambivalence of historical phenomena—both the shadow and the brightness alike betoken the future Advent, which will bear the surprising dual aspect of an irruption of light and an overwhelming catastrophe.

> The world still goes on its way. An age-long, immemorial procession of the strong and the oppressed, the wicked and the innocent whom they trample, towards the common grave of Eternity. History is nothing but a cry of pain in every century. *It is as if there had been no Redemption.* One would be tempted to believe that but for the appearance, at long intervals, of marvelous creatures who seem to say that the Almighty is in captivity for an indefinite term, that Supreme Justice is temporarily in chains, and that men of goodwill must trust their God. Creatures of consolation and hope whose actions are the earnest of the unimaginable magnificence foretold by the Scriptures.

Marchenoir's great meditation likewise ended with this dominant theme of Suffering "written for all eternity" in the texture of events:

> For these were the terms in which he framed his conjuration—that magician of exegesis who wanted all to appear together

LÉON BLOY: A STUDY IN IMPATIENCE

before the tribunal of his mind: "Everything on earth is ordered for Suffering." This Suffering was, in his eyes, the beginning as well as the end. It was not only the object, the ulterior comminatory purpose, it was the very *logic* of those mysterious Scriptures in which he presumed that the Will of God was to be read. The terrible sentence in Genesis, pronounced upon the departure from Eden, was applied by him in its strict sense to the *throes* which accompanied the birth of the smallest peripeteias in the ecumenical history of the earth.

And Bloy then limns an impressive vision of the passing of the ages. Without intermission, from the far-off beginnings, it is the same dreadful "sprouting of thorns," and a succession of happenings which repeat themselves, in "dreadful mockery of Progress," each foreshadowing in its own way "the Catastrophe which will explain everything and fulfil everything at the end of time." The whole course of the temporal adventure is thus pounced upon by its unimaginable end and seems to have no other meaning than to remind man that everything is rushing towards a consummation which has nothing to do with earthly hopes.

This interminable reign of Suffering is already familiar to us from the exegesis of Poverty. What is history but the reiteration of the "banquet of the strong," where they devour the Poor Man, whose amazing destiny it is to represent very God, the poor man, always conquered, mocked, buffeted, outraged, cursed, hacked to pieces, but not dying—kicked aside, under the table, like dirt, from Asia to Africa and from Europe all over the world—without being allowed so much as an hour to slake his thirst with his own tears and to scrape the scab from his sores!

And "the advent of the perfect Poor Man," the coming of the Redeemer, who has drained the full cup of suffering, has not put an end to this spectacle. It is from this point that the fundamental nature of history becomes apparent; for, once the sacrifice has been accomplished, the reign of Suffering is prolonged, despite the charity of the early Christians, despite chivalry and the crusades, despite the permanence of the Papacy and the mission of France. Marchenoir makes himself the mouthpiece for the desperate cry of the oppressed of all the ages and "in a mind-shattering algebra" sets down the universal sum of suffering. And so, because he has taken, upon himself this unspeakable torture and "given his heart to ancient, things," he has really found the key which opens the secret of all history:

> From that forest came roaring forth an unknown Symbolism which he might have called *the symbolism of Tears* and which was to become his language for addressing God. It was like an endless clamor of all the piteous voices of the downtrodden of all the ages, miraculously reduced to a formula explaining—by the need for a kind of divine ransom—the interminable delays of Justice and the seeming inefficacy of the Redemption.

Thus the principal themes of Bloy's life are rediscovered in the contemplation of history: the theme of the Kingdom of God delayed by human disobedience; the theme of Salvation offered, given, but not accepted, the theme, above all, of *Expectant Waiting* for the final catastrophe. For history is not only revelation, it is first of all *prophecy*. But Bloy came to perceive, at the end of his life, a new and important difference between the two languages of the revelation when, in 1917, in the preface to *Constantinople et Byzance* (a revised edition of *L'Épopée byzantine*) he compared the prophecy of the Old Testament and the prophecy implicit in the events of history. He was then able to assert that the Scriptures announce the coming of Christ while history outlines the shape of the future Advent. And that is why this second revelation remains more impenetrable, "since a divine law prevents all natural or supernatural warnings from being understood beforehand":

> The history of a multitude of centuries lies before us like a poor woman about to die of starvation without having been able to

make herself understood. The Symbolism which was always her language will vanish with her, and no human mind has succeeded in unriddling it.

All that it is possible to divine or believe is that universal history—read to so little purpose by Bossuet!—is a mysterious and prophetic foreshadowing of the Drama of God, resembling in this the collection of prefigurative images which make up the biblical Revelation, impenetrable until the High Mass of Calvary; *with this difference, however, that Jewish prophecy concerned the Redemption, while the universal prophecy of history concerns the* CONSUMMATION *of the redemption by the triumphal advent of the Holy Spirit.*

Hence the obscurity of history. It cannot serve as a "lesson," in the usual meaning of that term, since none of it will be clear before those things have come to pass which is merely foreshadows. From 1917 we have this further passage, written in face of the enormity of events:

> Here we are today, on the brink of the gulf, destitute of faith, totally devoid of the power to see, and incapable alike of loving and of understanding. Yet all that can be known of the past, for six thousand years, lies before our eyes: the Patriarchs, the Kingdoms, the Empires, the migrations, the wars, the exterminations, the infinite adventures of Suffering—to say nothing of the enormous blanks, the immeasurable waste lands of Tradition, for which we have to thank the cataclysms; but we are no further than before. Having never observed anything but the external and the transitory, we have absolutely no understanding of the new Deeds of superhuman aspect, which have no parallel in any past and seem already to form part of some indiscernible Future.

The historian after Bloy's own heart—and the historian Bloy himself—will thus steer his course according to that symbolical "algebra" which enables certain hypothetical soundings to be taken in the depths of the world of events. He will not venture there without laying down exact rules of procedure for himself.

First of all, when considering any happening he will bear in mind that it is inserted in the infinitely complex web made up of all happenings, present, past and to come, and that these happenings are simultaneous and closely inter dependent.

In the next place, everything must be viewed in the light of a knowledge of Suffering, which alone provides the true key, the understanding of the heart. This makes it possible—and there is no other way—to perceive the universal connection between souls linked in the fellowship of the mystical body, and consequently the secret universal connection which threads all the moments of time. And, above all, it makes it possible to discover, in the most illustrious and exceptional man, the changeless face of misery that is common to all creatures. Bloy found a magnificent way of putting this in his *Jeanne d'Arc* in 1914:

> Once again, there are only tears when we are sufficiently loved by God to have any: *Beati qui lugent*. Tears, it is true, blur eyes that are already so untrustworthy; but they are more than replaced by the *clairvoyance of the heart*, and the meagre historian can be illumined by a magnificent divination.
>
> Moreover, at a certain depth, the depth where the great dead have their resting-place, we are bound to come upon *the universal Fellowship* which is hidden from us by the social lie, and which the dust of the great dead so eloquently proclaims! For that, above all, we must needs weep!
>
> We feel on a level with this extreme misery of all mankind. The dazzling effect of Heroism or Beauty has worn off. Whether it be Charlemagne, Napoleon, or Joan of Arc, they seem no more than neighbors, very humble brothers in the immense

LÉON BLOY: A STUDY IN IMPATIENCE

flock of co-inheritors of the Expulsion. Hymns of glory, cries of enthusiasm, the cheers of the crowd no longer exist, and never did exist save in a dream that has faded. There is nothing left but tears of penitence, of compassion, of love or of despair, luminous or dark rivers flowing down to unknown gulfs...

But, if history is considered in this light, the means of expression and the method which it demands of the historian are rather those of art than of "objective science," and it calls for the resources of the most unfettered imagination. And Bloy justifies his recourse to hyperbole in an entry in his diary (dated September 11, 1912), where he speaks of his book on Napoleon:

The evil of this world cannot be seen clearly unless it is exaggerated. I wrote that, I don't know where. The Absolute admits of no exaggeration and in Art, which is the search for the Absolute, there is none either. *The artist who only looks at the object itself does not see it.* The same applies to the moralist, the philosopher and even the historian. *Most of all, perhaps, to the historian.* In order to say anything of value, as in order to give an impression of Beauty, apparent exaggeration is indispensable; in other words, the eye must be fixed on a point beyond the object, and the result will then be accuracy itself without any exaggeration, as may be seen from the Prophets, who were always accused of exaggerating.

I felt this in writing *L'Ame de Napoléon*. That great figure eluded me whenever the images and expressions which occurred to me were not vast enough. I saw quite clearly that, somehow or other, I must go after my own spirit, mine, which flew off beyond the historical character in every direction, following an orbit traced by its profound sense of a divine presence surrounding that incomparable man. Of course, I expect to be roughly handled by the critics; but later on, when my work can be viewed from a distance, it will be seen that I have not exaggerated, and that I may even have fallen short of what should have been said.

Hyperbole is a microscope for the perception of insects and a telescope for drawing near to stars.

II.

None of Bloy's historical works are unimportant and all are strictly in keeping with his philosophy of history. But, if the writings of his youth on Marie-Antoinette and Christopher Columbus, his works on Louis XVII and on Byzantium, and then his book on Joan of Arc, all contain illuminating passages, *L'Ame de Napoléon* must undoubtedly rank as his masterpiece in the exegesis of Events.

Twenty years or more had gone to the preparation of this book, which was written in haste, between January and April 1912, in one of those bursts of activity that nearly always came to Bloy at the actual moment of composition. From childhood he had loved this great figure, and from 1895 to 1911 his diary bears witness to the reading of innumerable memoirs and learned works on the First Empire. From the notes he took in this connection, the genesis of his own ideas can be followed fairly closely, and it may be said that all this meditation and careful study had the one object of heightening his sense of *stupefaction* in face of a destiny which fascinated him. It was by cultivating in himself this capacity for surprise, and by seeking in the Napoleonic adventure those elements which harmonized with his own intuitions and his own spiritual experience, that he gradually breathed life into the imposing portrait of the Emperor traced by his own pen. Knowing full well that "no man can *see* anything but what is in himself," and believing that we should "*turn our eyes inwards* and practise a sublime astronomy in the infinitude of our own hearts for which God chose to die," he wrote in dedicating *L'Ame de Napoléon* to his daughter Véronique: "*I saw no other way*

LÉON BLOY: A STUDY IN IMPATIENCE

of considering this extraordinary man than by imputing my own soul to him."

A proper understanding of this confession is indispensable, since it throws light upon the whole book. Needless to say, it does not enter Bloy's head to imagine, in the crudely unsophisticated fashion of a Julien Sorel, that he resembles Napoleon in his glory. On the contrary, confronted by this most spectacular of destinies, he never for one moment forgets that, strictly speaking, there can be no such thing as an exceptional soul.

> Obviously when you are a Christian you must be aware that every man has a soul and that this invisible creature is made in the image of an invisible Creator. Knowing that, you must also be aware that the soul of anybody whatsoever, the soul of an imbecile or of a savage, is infinitely more precious than all the treasures imaginable, and incomparably vaster than the star, Canopus, which the most cautious astronomers admit to be eight million times the size of our sun.

He also noted that exactly the same thing might be said of the soul of a bailiff: "but where is a bailiff's soul to be found?" The soul of Napoleon, at any rate, left a visible trace of its actions, but in secret that soul experienced *the same* loneliness as any other creature's, and a loneliness that was intensified by genius and by success before it became intensified by adversity.

In order to make of Bonaparte a gigantic figure and a Foreshadower of the Kingdom of God, Bloy did not need to shut his eyes to, his hero's weaknesses, which in no way cramped his argument. It is in his diary that we have the clearest proof that he cherished no illusions about his great man, and that the hyperboles of his exegesis betray no tendency to deification. The severest judgments alternate with expressions of a peculiar veneration, which goes much deeper than enthusiasm for success or brilliance. Bloy carried on a veritable dialogue with himself on the subject of Napoleon:

February 17, 1895: Surprising intellectual mediocrity of Napoleon. That great man is the father of all the platitudes of the nineteenth century, and the more abject they are, the more patent their origin.

November 2, 1902: Divorce. When Napoleon wanted to provide himself with an heir, what he chiefly begot, it seems to me, was the modern Bourgeois.

January 20, 1903: Napoleon's shoddy side. His lack of greatness...

February 24, 1903: Napoleon...besotted with the bourgeois urge to reign at any price...

January 11, 1903: Napoleon was, if not the father, at least the uncle of the contemporary Bourgeois, and he must definitely be regarded as *a fool of the most overwhelming genius.*

And on the other side:

December 4, 1897: I seem to have Napoleon in my blood. Every book concerned with the glory of this Prodigious Man leaves me gasping, panting, almost sobbing, *as if God were passing by.*

July 10, 1902: Looked at from above, Napoleon is the superb Failure, the colossal Weakling. From a certain point onwards, everything he attempts miscarries with a resounding crash, and he is no longer the man of achievement but *the wonderful instrument of the Prefiguration*!

October 25, 1903: At the very name of Napoleon my heart breaks with love, as if it were the name of God.

LÉON BLOY: A STUDY IN IMPATIENCE

February 3, 1904: I have this great man so much in my blood that I can hardly hear him mentioned without having my balance in some way upset or restored.

August 23, 1908: The first thing to be noticed in any known circumstance of Napoleon's life is his immense superiority over other men. That is not disputed, but very few people really feel this unprecedented superiority, which makes him a prophetic figure, a foreshadower. His superiority is so assured that even his mistakes have a depth and breadth beyond any other man's mistakes. What is disturbing is his want of energy in both abdications. Even the most discriminating historians have undoubtedly left something undiscovered and unsaid, something immense, which would come like a divine revelation.

And in 1904 we find Bloy making a novena for the soul of Napoleon, fixing the Emperor's death-mask in front of his desk, marveling over the great man's handwriting. To read accounts of the campaigns in Russia, Spain and France is deeply distressing to Bloy, and it is his compassion for Napoleon, rather than his admiration, that calls for remark. Yet, when Albert Vandal's pen seems to confer upon the Emperor a sovereignty which belongs only to God, Bloy is shocked and protests:

February 15, 1907: ..."Napoleon," says the writer, "is the type of integral humanity." Up to now I had thought that this could be said only of Our Emperor and King, Jesus Christ.

Greatness and wretchedness of Napoleon—greatness of the "colossal Failure" *because* of his weakness and his defeats—supernatural "greatness" which in no way blurs his natural mediocrity: such is the complex picture in which Bloy claimed to discern one of the most visible manifestations of the human soul in the situation assigned to it between the Redemption and the End of Time.

ALBERT BÉGUIN

To come to the heart of this book—parts of which show Bloy the writer at his most dazzling, besides containing his most essential views on the human mystery and the meaning of history—it is necessary to bear in mind not only his principles as a "symbolist" historian, not only his ideas on universal fellowship, suffering, prophecy and preoccupation with the Second Coming, but also, above all, his conception of the freedom granted to man in God's infallible design. Remember that for Bloy every creature symbolizes something—it knows not what—and every destiny necessarily plays its part in the revelation by history, but does so on condition that it offers itself *freely* for that purpose. Remember too that, if we were able to grasp what one single man, the most undistinguished or the most illustrious, really *is*, we should straightway catch a glimpse of the divine plan itself, since all things are interdependent in it and the whole meaning of God's discourse is hidden in every syllable of it. But each of us is ignorant of his own real *Name*, "his imperishable name in the register of Light." It is the mystery, impenetrable here below, of our *identity*, which will not be revealed to us until after death, but to which we already conform, in "freely" answering the call addressed to us in the most cryptic but the most imperious fashion. Thus we are told of Clotilde, when she reappears, remolded by misery, after the catastrophe of the first part of *La Femme pauvre*: "She has not changed... But she *hears a greater resemblance to* herself. By force of suffering she has so far *won her identity* that sometimes, in the street, the tiniest children, those born not very long ago, stretch out their arms to her and seem to *recognize* her..."

Let no one expect, then, to find in *L'Ame de Napoléon* an "explanation" of his unparalleled career by what historians call causes—economic, political, social or psychological. In this book more than in any other Bloy keeps to the absolute point of view, leaving on one side all considerations of a relative order; and more than ever his sole preoccupation is with "the presence of Mystery." Thus he had achieved his object, and he considered that he had really dealt with *quod erat demonstrandum* about Napoleon, when, in the chapter which he devoted to the Emperor, as far back as 1900, in his *Le Fils de Louis XVI*, he exclaimed:

> I have named Napoleon. Why not state immediately that *I know nothing of that Personage*, who seemed to be Emperor of all the West and who for ten years appeared to command fifty million men?
>
> Everything has been written about him except, I think, the fact that *nobody has ever been able to find out his name*. It must be very well hidden, that formidable Name!"

L'Ame de Napoléon ends with a confession of the same kind: musing upon the Emperor's Guardian Angel and their "amazing colloquies" together, Bloy is thrilled with the joy of having reached the incomprehensible:

> Who, then, are we *in reality*, that such defenders should be put in charge of us and, above all, who are these defenders? What are these beings who are linked to our destiny but of whom it is not said that God made them, like us, in his own image and who have neither body nor face? It was because of them that we were enjoined never to be "forgetful to entertain strangers," lest some of these beings should be hidden among those in need who come our way.
>
> Who, then, can have been more of a *stranger* and more *in need* than Napoleon? *As I do not in the least understand the apparition of such a man upon the earth*, I have nothing, to say about it; and what could I say of the Being charged to accompany him invisibly wherever he went? One might have expected him to have a Cherub, a Throne, a Domination, or at any rate a very great and very splendid Archangel. But I am inclined to think just the opposite: that he must have had as guardian one of the lesser spirits of the lowest order of the celestial Hierarchy...

What this extraordinary Personage needed was the guardian angel of a little child abandoned on the high road of the world, a humble protector to scare away roving dogs, to pick a path for him among the brambles and the stones that might have hurt him, a lowly and almost timid guardian angel for the greatest of all men!

———•◆•———

Napoleon, then, is the man of whom it is particularly *manifest* that his destiny is *quite incomprehensible*. Accordingly Bloy's exegetical approach—and we are beginning to recognize this as the favorite method which came natural to one who had been "dazzled by the Face of the Lord"—will not set out to tell us what Napoleon is (since that is what nobody knows) but to demonstrate that this is not known. A singular quest, indeed, which feels that it is nearing the light when it has succeeded in establishing the presence of darkness...

Nothing is known of Napoleon, as, for that matter, nothing is known of any other soul. But one may risk the assertion that the *obscurity* which envelops him in his glory is particularly *luminous*. Napoleon is, first and foremost, the Man of Surprises, the Incomprehensible. He is thus what we all are, but in a conspicuous degree. He is indefinable, unknowable; but this incomprehensibility of his is a very great discovery since, in the absence of any human explanation, a mysterious reason must be postulated for his deeds and his fortunes.

Bloy's exegesis *does* postulate this hidden meaning and, as twenty years of reflection had only brought him to the point of asserting that Napoleon was "prodigious" and "amazing," he took this man to be the symbol and foreshadower of that which will one day arouse the greatest of all Amazements. If the whole of history is a prophecy of "the fulfilment of the Redemption"—that is to say, of the overwhelming apparition of the Holy Spirit at the end of time—the most surprising figure in history cannot be the harbinger of anything but that apparition, which Bloy was awaiting so impatiently.

LÉON BLOY: A STUDY IN IMPATIENCE

Throughout the years, what else had he sought, in his contemplative life and in his work as a writer, than *images* sufficiently blinding to suggest the ultimate astonishment? This is, at bottom, the meaning of all those metaphors of fire, conflagration, furnace, gulf and abyss which he heaps up, albeit with no hope of ever doing more than very remotely suggesting that advent which he knows to be *unimaginable*, in all the literal force of that word. His constant "exaggerations" are an effort in the same direction, and so are his strange way of making contraries synonymous and his habit of choosing, among the figures and episodes of history, the most glorious or the most abject destinies. Radiant splendor and the depths of ignominy are alone capable, in his eyes, of representing, however feebly, the future effulgence of the light of God in his final triumph. Between the pit of deepest darkness and the peak of utmost light, mirroring each other as contrasting extremes, the intervening space is too commonplace, too incompatible with hyperbole, to suggest the prodigious Event. But the utter abasement to which, say, the son of Louis XVI or Christopher Columbus was condemned is akin to the Marvel and foreshadows it just as effectively as the glory of crowned and conquering heroes.

Bloy had long been conscious of this need for "extravagant" images to suggest what the glory of God may one day be like. As early as 1880, in one of his great, impatient letters to Hello, he said: "If I could write down cries, I might be able to express something of what I feel."

Now Napoleon—and that was his privilege—had a destiny which made him the man of splendor and misery, of glory and disgrace, of greatness and mediocrity: "a fool of the most overwhelming genius." The simple took him for a God come down upon earth, and in this naive belief they were mistaken; but in a symbolical sense they were right:

> Since the establishment of Christendom, as before it, expectation has always looked forward to the coming of *a great Per-*

sonage who is to fulfil everything. This personage, always imagined as puissant and invincible, could only be Napoleon and no other for the transparent souls of those who thought that, the Kingdom of God having come, his Will must be done on earth as it is in Heaven, and for whom that was the whole of the Lord's Prayer.

Assuredly the Master of this flock was not merely a man; he was, in the direction of the Absolute, the epitome of a line of Beings indispensable to enable the Third Person of the Trinity to be fittingly prophesied...

The century has gone on, the generations have jostled one another like beasts at the edge of a stream, and the One desired beyond all desiring, the One of whom Louis XVII was the faintest and Napoleon the most brilliant Image, does not appear.

How can such a daring parallel be sustained?

Bloy's exegesis, infinitely complex and full of surprises, must here be followed step by step.

———

A figure like Napoleon is necessarily *the instrument of the Divine Will*—but the sense in which Bloy affirms this must be defined very precisely, to prevent any possible confusion between his point of view and one which would be tantamount to deifying a man, a leader, as such. Bloy never thought that Napoleon's plans and ambitions were, in any degree whatsoever, of heavenly inspiration, and justifiable for that reason. Instead of increasing his stature and heightening the difference between him and other men, the fact of being an instrument of Providence brings Napoleon down into the ranks of common men and Bloy, despite his hyperboles, despite his admiration for the exceptional career of the conqueror, does not fail to assign the great man his place, humble and on a level with the rest, in the "universal fellowship." In the divine discourse of History

LÉON BLOY: A STUDY IN IMPATIENCE

Napoleon may have been "an iota sparkling with glory"; but this does not affect the possibility that such and such a battle of his was really won by "a little girl of three years old or a wandering greybeard, entreating God that his Will should be done on earth as it is in heaven." Bloy adds: "What is called genius, then, would appear to be simply this Divine Will, incarnate, if I dare express it thus, become visible and tangible in a human instrument carried to its highest degree of force and precision, but *incapable, like a pair of compasses, of going beyond its furthest circumference.*"

Nevertheless, if God, *obeying* the prayer of an unknown who called for the reign of his Will upon earth, permitted the rise of Napoleon, many of the acts in the Emperor's career remain irreconcilable with this hypothesis: not only the final failure of all his plans and the double abdication (which Bloy was to have no difficulty in accounting for in the logic of his interpretation) but above all Napoleon's conflict with Rome. How could he, willed and guided by God, be the persecutor of the Pope, Saint Peter's heir and Jesus Christ's vicar upon earth? In a chapter called "The Diadem," which is one of the most typical examples of his method, Bloy, facing this inevitable objection, replies to it by two assertions which he does not even try to reconcile, so little does he care whether reason considers them incompatible.

Napoleon's attack upon Pius VII is, in the first place, a weakness on his part and one of the immediate causes of his fall. Enraged at the thought that, in all the magnificence of his power, he was only reigning "over matter," while the Pope retained his "empire over mind," Napoleon could not resign himself to the limitations of his conquest. He wanted to go beyond the furthest circumference of "his compasses":

The priests keep the soul and throw me the corpse. What sudden flashes in that great man's night, but how unavailing! He was determined to disregard the point at which force should rein in its demands. Could he be ignorant, then, that in the natural course of events power, carried to excess, itself creates and finally encounters a *resistance* which it cannot overcome?

But that is not all: at a deeper level the persecution inflicted on the Church is likewise a part of the divine plan. And the Pope was well aware of it—he who, Bloy asserts, "loved Napoleon with a special predilection." Between them there was "something ineffable." To understand this we must go back to what Bloy discovered in 1870: "It is really when the Church suffers that she can be said to triumph... Suffering is her patrimony, her inalienable domain, her true treasure." At the particular moment in the plan of Providence when Napoleon appeared, it was doubtless necessary that the Church should once more be "prodigiously strengthened by the prodigious blows" which were to fall upon her, that she should once more experience the depths of suffering, and that the Pope in person should taste that salutary bitterness. Hence the words which Bloy puts into the mouth of Pius VII and the commentary which precedes them:

> In short, there are these two Souls: the *central* and inordinate soul of the one and only Napoleon, and the soul of the imperishable Papacy. Who, then, could think and who would dare to maintain, after a hundred years, that there was really any antagonism between them? *God had willed Napoleon, as he had willed all the Popes, as he had willed his Church. They were obliged to live side by side and in some sort of agreement, at whatever cost*; the one in order to hollow out to its fullest depth the chasm between the old world and the new, the other in order to say to all peoples: "Behold the *Fixer of Boundaries*! His hand is hard and his foot heavy; but He whom I represent willed it so and not otherwise. If I suffer through him, it will be in the infinite and abiding certainty of having done what had to be done, at that particular moment, for God and men. If this man of destiny overthrows me, it cannot happen until he has uprooted himself. But the Diadem which I have

LÉON BLOY: A STUDY IN IMPATIENCE

the honor to wear in succession to so many others will not be shattered. Recognize, then, *in him and in me*, the Will of our Father above, fulfilling itself upon earth at the same time as in the highest heaven."

Willed by God, Napoleon's appearance upon the scene and his providential success must have had a meaning. But what? How is that meaning to be divined? Are we to suppose that Providence sanctioned a domination gained at the cost of millions of human lives and in the name of principles which, it must be admitted, were monstrously unjust? Moreover, if Napoleon was incited and supported in his conquests by the will of God, why were these triumphs so quickly followed by the most terrible fall? Are we to conclude that the Emperor was raised so high only in order to point the moral of his catastrophe and to provide a spectacular object-lesson illustrating "the characteristic, manifest, constitutional, and capitulary inability of the majority of great men to establish anything capable of enduring for more than a day"? These lines occur in *L'Épopée byzantine*. But in *L'Ame de Napoléon* Bloy's train of thought, without disavowing them, takes a different turn.

Napoleon's mission was not to establish an earthly empire approved, as such, by Providence; nor was it, except incidentally, to demonstrate the brittleness of human conquests. His true, fundamental vocation could not be anything but this: to help to throw light upon the Mystery of history. This is what makes him both *commonplace*—since no historical figure and no event amounts to more than "an iota" in the Book of God—and *exceptional*—since in that Book he is a syllable startling enough to arrest and petrify our attention. But, on this plane of symbolical significance, to what particular aspect of the Mystery does Napoleon's destiny correspond? Which point of the Revelation does it transcribe more specifically in the language of historical events? Bloy's reply is as categorical as it is, at first glance, disconcerting:

ALBERT BÉGUIN

Napoleon...was the clearest image, unique and incomparable, of the infinitely strong Heart of Our Lord Jesus Christ...
 In him the Inscrutable Prescience had an adventurer, one who went to and fro carrying the Secret of God. *That more than strange being called Napoleon could never make a gesture without unconsciously betraying the Three Persons of the Trinity.*

He even wrote: "*Napoleon is the Face of God in the darkness.*" Symbol of God, of the Trinity, could Napoleon be that? How could any man have the temerity to make such an assertion? And how did he propose to give so great a hyperbole some sort of verisimilitude?
 Napoleon (here a step is already being taken in the direction of precision) is not only a figure that stands for something, but, in the sense in which history is prophecy, a *prefiguration*. He presages what will one day happen, the vent which Bloy invokes in his impatience, the Personage who will come to fulfil time. What he signifies in his glory, his solitude, and his very defeat, what he represents in an imperfect because terrestial fashion, is the Paraclete itself, the Holy Spirit. He stands for and foreshadows the Holy Spirit first and foremost by his strangeness, the things about him which are *surprising*:

Napoleon, endowed with strength and greatness as no other man had ever been, must have been a much bigger surprise to himself than to those whom he dazzled. Native of an unknown spiritual region, *a stranger by birth and by profession in all countries alike, he felt*, like Gulliver in Lilliput, *a genuine and lifelong surprise* at the excessive inferiority of his contemporaries; and his last recorded words, on Saint Helena, prove that this surprise, which had now taken the form of supreme contempt, went with him into the grave and before the Judgment Seat.
 What was he here for, in this eighteenth-century France which certainly did not foresee his advent and was even less on the lookout for him? For this and this alone: to be a *Deed*

LÉON BLOY: A STUDY IN IMPATIENCE

done by God through the Franks, so that men all over the world should not forget that there is a God and that he will come, as a thief in the night, at an hour which no man knows, *accompanied by a final Astonishment,* which will reduce the universe to emptiness. No doubt it was fitting that this deed should be accomplished by a man who scarcely believed in God and did not know his commandments. Having the investiture neither of a Patriarch nor of a Prophet, it was important that he should be no more conscious of his mission than a storm or an earthquake, so that his enemies could identify him with Antichrist or an evil spirit. What was necessary, above all and before all else, was that he should be instrumental in the consummation of the French Revolution, the irreparable ruin of the Ancient World. Clearly God had had enough of this Ancient World. He wanted something new and a Napoleon was needed to establish it. Exodus that cost millions of men their lives...

I do not think that in the whole of his life there was a single action or a single circumstance which could not be given a divine interpretation, that is to say interpreted as foreshadowing the Kingdom of God upon Earth.

Not only does Napoleon foreshadow the Astonishment which is to accompany the advent of the Comforter but, having attempted to unite the whole world under one single Domination, he adumbrates and heralds the final Kingdom of God! Here, above all, an accurate and just understanding of Bloy's symbolism is essential, if he is to escape the imputation of some sort of idolatry. Not for one moment does he dream of suggesting that the Napoleonic conquest was good in itself, or that its success would have been the starting-point for a mustering of mankind with which a future Ecumenical City would have been coextensive, and that it would have rid Europe of its internal frontiers, so that first this continent and then the rest of the world might be offered to God already united. Bloy's conception has nothing in common with the great idea which Péguy formed of an Ancient Rome preparing, by its military expansion, the material body of the future Christendom.

On the contrary, it was because he had imagined that his work was, in itself, Providential, and because he had forgotten or failed to realize that his mission was to *symbolize* and not to *fulfil*, that Napoleon went to his doom. He was intended for a herald and he wanted to be a performer, thus overstepping the humble bounds of his figurative function. Seeing the planet sick, humanity distraught and suffering, he thought himself called upon to cure it; but in this he misunderstood the very nature of the wound which sears the whole tragic history of mankind, and, like the rest of the modern world, he imagined that human resources, genius and strength, a good organization and a new order, could remedy that suffering. Madness! For the world will not be healed until the end of time, when He comes whom Napoleon should merely have announced, and whose place he aspired to take. Such an aberration of pride, playing havoc with all values and (though Bloy does not expressly say this) turning Napoleon into a foreshadower of Antichrist, could not fail to end in the most mortal catastrophe:

> Never had king or emperor fixed such an attentive, such a penetrating gaze upon the earth. Thinking perhaps that, with its volcanoes and its oceans, it resembled himself, he considered its distress, the horror of its sores, its bruises, its scars, its ghastly pallor; he even noted the beginning of its death-agony. Rash physician that he was, he undertook to cure it, to revive that dying face by infusing new life into it. He only succeeded in covering it with blood…"

God had to overthrow the Emperor. He Himself had to ruin that empire whose sudden success had been meant to make the beholders feel something of the stupor which will overwhelm men's souls when, in an instantaneous, unimaginable Triumph, His own Kingdom is established. And, in order that the mystery might be even

LÉON BLOY: A STUDY IN IMPATIENCE

more strikingly apparent in Napoleon's downfall than in his glory, Providence chose as his destroyer a people living on the outskirts of that Europe, which, despite the stubbornness of England, seemed already subjugated. The continental fortress collapsed under the blows of Alexander's army:

> He decreed the Continental Blockade, the vastest undertaking ever conceived. The whole continent of Europe locked and bolted, three hundred million men, if necessary, condemned to ruin and despair in order that England, outlawed by the nations, should be forced to surrender the keys and the triple bars of the gaol of the oceans—and it very nearly came to that... This recalls, on a large scale, the famous Interdicts of the Middle Ages, the memory of which is so disturbing. Apocalyptic decree! It might well be dated the eve of the Last Judgment. There are angels and trumpeters in all the wards of heaven.
>
> But the Scythians and the Sarmatians are newborn in western civilization. Does not justice demand that they in their turn should have time to rot? They refuse to sacrifice themselves! Napoleon falls upon them with ten armies. And lo! God protects these barbarians! The fabulous, unconquerable warriors are killed by the cold; the Blockade becomes impossible, and, with it, the Domination of the world.

And yet, the Empire was finally overthrown and the Emperor tumbled from his throne, what he undertook to do still remains fraught with meaning. Humanly unrealizable, the domination of the world is nonetheless a kind of rough plan of the future Kingdom, outlined before the eyes of men to give them a faint idea of the Divine Sovereignty that is to be. Napoleon's mad presumption does not alter the fact of his having, as it were, pointed out to God himself the strategy for his conquest:

It was beautiful, though. Too beautiful, no doubt for this jealous God who will not go shares. When he deigns to manifest himself completely at the end of ends, that is to say, when all symbols have been exhausted, *he will be forced to do something similar to this Design of Napoleon's.* Then, but not until then, we shall know how fine it was!

A daring thought, indeed, but a perfect example of hyperbole, with all the rectifications which Bloy does not fail to bring to this kind of bold assertion. For, if he alleges that God, when the time comes, will to some extent be obliged to imitate Napoleon, he leaves intact, between the two "designs" and between the means for their realization, the whole difference of "highness" which, by an infinite distance, separates the "symbol" from what it presages or represents. The weakness of Napoleon, who remains a mere creature, lay in his wish to *recreate* the world, without having the strength which would have enabled him actually to *transfigure* it. For the maintenance of his kingdom he had only poor human resources, fashioned from night and sin, conquest, violence, tyranny, and the external adaptation of laws and institutions. Lover of the earth, he imagined that he could *save* her by molding her in this way, and that he could give her unity by giving her laws; but he only succeeded in tearing her asunder and collapsing upon her bloodstained soil. For the union of all the members of Jesus Christ under a sole master is for all time the prerogative of the sole Master of men, who, when He wishes to establish his domination, is capable of transforming them from within and turning them into the really *new* men of another age. He will have, says Bloy, the resource which Napoleon lacked and which no man can have, the power "to make of his people, as it were, a new kind of people, but little lower than the angels."

Once again, one of Bloy's most enigmatic ideas has its application in an elementary law of human affairs. Once again it is clear that the "pilgrim of the Absolute," however strange and remote from the ordinary plane his ways of thought, is no visionary but a profound *realist*, whose mind sees the ultimate reality precisely because *it* goes straight to the heart of things. Thus he understood that the great conquerors, the great reformers of the earth are doomed to failure because they set themselves to change the world at surface level, by bringing "order" into it, whereas men's lot can be improved only by renewing their souls. As early as 1872 Bloy said: "*The only Politics are those which concern themselves with souls; for in the problem of Man it will not do to get rid of man.*"

But Napoleon's failure was not due solely to lack of moderation in his plans. Paradoxically, it was also the fault of their mediocrity and his own. For, if there is never to be any true kingdom before the Kingdom of God, that Kingdom is yet to be heralded, on the eve of its advent, by one last and well-nigh perfect prefiguration. This is foretold in the "Revelation of Saint John." It is the reign of Antichrist, who in evil will approach perfection, thus being the only Personage who, though *inversely,* can really typify Christ: Napoleon, despite his greatness and his audacity in crime, fell very far short of the perfection of evil, that abyss below which reflects the abyss above. Latecomer in a long procession of forerunners announcing more and more clearly the last one of all, he will be followed by others who will dare more than he dared and will not show the same hesitations. What prevented him from truly symbolizing the Astonishing personage in whom time will be fulfilled, was that he did not go far enough, that he did not take upon himself the whole evil in order to suggest the whole of goodness. There were pettinesses in him, a bourgeois streak of meanness, an upstart's ineptitude; he had a remarkable incapacity for cruelty, effrontery, barbaric brutality. What Bloy *reproaches* him with is that he was too magnanimous towards his enemies, accessible to pity and inclined to justice, according to his lights. He was a sentimentalist who disliked the sight of blood and made his soldiers stop wearing their white uniforms, on which the red showed up too crudely. He did not dare to let loose a war of extermination, the only war "which makes sense," the war which Bloy foretold as "very near at hand."

Thus he was not the monster which he should have been for *total*, apocalyptic *war* with all its consequences, the abyss of war called for by the abyss of turpitude, and *it was clearly not this devil whose precursor he was.*

Bloy was convinced that the world, by its own law, is hastening towards a terrible punishment, towards pitiless destruction, towards wars each more "total" than the one before, towards that absolute reign of Antichrist which will at last announce clearly what its forerunners suggested so timidly. At one time, however, it had really seemed to Bloy that in Napoleon Antichrist had already a harbinger who came very close to the thing he typified. In a prose poem dated 1894, *La Lamentation de l'Epée*, the Glaive speaks of him in terms which Bloy was later to reserve for the "devil" of "total war," still to come.

> Assuredly he did not pray, this Emperor of Death, but nevertheless I spread about him the ecumenical prayer of Sacrifice and Devotion—the terrible red prayer that lifts its cry in the slaughter-house of the nations.

Later, in 1916, confirmed in his expectations of more and more ruthless wars and catastrophes, Bloy was actually moved to withdraw some of his earlier assertions about Napoleon "as forerunner of the long-awaited Stranger who was to be astonishment itself." For he remembered that Napoleon "was not absolutely unexpected and was *commonplace enough to dream of world empire*. Thus he was bound to re-enact stale History and finish up like a rash adventurer exposing himself to the traditional vulture."

But in 1912 Bloy had not yet lost his illusions about his hero. Those aspects of his exegesis which we have so far considered do not exhaust its riches. *L'Ame de Napoléon* also contains, especially in the concluding chapters, the very profound reflections which justify the book's title and make it a masterpiece.

LÉON BLOY: A STUDY IN IMPATIENCE

Bloy discovered that Napoleon, dedicated to that strange destiny, was necessarily dedicated to loneliness. This is tantamount to saying that, while symbolizing the Holy Spirit under one of its aspects, and that the most visible one, he was at the same time, very humbly and in the privacy of his personal life, a figure in which *any human soul whatsoever* can recognize itself.

It is in this last intuition that Bloy's study of Napoleon goes deepest and develops its surprising dialectic, as well as that quality of compassion, of fellowship, which transforms this "historical" work into meditation of a wholly spiritual character.

Napoleon's infinite loneliness was the loneliness of a genius surrounded by people who were either hostile to him or cruelly inferior. "He was alone, absolutely, terribly alone, and his Solitude had an aspect of eternity." He who sought to be "the renewer of the World" and who confessed that he had wanted to "play Providence," found himself faced by adversaries who cared for nothing but their own ends—the kind of men who, by their materialism, are in all ages "the supernatural enemies of France." Around him, the marshals and his other creations had no understanding for the dreams of "this incomparable poet in action," and were only biding their time to betray him. Even the wonderful fidelity of his soldiers could not give him the warmth of companionship, for, deified, he was with them but not of them, separated by his greatness. "Alone forever; like the mountain or the ocean."

Visible to all, as few men have ever been, he remained unknown, in that "poor omnipotent wretch's" soul of his, isolated above happiness, "since what we choose to call happiness in this life is only a combination—and an illusory one—of paltry satisfactions and chance windfalls which are not suited to a great man, and least of all to the greatest of men." He had nothing of his own but his soul:

> There was no one so glowing and glittering as Napoleon, that is certain; but there is no proof that his soul *shed more light*

than the soul of a clown or a cobbler. The lamps or beacons of his genius spread a dazzling radiance which still endures and will not fade until the Day of God dawns; but his soul, forever unknown, could only light up itself, we know not how. His own soul, sad or joyous, dark as the pit or tortured by the light; his soul of a sinner, proud, ruthless, sentimental, affable; his soul of changing fire, smarting or triumphant; his inconstant or desperate soul always telling him: "You are alone, Napoleon, eternally alone; there is none to go with you, none to know what you love or what you hate, or whither your steps are leading you. Poor omnipotent wretch, weep in the depths of me; I will hide you, I will protect you."

Bloy then begins to picture that solitude, to see the whole life of Napoleon, not as a succession of outward deeds but as the mystery of a destiny unfolding itself *within* his lonely soul. Recalling the popular engravings which show Napoleon asleep on the eve of Austerlitz, Bloy imagines him sleeping like that throughout his life, a slumber haunted by visions:

> *Napoleon was a sublime sleeper, a somnambulist conqueror* crying out in his sleep at the sufferings of others and his own, and, by his cries, spreading terror to the ends of the earth. One day he would wake up, without his sword, but only when the moment came to appear before God...
>
> Into what fathomless depths meditation plunges at the thought that this mighty man of war could never win a final victory; that after Austerlitz there had to be Jena, Eylau and Friedland, and that Wagram, too, was needed before fate could confront him with the fearful dilemma: either to win an unprofitable victory at Moscow or to be crushed, elsewhere by the coalition of all the nations! Whichever you do, you are ruined and there is no help for it. You are in the bonds of sleep, in the torment or rapture of dreams. A higher and wholly infalli-

LÉON BLOY: A STUDY IN IMPATIENCE

ble Will has decreed that you should be *the troubled spectator of your own incomparable life...*

Thus everything, his battles, victories or defeats, his greatness, the coronation, Europe crushed and then rebelling, the apocalypse of his double fall and his exile, a death island to match his island birthplace—all this is represented as having taken place "in his soul," and as having been seen by him "with boundless anguish, as a prodigious poem conceived by one greater and more terrible than himself."

Poor man, alone like all men! Do what he would to believe, and make others believe, that his actions were his own choice," that he was their author, he knew in reality, being endowed with a clear understanding of his fate, that everything, absolutely everything, is always played out between the creature and his Creator. This adventure of life, which seemed to be taking place in the world of men, with visible, tangible things as its substance and as its obstacles—this was, in reality, the eternal spiritual adventure. It was nothing else than what God was making of him, working out through him, requiring of him, the intoxicating bliss and the afflictions which God was sending to rouse his soul to consciousness and to make him understand the hidden meaning of all human destinies.

What, then, could he learn about himself, by reading this picture language which was a definition of himself pronounced by God, the name which God gave him, the call he was summoned to answer? He understood at last that—at the height of his splendor as at the depths of his fall—he would never be anything but a Poor Man, *a man of Longing*. Incited to daring deeds and to extraordinary actions by a strange inward force, the whole of his active life and the long meditations of his exile were no more than he needed to divine what this force was: it was Longing, a "great desire like that of the poor, which could not be appeased because, taking it for the craving to possess power and empire, he tried to sate it with that misery. He did not know, or only very dimly realized, that he was actually listening to the great impatient cry of every human soul, which has no other object than the possession of God in the perfection of Love. Thus, in order to go beyond commonplace appearances in the understanding of Napoleon, one must be devoured by that same unquenchable thirst:

> Those who have never legged can tinder stand nothing of Napoleon's history. He was, on the threshold of his soul, the Beggar of the Infinite, the Beggar always uneasy about his own borne, which he did not know, which he was unable to comprehend; the extraordinary and colossal Beggar asking the passer-by for that spare copper, the empire of the world, for the signal favor of contemplating in himself the Earthly Paradise of his own glory; and dying, at the other end of the earth, empty-handed and broken-hearted, with the weight of millions of death agonies!

Comparable in every way to any other soul—but "any soul, be it that of an imbecile or a savage, is infinitely more precious than all the treasures imaginable"—Napoleon understood something of his own mystery when he spoke of his star and accepted the exigencies of a "Plan which went beyond the comprehension of his genius." But, again like any other soul, he rebelled against his vocation and, just as we all flee from the very thought of our supernatural destiny, he often sought to "escape from his own greatness." Bloy pictures those moments when the soul of Napoleon refused to hear the voice of his "invisible companion," his Guardian Angel:

> What amazing colloquies between these two Imperturbables; the one of this world, the other of heaven; the one visible, the other invisible! And Napoleon, was not he also invisible after his fashion? Invisible indeed! to his servants, who were incapable of suspecting or even of imagining his anxieties when he conversed with the translucent Companion through

LÉON BLOY: A STUDY IN IMPATIENCE

whom his anguished soul saw the storms gathering. "*Do not go that way,*" said the angel. "*My destiny bids me,*" said the emperor. So Destiny went against God, and Napoleon was lost! But no one in his circle could see *that*. Thus there were moments, hours, long nights when this Master of the world, not knowing what to do, passed from one resolution to another, leaping over the rocks, to be hurled back upon them by the insolent waves until, exhausted by the effort, he let himself fall, and five or six hundred thousand with him, murmuring something which, whatever the actual words, may have meant "God have pity on me!"

By degrees we recognize the features of this portrait of Napoleon. They are the characteristics which Bloy had already ascribed to the Poor Man and to Israel: longing and impatience; endless expectation; "absence from everywhere"; a destiny which the one who received it did not understand, but which had the greatness of being a *vocation,* with a place to fill in the divine plan of History... Incapable of understanding that he is being led, man nevertheless divines it; and it is useless for him to struggle against "his star," something makes him *freely* follow the course set by it.

"*I have given him my own soul,*" said Bloy. "*The apparition of such a man upon earth is beyond my understanding.*" In very truth Bloy was himself a man of longing and impatience, anguish and obedience, a man who saw everything by looking inwards and who, whatever the object of his contemplation, always ended with the same cry: "*I can't understand it!*"—which was for him a kind of cry of triumph.

Thus his *Napoléon,* like all his other historical exegesis, is deeply rooted in his spiritual "identity." The symbolical method of interpreting history (a method which, while readily acceptable as a general principle, is always problematical in its particular applications) is extraordinarily fruitful when someone like Bloy adopts it. True, another man, whose inward life was "specialized" in a different way, might explain the mystery of Napoleon with reference to other aspects of Mystery than the End of Time or the Longing of the Lonely. But that in no way impugns the *truth* of Bloy's *Napoleon*, provided that it is clear what kind of truth is concerned, and that the sole point here is to show, through a fragment, of the visible and the temporal, "the footprints of the Invisible." Nothing could be more subjective at the outset; but nothing can claim a more fundamental "objectivity" than this gaze which passes over everything accidental in order to *imagine* and *suggest* the Absolute.

And one of Bloy's supreme intuitions lends confirmation, to this quality of truth in his book. The man who, as Napoleon, is haunted by the vision of Mystery, finds himself, by that very fact, introduced into the fellowship of souls, where by mutual divination he knows and is known. That is the meaning of the chapter called "The Battle"—a wonderful poetic synthesis of the Napoleonic wars. At the mere presence of Napoleon we see his soldiers *becoming* souls, an immense throng of fighting souls, because they receive from him an unexplained revelation, recognizing and realizing, in this being who was more "visible" than any other, their own anguish and longing as living souls confronted with death:

> A pallid day dawns over the dreary plains of Poland. The bugle calls have been answered by the neighing of forty thousand horses. The cold, black night had weighed oppressively upon the army, whose sleep was perforce broken, how many times! by the near or distant groans of yesterday's wounded, or the day before yesterday's. These lamentations have mingled with the memories or the dreams of one and all, for each of these fighting men has a soul which will probably leave its body a few hours hence. *It is an immense herd of souls, beasts of the field of Eternity.*
>
> Some of them, many of them I dare say, have thus beheld once more their families, their fields, their villages, in Bur-

LÉON BLOY: A STUDY IN IMPATIENCE

gundy, in Périgord, in Normandy, in Brittany; others in Holland, in Germany, in Italy and even in Spain, for the armies of the Emperor are recruited from everywhere except Russia and England.

They have been fighting for ten years, they will doubtless fight for another ten, and nobody can tell when or how it will end—Napoleon less than anyone. The most intrepid leaders have begun to murmur. What they all feel is that the whole of Europe is against them simply because they are France, which is the living soul of all the nations, and because it is a law that the human animal makes war against its own soul.

For the common soldiers *this soul is visible in Napoleon,* so visible that, if he were to die, it would be the end of France and the end of the world. Is there anything more tragic, I wonder, than the tears of this poor grenadier, weeping on the Beresina because he has seen Napoleon walking among the specters of his old guard? I don't rightly know whether I'm asleep or awake. I am crying because I saw an Emperor on foot, with a stick in his hand—and he so great, who made us feel so proud!

But the moment has not come. The humiliation of the peoples has not yet been, sufficiently fertilized, and other victories will be needed to bring the disasters to birth.

Meanwhile here is the opening roar of the artillery, the resonant voice of the guns. The Great Army stretches, straightening its mighty limbs, yawning at death. To waken it completely the icy wind sends gusts of snow into its face. It is on its feet now, shivering and shaking in the valleys, on the hills, on the frozen lakes, in the midst of the woods.

Here and there on the chessboard of the Infallible there are the formidable wild beasts at his disposal: Davout, Augereau, Ney who knows neither fatigue nor fear; Murat who rips up whole battalions, the Achilles of every fight; the sublime Lannes, the terrifying cuirassier Hautpoul, the epic generals Saint-Hilaire, Friant, Gudin, Morand and fifty more.

Swift and sure, like angels of war, they carry out their master's last orders and the carnage begins.

By this evening there must be at least twenty thousand dead and thirty thousand wounded, and there is no time to lose; for it is God who makes Man's Daytime that he may fill it with his works, good or evil; and in February, so near to the pole, the day is not even eight hours long.

Only those who have beheld one of these mass conflicts know how true it is that life is a dream. Here a whole division is mown down by grape-shot. What of it? And, anyway, who has time to weep? Thirty squadrons, hounded by the Furies, trample it under their horses' hoofs to get at the gunners and the foot-soldiers and hack them with their sabres before going down themselves into the luminous night of the dead. The battle surges to and fro continually, in systole and diastole of the armies at grips. A position stormed by a mighty effort is lost and recaptured, time after time! A heroic charge (surely this will carry the day!) is checked by a cyclone of fire; the troopers—what is left of them—are pressed back upon the infantry, who will protect them as best it can, being sometimes itself in desperate need of protection. *But the dead are strewn more and more thickly and the souls emerging from the tomb of the body, the poor souls hitherto so much in the dark, knowing at last for what and for whom they fought so fiercely, have floated down there, invisibly, upon the imperial mound, around the visible Master who brushes them away with his hand like importunate thoughts...*

CHAPTER IV

A Prophet of Our Catastrophe, and His Impatience

―◆▶―

"I am waiting for the Cossacks and the Holy Spirit."

I.

We know in what sense Bloy can be called a prophet: he is one who sees the hidden Meaning of things and who interpreting everything that happens in terms of the universal symbolism of history, considers it both within and outside time. Within time, since it is on its own date and by its relation to the succession of the ages that an event receives its significance and "keeps its place" in the Book of God. But outside time, since in a certain sense all facts are synonymous, as are the words of Scripture, none of them being anything but a revelation of God about himself. For the prophet, then, any scene presented on the stage of history has always to be interpreted according to its temporal character but, at the same time, according as this temporal "datum" denotes a Truth which is beyond time. But a by-product of this insight is the gift of prophecy in the common acceptation of the word: the fact that events "are not successive but contemporaneous and simultaneous" accounts for the existence of prophets, that is to say of men capable of "taking in, at a single glance, the multitude of concomitant gestures of Providence"—and thus of looking through the present into the future.

Without dwelling upon specific prophecies (in the commonplace sense) which are not more infrequent in Bloy than in Péguy (or in the Claudel of *Tête d'Or* and *La Ville*), suffice it to quote a surprising passage dating from 1900, in which Bloy, remembering the great disaster of 1870, predicts that it will happen again, magnified a hundredfold thanks to the invention of bicycles and motor cars:

> ...Never did the bourgeois take to his heels as he did in 1870. It was a tumultuous, screaming, headlong flight, an immense panic emptying the houses and emptying the towns as night-soil collectors empty cesspools. It was the crude, craven, traditional fear of the rentiers, trampling the weak in their frantic stampede. Today it is a procession along the highway of silence.
>
> What did you do in 1870? After all, it was the moment when one should have been doing something... When there were a hundred thousand of us in the field; without fire to warm us under an icy sky; without bread to eat in the heart of France, which had become the eldest daughter of Gambetta; without even the enemy, whom we were never lined up to meet, we had the right to enquire, perhaps, and to ask the well-dressed and well-fed what they were doing in their trousers. We had some funny answers, now and then, and sometimes they were drowned by belly rumblings—that time, for instance, when we sent the only son of a notary of Château-Gontier into La Mayenne. Today, as I said, it is the highway of silence. Go and ask those of our great men who are over fifty what they did in 1870...
>
> That date has become a kind of code sign for all the postures of contemporary dishonor. It stands for every kind of

LÉON BLOY: A STUDY IN IMPATIENCE

cowardice, every kind of shame, past and to come. The most perfect form is silence, the universal silent flight now in progress or in preparation. Bicycles and motor cars are the precautions being taken in readiness for an immeasurable rout, of which the disaster of thirty years ago will prove to have been but a humble forerunner, a timid prognostication with downcast eyes. Will it be a rout of bodies or of souls? Nobody knows. Both, most probably. But the imagination boggles at this world in flight, this deluge of deserters and panickers..."

Incidentally, what makes this prediction interesting is not so much Bloy's clairvoyance in describing in advance the spectacle which was to be presented by the roads of the defeat, but rather his exact diagnosis of its underlying causes. He sees in it the outcome of bourgeois cowardice (and for him the word "bourgeois" denotes a spirit by no means confined to one class of society), the secret daily flight of peacetime simply transformed into sudden overt panic.

The present war was repeatedly foretold by Bloy, relying, as he constantly does, on the threats uttered in the "Secret" of La Salette, from which he culled the following:

> This peace among men will not last long. Twenty-five years of abundant harvests will make them forget that the sins of mankind are the cause of all the troubles that come upon the earth. A forerunner of Antichrist, with troops of various nationalities, will fight against the true Christ, the only Savior of the world; he will shed a great deal of blood and will seek to destroy the worship of God, that he himself may be looked on as a God.

But above all Bloy regarded the coming catastrophe, which had been foreshadowed, for him, by 1870 and 1914, as *a sign* to be interpreted, as the symptom and at the same time the sanction of a crisis of the modern World, rushing to the doom brought upon it by its gross infidelities. Every upheaval in history was, in his eyes, at once a punishment inflicted upon disobedient man and, more essentially, the foreshadowing of an event to come. What is peculiar to Bloy and to his spiritual life is not so much the idea of expiation as the interpretation of the premonitory symbols contained in visible facts.

Once more he appears in the same guise as on three previous occasions, with his love of Suffering and of Poverty, his supersensitive feeling for Christ's agony stretching out across time, and his impatience, above all his *impatience,* for the unutterable epilogue which is to put an end to that agony.

It might be said that this impatience of Bloy's, as 1914 drew near, was something that had been going on for centuries, and that, if the modern world exacerbated his expectancy, it was because he, Léon Bloy, had known ages in which men were still, in their awareness, *contemporaries* of the Passion; men for whom it was part of their daily life and not a thing of the past. He measures the frightful despiritualization of our era only by comparing it with another state of mind, in which men were still able to read symbols and thus transcend, in time itself, the destructive work of time. Twenty passages could be quoted bearing witness to this age-long memory which really seemed to make Bloy the multicentenarian judge of the present age. "I am a contemporary of the last men of the Byzantine Empire and consequently a complete stranger to what followed the ruin of Byzantium," he wrote, for example, in *Le Désespéré*. And in the preface to *L'Épopée byzantine*:

> History is to me like *a ruin in which I had lived most intensely* before it became a ruin. I have the painful and paradisal sensation of *having put my heart into very ancient things which seem no longer to exist.* I visit Byzantium, as Schlumberger visited the ruins of Ani, the ancient capital of the kings of Armenia, holding up the whole starry firmament with my feeble hands above *this great vestige of my soul.*

LÉON BLOY: A STUDY IN IMPATIENCE

"This great vestige of my soul!" We are inevitably reminded of Bloy's Napoleon and his inward vision, of that "dream" which makes him see *in himself all* the adventures of his life. Speaking, in his last book, of the coming of the Paraclete, Bloy wrote quite naturally: "*When I saw Napoleon pass, last century,* I thought he was it..."

Thus he "saw" the whole history of the Christian ages "pass," within himself, like "those who, fretted by the clamor of Disobedience, *live in retirement in the depths of their own souls.*" And it is this inward picture of successive epochs that we must grasp if we are to avoid misunderstanding the curses hurled by Bloy at his contemporaries. We have already had a glimpse of the broad lines of this picture, as traced in the historical vision of *Le Désespéré* and in the two "foreshortened" delineations—*Le Salut par les Juifs* and *L'Ame de Napoléon*. Let us recall, in addition, Bloy's view of the Middle Ages and, by way of contrast, his vehement satire upon the eighteenth century. We shall see more clearly why he could not be the reactionary and traditionalist that people have called him and that he believed himself to be at the time when he drew his inspiration from Joseph de Maistre; why he was gradually to reveal himself as the most daring of revolutionaries. Not someone who dreams of a return to the past, of restoration in some form or another, but a man who, with eyes bent on the profoundest, most hidden aspect of the future, knows by experience that a Christian is necessarily one who does not conform.

———•••———

Bloy repeatedly dwelt upon the Middle Ages in *La Femme pauvre, Le Salut par les Juifs, Jeanne d'Arc* and *L'Épopée byzantine*; and always as "Christianity's great time of mourning."

The Middle Ages, my child, were an immense church, such as will not be seen again until God comes down once more—a place of prayer as vast as the whole Occident, and built upon ten centuries of ecstasy, recalling the Ten Commandments of the Sabaoth! The whole world knelt in worship or in terror. Even the blasphemous and the bloodthirsty were on their knees, for there was no other attitude to adopt in the formidable presence of the Crucified who was to judge all mankind... Outside, there was nothing but darkness, full of dragons and satanic rites. The Death of Christ was still going on and the sun remained hidden. The poor country folk tilled the soil in fear and trembling, as if they were afraid of waking the dead before their time. The knights and their squires rode silently by in the distance, on the horizon, in the twilight. Everybody wept in praying for pardon. Sometimes a sudden gust blew open the doors, pushing the dark figures from outside into the heart of the sanctuary, where all the tapers went out and nothing more was heard but a long-drawn cry of horror reverberating through the two angelic worlds, as they waited for the Vicar of the Redeemer to lift his terrible Hands in exorcism... The thousand years of the Middle Ages were Christianity's great time of mourning, from your patron saint Clotilde to Christopher Columbus, who took the zeal of charity into the grave with him—for only Saints or their antagonists can serve as landmarks of history...

As for us, the rabble, we are the children of that marvelous patience, and when, after Luther and his captious crew, we denied the great Lord of Paradise who had consoled our fathers, it was right that we should be shut out, like dogs, from the banquet of poetry to which simple souls had so long been invited. For those men of prayer, those ignorant men, those unmurmuring victims of oppression whom we have the foolish presumption to despise, had the celestial Jerusalem in their hearts and in their brains. They expressed their ecstasies as best they could, in the stone of cathedrals, in the glowing stained-glass windows of chapels, on the vellum of missals, and our one endeavour, if we have a tincture of genius, is to lift ourselves once more to that source of light...

LÉON BLOY: A STUDY IN IMPATIENCE

For centuries, if suffering ceased it was only to give place to supplication, for they lived on *compassion,* for the Lord, and the hosts of the poor "gladly added to their own load of misery as much as they could carry of His burden." That age took up the Cross, like Simon of Cyrene, like La Fontaine's woodcutter collapsing under the weight of the "tree of Salvation" and begging Death to put it back upon his shoulders for him.

"Jesus will be in agony until the end of the world," wrote Pascal—the most lamentable, I think, among the great men who have been greatly mistaken. There is a sad, exalted beauty in that thought, which the farouche Jansenist could certainly not have explained and which, in his own eyes, could only have been a devout hyperbole. But it would not be easy to convey the haunting power of that combination of syllables over a profound heart which sees in it something superhuman. By force of loving, the Middle Ages had understood that Jesus is always being crucified, always bleeding, always expiring, mocked by the populace and *cursed by God himself* in accordance with the precise wording of the ancient Law: "He that is hanged upon the tree is accursed of God."

This, then, was the time when Christ's sufferings were felt to be happening at that very moment, before the modern mind, to distract attention from those sufferings, had invented the distances of historical computation. And all these torments, assumed by millions of souls, had their crown in "the marvelous passion-flower of the Middle Ages, whose name is Joan of Arc."

Bloy's *Jeanne d'Arc,* appearing shortly after Péguy's, bears little resemblance to that work (which Bloy never read). Instead of that instantaneous birth of the virtues of holiness, and that marvelous childhood of a creature who was carried up to heaven before the age at which temporal purity withers through the process of "growing old"; instead of that embodiment of hope and that childish familiarity with a God full of tenderness, Bloy's Jeanne d'Arc is "a monster of holiness." He did not love her, as Péguy did, with a young and spontaneous love; but, having come to understand her late in the day, his reverence for her in the end was as great as that which inspired the author of the *Mystères*, although Bloy's view of her was colored by the preoccupations of a spiritual life based on very different data. The Maid's vocation certainly seemed to Bloy "the greatest miracle since the Incarnation," just as Péguy hails her as "the saint nearest in holiness to the Holy Virgin" and "the most perfect imitation of Jesus Christ." But for Péguy that is a very simple conviction, fitting in with his great idea of the presence of the eternal in the temporal. For Bloy it is an overwhelming mystery, a dazzling experience before which the mind falls prostrate, and one which links up with the unfathomable promise of the End of Time, when "it is through Woman that all shall be accomplished"; this attitude bespeaks the author of *La Femme pauvre* and of the *Lettres à la Fiancée* no less than the devotee of the Virgin Mary in *L'Introduction à la Vie de Mélanie*. So true it is that every great contemplative expresses his astonishment, face to face with mystery, in a style which is dictated by his own "identity," by that peculiar knowledge which it is his special vocation to seek. It is impossible to imagine anyone but Bloy writing, for example:

> Joan of Arc is the very palpable foreshadowment of that victress over men and devils, and in all history there is no other who so exactly plays this part. Her contemporaries were vaguely aware of it. Very often *it* took all the ingenuous singleheartedness of this shepherdess of Paradise and all the strength of her unconquerable faith to withstand the boundless enthusiasm of the simple soul's who saw in her an emanation of the Godhead.
>
> Full of the Holy Spirit, as her life and above all her death have shown, absolutely alone in the midst of the crowd, she was akin to *Fire*, the visible and terrible symbol of Love, in the same way that Napoleon, later, was akin to Thunder, and it is

LÉON BLOY: A STUDY IN IMPATIENCE

a holiday for the mind to forget for a moment the intervening centuries and bring together those two incomparable destinies: Joan creating the very special kingdom of Jesus Christ, and Napoleon enlarging that kingdom miraculously in order to establish in it the mighty image of the future Empire of the Holy Spirit!

But to whom is such a vision vouchsafed? *Looked at thus, History resembles a gulf, vast as space itself in which whirlwinds of darkness continually alternate with whirlwinds of Light, to dazzle the terrified beholder.* However intrepid one may be, one envies at such moments the simplicity of those babes to whom, says Jesus, these things, so profoundly hidden from the wise and prudent, will one day be revealed by his Father who is in heaven.

Yet Bloy is by no means incapable of that childlike simplicity which he seems to envy here. With much more tenderness in his disposition than is commonly believed, he can recognize the miracle of a sainthood made up of the most natural behavior, transfiguring everyday life without any violent upheaval and going along in the same homely guise until the final holocaust:

> The historical figure of the Maid resembles a stained-glass window of the Annunciation, infinitely gentle and pure, which time and the vandals have respected. Around this martyr figure, the azure blue of France and the red of her fiery ordeal are softened by the filtering light. Through a sublime coalescence, she seems at once the angel of the Annunciation and the very obedient maiden humbly receiving the formidable sword which is henceforth to replace her pretty distaff. At first she does not understand what is required of her. She does not know the history of France, she is ignorant of war and loathsome politics. She knows nothing save that God is suffering in his people and that there is great wretchedness in the kingdom which he chose for himself long ago, at the time of his grievous

Passion, in the paschal night, when the Cock began to crow. So she rises to her feet, quietly, resolutely, like a good daughter of God and, led by her Voices, at once becomes an invincible strategist, guide and unerring counsellor of the highest princes. When she had delivered France, she had nothing left to ask for but her own release from her mission; and, because she is of the Holy Spirit, this other, more glorious deliverance can be accomplished only by fire, after the preliminary horrors of the most infamous trial that has ever appalled mankind since the unspeakable trial of Our Lord Jesus Christ.

Foreshadowing, by her death at the stake, the "deliverance of the Holy Spirit," Joan of Arc is also, for Léon Bloy, the clearest example of that liberty which is left to the human being of whom God makes his overt instrument For, though doubtless strengthened in her determination by the comfort of the heavenly voices, and "commissioned" by them, she yet remains sole mistress of her own actions and, in particular, of her warlike enterprises. "In common with all other human creatures she had the *intangible liberty of the children of God*, the power to accomplish of her own accord acts of supererogation, though encompassed within the eternal Prescience. Incontestably she always wanted what God wanted, but she wanted it *in her own way*, which was her own and nobody else's."

As Péguy also is at pains to point out, Joan of Arc had not the advantage of any immediate supernatural aid. She was alone responsible for the great resolutions which she had to take, with no sort of preparation, humanly speaking. The miracle which God wishes to perform through her was accomplished not by means of celestial armies and flaming swords but by making use of Joan's freedom. For such is the mystery of Christian sainthood: the creature destined to become a particularly clear "word" in the revelation of History is not reduced to the role of a mere pawn moved by the hand of God on the chessboard but is rather endowed with an unusual autonomy. In her free choice Joan has no need of ceaseless counsel, for sainthood in itself implies a knowledge which has no bounds and requires no apprenticeship. This "infused" knowledge can make its appearance in any field whatsoever, as in Joan of Arc it takes the form of military genius, so unexpected in a child of her years and one so much a stranger to that calling. According to Bloy's fine definition, sainthood is "a kind of return to the primordial Integrity which existed before the Fall, but with the great complement of beauty that Suffering adds to it."

In the story of the Maid, Bloy reads yet another lesson—and one that had not escaped Péguy either. The saint of France is linked with the people, which remains faithful because, living in Poverty and knowing Suffering, it is near to God and *supernaturally* preserved from treachery. On the other hand, Joan of Arc's mission was continually thwarted by the great and the powerful, the courtiers and prelates, clouded by their earthly "consolations" and ready to deny God and their country in a single betrayal...

Thus, contemplating Joan of Arc, Bloy finds in her the confirmation of his convictions regarding the role of Suffering, Poverty and transparence to God and, in a singular degree, his convictions regarding the impenetrable but manifest alliance of human Freedom with the Will of God expressed in the facts of History. In Joan of Arc, too, the medieval spirit found its last and highest personification: like all her contemporaries—and this is what our age has lost—Joan lived with the constant idea of Christ's Passion *present* every minute; and that is one more point of contact with Péguy, who makes Jeannette and Madame Gervaise exclaim together: "He is there, He is there as on the first day..."

After Joan of Arc nothing of the same sort was ever to be seen again. There was still Christopher Columbus, of course—that other Poor Man, that other "envoy," who was also sneered at by the great and the rich and bore his high destiny quite alone, dreaming of bringing Christ to numberless men who, plunged in the darkness of unknown lands, had lived for centuries in a state of expectancy, of unsatisfied Longing.

ALBERT BÉGUIN

But from *Le Révélateur du Globe* to *La Chevalière de la Mort* the downward slope is painfully apparent. Bloy had written his book on Marie-Antoinette at a time when, under the influence of his earliest masters, he still looked back with nostalgia upon the splendors of the French monarchy. Much of the work bears obvious marks of that political heritage. But what is peculiar to Bloy in this prentice effort, and what makes it in spite of everything a work full of flashes of light, is the already emergent idea of the grandeur of Suffering. The Queen who mounted the scaffold after having been subjected to the foulest insults, and who experienced a human anguish comparable to that of Joan of Arc, had a mission too, but one adapted to the mentality of her age. To enable us moderns to understand her martyrdom, it had to be disguised as simple human heroism, with nothing of sainthood about it. God himself, because of the darkness of human minds and hearts, is constrained to speak in history a language which rules out direct allusions to the supernatural. The only means by which the kingdom of Suffering, cruelly misjudged, could now be restored and re-established was through this figure which the modern world could already claim as one of its children: Marie-Antoinette, born on All Souls' Day, the day of the dead; accompanied throughout her life by echoes of the Dies Irae which was to thunder in her ears at the point of death; expiating the sins of a number of kings, and attaining to "the supernatural poetry of the Passion of Our Savior"—but all this without any other support than a courage wholly of this world:

> What makes Marie-Antoinette so profoundly moving, what grips our souls with such overpowering emotion, is *the fact that she is not a saint*. She is not one, at any rate, as the Church understands it, and therefore the grim ordeals she had to face as queen, wife and mother cannot strictly be called a martyrdom. If she had been truly a saint, in the manner of Saint Elizabeth or Saint Radegonde, and if her earthly anguish had been coupled with the supernatural anguish of a soul which thirsts

for Heaven—our own misery would soon have turned away from that crucified Misery, whose splendor would infallibly have escaped us.

Modern reason has an aversion for the Supernatural. Everyone knows that; and the Saints, perpetually outsoaring time, offer little for our earthbound enthusiasms to clutch at. But, fortunately for the sensibility of that cheerful crocodile known as public compassion, Marie-Antoinette was not a saint and in her afflictions there is no suggestion of the supernatural. They come to us simply from the midst of her solitary throne and from the midst of her still more royal and solitary soul. They spring from every part of her life, as streams of blood escape from every part of the body of a brave man who, overpowered, lets himself be hacked to death. If the august beauty of the Queen's sufferings sets her at an infinite distance from us, their essence and their very nature bring her *near to us as a sister, almost one of us and on a level with our hearts...*

To be sure, there is no really godlike beauty in that. The mystic flower does not spring up, in a sudden burgeoning, from the streaming wound of this beautiful body as from the bodies of holy Martyrs in the naive portrayals to be found in old antiphonaries. *But human beauty, bankrupt human beauty, is there in plenty, breaking all hearts with compassion.* Earthly affections and fidelities stand in silence round this poor, wretched coffin, from which no trappings will keep away the expiatory tears of the true poor and the truly wretched to the last hour of the world.

From Joan of Arc to Marie-Antoinette, from the Middle Ages to modern times, the descent is formidable. The first serious falling-off came with the Renaissance, but the eighteenth century had the sad privilege of ushering in the flatness of the present day. In *La Chevalière de la Mort* and *Le Fils de Louis XVI* Bloy gives a grimly satiric picture of it. It would be a mistake not to realize that his vengeful virulence hides the bitterest grief, which Bloy always feels when confronted with the state of contemporary souls, and which is nothing but the infinite heartbreak of wounded love. His frame of mind recalls those words which he wrote with reference to the men of the Middle Ages and their outbursts of anger against the Jews, obstinate in non-recognition of the Messiah. "If they sometimes hurled themselves upon the traitors, it was because the Jews refused to put an end to the lingering agony of Christ. They were moved by *a feeling of ineffable tenderness* which nobody now will ever understand."

It is this feeling of compassion for the God of Tears that inspires Bloy with the fierce vehemence of those *Bucoliques de Moloch* in which he depicts the world of the "absence of God." In them the eighteenth century appears as the age of universal prostration of souls: "A whole society flat on its belly before God, not in worship but *in order that he may pass without touching anyone.*" People at that time nursed a furious hatred, "of positively Punic proportions," for Heroism and every kind of greatness. In that "marvelously superficial" age everybody seemed to be born with "*the gift of understanding nothing of higher things.*" In a vast carnival of frivolity, amid foolish pastorals, these "fanatics of littleness" had no suspicion that their puerile antics presented the frightful spectacle of a death-agony. "Unparalleled night of the French mind," the age of "enlightenment" was embarking "with the calmest confidence on the philosophic capture of despair," while, in a real flash of genius, the century chose as its fetish the Monkey, which was to be found everywhere, on hangings and in pictures in novels and in salons, and even in the grimace of Voltaire...

And since then? What but a more and more definite refusal of God and a growing fear that he may reappear to disturb the ominous optimism of humanity left to itself. The whole of the modern world, through all its gradations from triumphant atheism to shamefaced piety, is a world that has banished God. In 1900 Bloy, in *Le Fils de Louis XVI*, summed up his merciless diagnosis in a very

LÉON BLOY: A STUDY IN IMPATIENCE

eloquent passage:

> It is remarkable that, at a time when meticulously exact information has Become the Wizard of the world, it is impossible to find anyone who can give men news of their Creator. He is absent from the towns, the country, the mountains and the plains. He is absent from law, science, art, politics; from our upbringing, our manners and our morals. He is even absent from religious life, for those who still claim to be his closest friends have no need of his *presence. God is absent as never before.* That recurrent theme of the Psalms, at which the ancient Hebrews trembled, the *ne dicant gentes: ubi est Deus eorum*? has at last been realized to the full! It took not less than nineteen centuries of Christianity.
>
> Of course, Christians will not fail to protest that God is everywhere, in heaven, on earth and in hell. But that ubiquity, so reassuring for the multitudes who no longer believe in heaven or hell and have consequently even ceased to have any very clear notion of the earth, is equivalent to infinite absence. *This absence has become one of the attributes of God.* That is the consummation given to the dismissal of a Creator of whom men have no further need, since something better than Paradise has been found. God is absent in the same way that he is worshipful—so much so that it looks as if the catechism should be understood in the reverse sense, and that eternal Beatitude consists principally in *not seeing him*. Anything, in fact, rather than that. It is mankind's great Fear. *Non poteris videre faciem meam*—"There shall no man see me and live," Moses was told. The human race has never recovered from that Saying. If it was hardly bearable in the days of the Saints, how could it be in our time? Without supernatural life—and the nations are moving further and further away from that—the desire for the Sight of God is not even conceivable, and the mere idea that a God might be *seen* could only strike terror, were it not so absurd.

It is said that the pure in heart are blessed "for they shall see God." If that is so, long live the impure in heart, the rotten hearts, the hearts inhabited by the spawn of the devil!... To be sure, those who still count themselves Christians do not say that; but it exactly sums up the choice they have to make!...

A day will come—and it looks as if it is near at hand—when all hypocrisies will be brought to bay and when the whole world will be forced to recognize its utterly godless state. There is reason to think that this festival has been fixed for the beginning of the next century. But, since the whole world will by that time be in motor-cars or on bicycles, hardly anyone will mark the occasion by jumping for joy. People will content themselves with carefully running over the few penniless pedestrians who have escaped from previous exterminations, and they will continue to bowl along at top speed towards the double abyss for which they have to thank the hideous contraptions: the twin gulfs of imbecility for men and sterility for women. They *will take their fun* in rottenness and insanity.

And now, while awaiting these events, while the tocsin of the end of the century has still to ring out, at almost the last moment in which something still remains of what was once the Passion of the Son of God in all his members, and when a few souls lagging behind the horrible multitude can suffer, as they suffered in the olden days, at the thought that the God of heaven and earth is not to be found;... at such a moment, which is almost that of death, it is surely permissible to wonder whether, in reality, the Image is not just as *absent* as the Prototype, and *whether there can be any men in a society without God*!

A world without God is a world without men. How could Bloy, convinced of this inference and haunted by the torturing thought that humanity was committing suicide in exiling God from its history—how could he for an instant have shared the euphory of his

LÉON BLOY: A STUDY IN IMPATIENCE

generation and believed that "Progress" guaranteed, for nations and classes alike, a coming age of peace and prosperity? For him this happy blindness was a cause of grief and rage, the very sign—where others saw the earnest of "better times"—that the cataclysm of the "Revelation" was not far off. He longed for this with all his heart, and it was one of the bitterest disappointments of his life to see the first year of the new century go by without its advent. As before, in the days of Véronique, he felt personally frustrated by the lie thus given to his prophecies. And when the war of 1914 came, he did not straightway hail in it the vastness of the event which he had not ceased to invoke. Convinced that that event must be unlike any other, he felt that, in spite of such immensity of suffering, this could not yet be the Astonishment which was to bring about the final conflagration of the world.

Before following Bloy in his wartime meditations, full of allusions to a future of which we are now the witnesses or the victims, it behoves us to know what love he had felt for his country from his youth upwards, and what idea he had formed of the special destiny of France. For he steadfastly believed that in the epilogue to temporal history hers would be the part of a privileged witness and a martyr.

Critics have not been sparing with accusations of "national messianism" and with the reproach that Bloy's eulogy of France is a projection of his personal pride. The only thing that lends color to that accusation is the comparison between what he had to say of his own destiny and of the fate of France. Both serve him as an example and a symbol; because they are near and familiar to him, he looks to each for striking images to throw light upon all personal or national vocations. But, whether he is speaking of himself or of his country, Bloy *goes beyond* pride (if at moments he passes through it) and always arrives at that humble contemplation of facts which leads him to accept misery as well as glory, provided that this is the path of fidelity.

ALBERT BÉGUIN

France is, for him, the eldest daughter of the Church and the country to which Our Lady brought her tears. He has the greater urge to repeat this since he feels himself alone among his contemporaries in the realization of these things—for jingo nationalism was something far removed from his own love of France. Indeed it may be said that at the end of the nineteenth century nobody loved France—I will not say to the same extent but in the same way—as Bloy, who was neither a Jacobin carried away by the stirring words of '89 nor a man of the "right" disposed to regard patriotism as the prerogative of the conformist bourgeoisie. True, the contemporaries of his old age included Claudel and Péguy (not to mention hundreds of thousands of nameless Frenchmen) whose attachment to the fundamental France was as great as his own and equally remote from partisan allegiances; but he did not have the luck to know them or their work. He would almost certainly have had more in common with his compatriots of today, thanks to these two poets and their readers, thanks to Bernanos (so akin to himself) and to several others I can think of, thanks to the compulsion of events which has awakened both an awareness of France and an awareness of true Liberty...

Bloy never ceased to pore over French history in order to wrest from it the secret of its splendor and its misery. He dared to speak in terms of hyperbole, which will seem exaggerated only to those who do not know either his method or the true face of France, a face which remains consistent no matter what appearances or masks are imposed upon it by successive stages of its development. Bloy thought that, in the symbolic web of human history, France presented a more *legible* tapestry than any other people; but he did not suggest that this peculiar clarity gave her any right to power. He claimed another respect for her—that which love inspires. In his eyes this national history could only mean *the same thing* as that of all the nations, taken together or separately, since the whole history of mankind is a "revealed" text, the line of which, tortuous in our eyes, is perfectly clear to the eye of God. But it was the unique privilege of France to reflect more distinctly and more continually, in her

LÉON BLOY: A STUDY IN IMPATIENCE

days of magnificence as in her days of affliction, the meaning of the revelation through temporal events.

Therein lies the true pre-eminence of the French and that is what Bloy always has in mind when he asserts that, on the same footing as the Jewish people, France is "forever associated with the vicissitudes of Providence," or that her history is the immediate sequel of that related in the Scriptures, "something like a continuation of the New Testament, like a vast parable omitted by the Four Evangelists." If, across the span of time, the centuries unfold a revelation which "corroborates" the written Revelation, this is particularly clear in the succession of events that make up the history of France. And, be it specially noted, Bloy bases this conviction upon the fact that France has testified by suffering, after having testified by praise of God and by a prodigious work of Christianization. Essentially destined to bear witness, France began to testify by being, in the Middle Ages, extraordinarily productive of saints, of works, of songs, and, above all, of civilization; but she renewed her testimony when, gathering darkness about her, having lost her first transparence, she took up the load of martyrdom.

We need not dwell upon the attempts at exegesis in which Bloy, noting that the crow of the Cock rings through the Gospel at the moment when all is about to be consummated, concludes from this that France is to be a witness of the last days of all, and that, having been very mysteriously singled out by the words of the Gospel, she was "the secret of Jesus, the profound secret which he did not impart to his disciples and which he left it to the nations to divine..." (*Le Fils de Louis XVI*). The great testing years, 1870 and 1914, prompted him to utterances that were more simply moving and more readily intelligible. He had taken part in the Franco-German war as an irregular (and there is evidence that he was not boasting when he claimed that he and his comrades had been "a tough lot of terriers before the Lord"); but, in taking this step, he was very conscious of acting as a Christian. Right at the beginning, on July 26, he sent his friend Georges Landry some lines which are an almost verbal anticipation of Péguy's celebrated *Prière pour nous autres charnels* ("Happy are those who died for four roods of earth"):

"*The Mood of men who died for God in battle,*" Bloy wrote, "*comes nearest to the divine blood shed for the salvation of the world.* The gift of ourselves must surely be what is most pleasing in the sight of that greatest Giver of himself. Offer your life as a sacrifice. Beseech God to take it in exchange for the conversion of your kin. You know that this reversibility of suffering and acceptance is the supernatural foundation of the Christian edifice. There is nothing in the world more sublime. Such an impulse of the soul always finds hearkening and goes straight to the heart of God. I should envy him who died such a death, and all the ardent faith that God has given me thrills at the very thought."

But when about to take the field, on the Loire, he wrote these lines, to which he would certainly still have subscribed at the end of his life: "When people talk to me of patriotism, I don't know what they mean. *My own country is, first and foremost, the Church of Rome, and I mean to be a soldier of Christ.* Time will perhaps show that they are not the least formidable."

It is the spirit of Joan of Arc and the same hierarchy of the affections: to fight first of all for Christ, and then for one's country in so far as God has willed that country's existence for purposes of testimony. Thus it is in his book on the Maid, begun a few days before August 1, 1914, and finished during the early months of the war, that Léon Bloy has given most complete expression to the image of France which he had always kept in his heart. As we have seen, Bloy, while inheriting all the romanticism of Suffering, traced it back to its Christian sources, deepening it immeasurably in the process; even so he accepted that sense of nationality which had been rediscovered and revivified by the children of the Revolution, but placed it in an entirely different light. I scarcely know any point on which his example is more salutary. There is certainly every reason to be mistrustful of nationalist idolatries—that hardly needs stressing in 1943!—and to denounce the perils of a certain idea of national

LÉON BLOY: A STUDY IN IMPATIENCE

"vocation" or "mission" which may betray the worst kind of pride, the will to power, and the rejection of all universal truth. Romanticism offers only too many examples of these errors, and history has since then sufficiently demonstrated their fatal consequences. But when timorous Christians, afraid of falling victim to such fanaticisms, deny all possibility of belief in a vocation for one's native land or of a divine predilection for such and such a country, the caution they display is perhaps just as great an aberration, however correct the theological formulas on which it is based. If is not even necessary to cite in this connection the unmistakable message of Joan of Arc, whose claim to sainthood must be denied if we are not prepared to admit that she was sent by God to attest that the existence of "carnal cities" is precious to Him. Quite apart from that striking confirmation, it may be said, in the words of Bernanos, that in earthly life nations, like men, run "the immense risks of Baptism," or that, as Péguy puts it, they ought not to be "constituted in a state of deadly sin." Admittedly the resurrection of the "fatherland" idea, in the wake of the Revolution, had, in a case like Michelet's for instance, no concern with Christian justification. But it is not the first time in history (witness the beginnings of chivalry, originally secular, then Christianized) that mankind has made the apparently spontaneous and purely emotional discovery of something which, far from being necessarily dangerous, is capable of entering into the spiritual life of nations, as a treasure of great value. Those who know, as Bloy did, that nothing in history is in vain, can understand that these discoveries have their underlying meaning and that in each of them, as in every event that comes to pass, a word is hidden which is not of man. The peculiarities of a country, the personal character of its genius and of its awareness of mysteries—of which each nation, in the continuity of its saints, its mystics and its poets, seems called upon to know more especially one particular aspect—these things really make each people into a "person," as Michelet put it. It may be said of a nation, as Bloy said of every human soul, that it has its own "identity," "written and signed by God on each face"; that this personality is "a strictly private door into Paradise, which cannot be confused with the other doors"; and that what determines it is the vision which that nation has of God. It is only this underlying recognition of the diversity of the created world that enables the creature to accept the conditions of our incarnation. And, in opposition alike to a humanism that tries to disregard national differences and an idolatry that sets up one particular people above the rest in defiance of human universality, this submission to the real alone brings a true sense of the fellowship of all mankind. It is necessary to have this exalted idea of one's own country, and to believe that its very difference imposes the duty of humble testimony, before one can say like Bernanos: "There is nothing to be proud of in being French..."

It is in this spirit that Bloy should be read—Bloy who said that his only true fatherland was the Church and who was nevertheless more convinced than anyone that France had a vocation—if we are to understand him aright when, for instance, he makes Joan of Arc speak of the kingdom of France as a mere "lieutenancy" and remind the astonished Dauphin that "the real king of France" is Jesus Christ. The same thing applies, of course, to all countries; but Joan meant that the greatness of the French monarchy lay in its clear realization of this truth, in the fact that it rested on the Anointment, and that throughout the ages its governance was at pains to make the kingdom a truly Christian land and its policy and daily life a life of Christianity. Bloy had only this in mind even when he wrote these impertinent lines:

> Jesus Christ, the sole legitimate monarch and sovereign of all the monarchs of mud and ashes, could have no other earthly kingdom than France. One cannot imagine him king of Spain or of England, and it would be the height of madness or of absurdity to conceive him reigning over Prussia or Bulgaria, for instance...

Or when, with even greater audacity, and this time without

the least conscious paradox, he declares: "Integral, homogeneous France, the geographical France of the last three hundred years, was necessary to God, because *without her he would not have been completely God...*"

But he never came nearer to Péguy than in the passage in which, probing the mystery of divine predilection and speaking of France obedient and submissive, he saw in her pre-eminently the land of *hope* and *youth*.

> This exclusive privilege of France is a mystery. Whatever her infidelities and her crimes, she has come back to life under the knife of chastisement... Consider and reflect for a moment. God has only France! If she perished, Faith would still survive perhaps, somewhere or other, if only at the North or South Pole, along with shivering Charity; but there would be no more Hope!...
>
> She remembers having worshipped and broken all her idols including her own image, being both *indocile and quickwitted, unruly and repentant*, like those children of love whom it is difficult to punish.
>
> She has been punished, however—severely punished sometimes. That is the case today as it will be tomorrow, very probably; and the Arm upraised to strike her will be heavier than the withered arm of the German Emperor. No matter, all will be forgiven her in the end, because she has loved more greatly than any other, and because *her radiant youth is as irresistible as her courage.*

"We are not a nation of idolators"—it is again Bernanos speaking. And how can I refrain from quoting here what he wrote recently in his *Lettre à M. Roosevelt*, in answer to those who talk of ageing nations:

Old Europe is not so old as all that. You are too easily impressed by a few centuries—a mere trifle. Admittedly, comparisons do not prove very much; but I may make my ideas a little clearer if I ask you to consider that the cathedral of Chartres, for instance, is in reality much younger, that is to say much more in harmony with young hearts and young minds, than many of the monuments which seemed to your millionaires of fifty years ago the last word in modernity. Europe is not old; it is her institutions that were too old for her. The peoples of Europe are not old; it is the European *elites* that need renewing but won't hear of it, and encumber us with their refuse... *It is absurd to believe that nations pass from infancy to old age, like animals, by an ineluctable process.* The spirit of old age and the spirit of youth can dominate them in turn, and if the spirit of old age, that is to say the spirit of avarice, prevails too long, what does it matter how many centuries are recorded in' the calendar of history?... Europe has been an incomparable well-spring of the spirit; she will never abdicate the rights which she claims, rightly or wrongly, over the spiritual destiny of the world. I am speaking here of the peoples, not of the governments or of the privileged few. The *elites* have doubtless a much clearer notion of these rights. Only, they do not set store by them; they will gladly sell them to you for a mess of pottage...

II.

Twice over, in 1870 and in 1914, this man who had such a lofty conception of the destinies of France, and whose grief it was to look oh, helpless, at the downfall of a world without God, had cause to believe that the great catastrophe had come. Twice over, he might have thought that the hour had struck when France was to be punished for her infidelity and to know purification by fire. But twice over, except in a few moments of profound sadness, he conquered this temptation, great though it was for a mind so engrossed in apocalyptic prophecies; and the testing of his country and of mankind as a whole served to add new depth to the views he held.

We have already seen how 1870 revealed to him his own love of France. The sight of the disaster brought him other lessons too, and very soon he came to understand the futility of human calculations. "Realists," no doubt, judging by the disproportion in manpower and material, had already come to the conclusion that there was nothing for it but complete surrender; and their attitude was logical, since they thought that the events of history were exclusively governed by relative strengths. In a great letter published by Hubert Colleye, Bloy countered such ideas with the protest of a Christian, for whom the breakdown of the balance of power is a reason for casting oneself heroically upon the sole resource of hope:

> May very Christian France become once more a flaming sword in the immaculate right hand of the Queen of Heaven. May all hearts be possessed with the madness of divine love; there is no other means of salvation.
>
> *Those who count the number of soldiers needed for our defense, those who reckon, from afar, the material chances of triumph or overthrow—it is they who are the real madmen.* The absolute truth, which should be glaringly apparent to the least of Christians, is that God means to undo us and that he has already made a beginning. To think anything else is daydreaming and criminal blindness. Let us bow our heads in the dust; that is all that is left for us to do. And may God's holy Will be done upon the earth of France.

Against "political realism" the language of Joan of Arc, from the depths of the ages, comes quite naturally to the lips of Bloy, who at that time cannot have known much about the Maid's history. Shortly afterwards, in a letter to Georges Landry, he was even more explicit in detailing what were for him the real causes of modern chaos: the man who sets out to live on the single plane of "realities"—as he calls the material world, robbed of all its mysterious depth—necessarily condemns himself to error and rushes upon his doom. For, by closing his eyes to his own spiritual being, he becomes incapable of directing his temporal life, and any "order" which he sets out to establish is nothing but misery and sham, since it is not irradiated by the only real Order, the invisible order of creation:

> Oh! when I think of the two aspects of man, when I think that behind that rampart of flesh there is a whole world of souls, so different from that of bodies, a whole immortal hierarchy with its Kings, its Aristocracies, its Magistracies, hereditary and of divine right, its Soldiers, its Executioners, its People and its Rabble! and that this world manages its affairs under the eye of God by a *real* and infallible *policy,* nothing ever getting out of place and disturbing the primordial Order! Few give a thought to all that. And yet!!! It is only when the human eye is withdrawn, and turned towards these underlying depths, that it begins to perceive the divine lineaments of the supreme order, and *modern excesses come from the fact that men have lost the power to look at things in this way.* The only Education, the only Politics are those which concern themselves with souls; for in the problem of Man it will not do to get rid of man.

In the war of 1914 a recurrence of this same situation confronted a Bloy who had in the meantime "won his identity" and deepened all the spiritual intuitions of his youth; instead of the "convert," still groping his way from discovery to discovery, the emergency this time found a man who for thirty years had not ceased to worship certain aspects of the Christian mystery which had become the solid foundations of his inward life. But it would be a mistake to picture him as completely "withdrawn into his own soul" and as a stranger to an age which he certainly detested but in which he nevertheless

LÉON BLOY: A STUDY IN IMPATIENCE

remained actively present, with all his hostility and all his sorely wounded need for love. In his own heart he never accepted the defeat of 1870; nor did he, any more than Péguy, yield to the spirit of abdication which spread through the bourgeois and intellectual *elites*. He denounces this acquiescence in national mediocrity in one of the bitterest and most virulent passages in *Le Désespéré*:

> Oh, we are beaten, and no mistake! Beaten flat in heart and spirit. We take our pleasures like a conquered people and we work like a conquered people. We laugh, weep, love, speculate, write and sing like a conquered people. The whole of our intellectual and moral life is explained by this single fact that we are a cowardly, dishonored, conquered people. We have become tributaries of anything that has an impulse of energy in this crumbling world, which is appalled by our unutterable degradation...

When the war of 1914 broke out, Bloy had crossed the threshold of old age, and for some years his daily lot had been sweetened by the presence of friends. But events were destined to affect his personal life, to scatter the circle of intimates whose frequent visits he loved, to bring back his old solitude and even to deprive him of the material aid which, without putting an end to his poverty, had saved him from want. Several of the men for whom he had a warm affection, Philippe Raoux, André Dupont and Jean Boussac, the son-in-law of his dear Pierre Termier, were killed in action, and his *Méditations* show how deeply he felt these bereavements. But, above all personal afflictions, the common suffering of his people saddened his days, together with the oft-expressed regret that he was no longer of an age to offer his life. The massacres at the beginning of the war, partly due to un-preparedness, haunted and agonized him; and later on, throughout the long war of positions, his imagination pictured the vast unmoving front, that frontier guarded by the living and protected by thousands of dead, a sacred rampart always in danger of being breached. The melancholy pages of his two last, and perhaps finest, books, *Méditations d'un Solitaire en 1916* and *Dans les Ténèbres*, are filled with this infinite compassion for others—for those who die untended, for generous youth feeling itself in honor bound to take part in a hideous struggle, though the reasons officially proclaimed offered no acceptable meaning to grace their sacrifice. One of the *Méditations* voices, with admirable poetic restraint, the lament of France, the mother, for her children. On August 30, 1914, Bloy had described in his diary how, waiting all night at a railway station, at the most dramatic moment of the great retreat, he had seemed to hear the wailing of an unknown voice. But it was during the last few months of his life, in the summer of 1917, that he wrote this *Sanglot dans le Nuit*, which must be quoted in full:

> "Why art thou cast down, O my soul, and why art thou disquieted in me?" I was travelling in Normandy or in Brittany. With a muffled roar the train sped through the thick night and my sadness knew no bounds. I had been reading an account of one of those terrible holocausts which are turning France into a fountain of blood welling from a seemingly exhaustless spring. Some of those dearest to me had fallen, and I was inwardly praying My Lady of Compassion and all the Angels of Lamentation for tears enough to wash all those poor bodies abandoned by their souls and denied even the charity of burial.
>
> Suddenly there was a great silence. The train stopped in the middle of the wilds, as so often before—no doubt to let a convoy of wounded or dying go past. Then, oh then! a terrible thing happened. From the breast of this unknown landscape, shrouded in darkness, there rose a human cry, expressive of unutterable pain. This sob, feeble at first, and mistakable for the gasp of a bird in the clutches of some night marauder, soon grew louder, heightening, as it swelled, the note of human suffering in its agony. And it was not bodily suffering, oh no! but

suffering of the soul, the wild desolation of a mother who has seen her children butchered, and for whom there is no comfort. I cannot express the anguish born of this lament, breathed out into the darkness and spreading through the whole of that invisible countryside.

It was not an articulate plaint but, as I have said, a great convulsive sob, drawing new life from its own dying breath; a frenzy of weeping, with something universal in it, recalling, perhaps, what ancient writers tell of the nightlong lament of barbarian women wailing over their dead. But this classical parallel, which my mind was loath to admit, was belied by a strange something that was august and Christian, that raised the agony above nature and made my heart burst with compassion...

The train moved on and I no longer heard the terrible lamentation. I had travelling companions who were sound asleep, and it took me, I remember, some time to discover that this sob had been *for me alone.*

Later I passed through a number of provinces, Orléanais, Touraine, Périgord, Auvergne, and the departments of the South. Everywhere the miracle was repeated. Everywhere the same sob in the blackness of the night, and my travelling companions sunk in the same profound torpor. At last I understand that it was the great France of long ago that was weeping in me, the poor aged mother of all the children of France!

Yet however apocalyptic events might seem, Bloy from the outset would not let himself interpret them as the beginning of the last great calamities. It may even be that, in laying such stress upon the inadequacy of the present punishment, he was protecting himself against that hope and impatience to which he had given way too readily in the past, in the days of Véronique, or when the new century was just round the corner. In the quiescence of old age he had lost confidence in his own prophetic sense. But, above all, having so often imagined that the supreme events of temporal history would be beyond all human prevision—and having so thoroughly convinced himself that the hardness of human hearts called for suffering beyond any known affliction, in order that the eyes of the blind might be opened—he could not be satisfied with the present horror. While, all around him, some were despairing, unable to reconcile such a mass of destruction and murder with their own optimism; while others were proclaiming that a conflict involving so many peoples and causing such loss of life must needs be the last of all wars and the herald of a world shocked into peace by the very horror of what it had seen—Bloy remained skeptical. Nor did he let himself be carried away by the slogans which presented this enormous combat as a struggle for Justice, Right, Democracy; Bloy did not believe in these capital letters and would not consent to reduce the mission of France to this idealism of high-sounding words. It was not in the camp of jingoism that this patriot was to be found and, entering with all his soul into the defense of his country, which for him made the war a holy one, he suffered grievously at the sight of men being sent to their death without receiving more human and concrete reasons for fighting, reasons more worthy of their courage.

Tirelessly he recalled the threats of La Salette and voiced his prophetic conviction that this trial would not suffice, because men had fallen so low that it would take more than that to rouse them to real consciousness, and because the Supernatural, when the time came for it to burst forth upon the world of history, would show a far more terrifying countenance. From the very outset this was the language he used; on September 10, 1914, for instance, he wrote to Jeanne Termier:

> France has much to expiate, having so greatly scorned the tears of her Sovereign Lady. True, she is expiating at this very moment, but it is an expiation *without repentance*... But the time has not yet come. I see no *signs*. God is not showing himself

LÉON BLOY: A STUDY IN IMPATIENCE

visibly, indisputably... I, for my part, am waiting for Signs, and so far I have not seen any. So long as the Supernatural does not appear manifestly, incontestably, terribly, exquisitely, *nothing* will have been accomplished.

God cannot be commonplace. Now, what is happening at the present moment, this European war, the like of which has never been seen before, with its fifteen or twenty million fighting desperately, with its apocalyptic *appearance,* with the great tribulations it has brought and is bringing in its wake—all that is quite commonplace. All that is an *illusion produced by the Devils* horrible, if you like, but merely an illusion to hoodwink men, and especially the Catholics of France and Belgium, into thinking that they are at last being punished in earnest and that they have paid their debt.

...Streams of blood, infinite miseries, the collapse of two empires, all the nations in at the death falling tooth and claw upon the quarry; *the historical banality of all the ages*; and then nothing—nothing but a poor man of sixty-eight to seventy, a writer through necessity or weakness, who is waiting on his knees for God's deed.

I repeat, Jeanne, that what is happening is nothing more than a hideous grin on the face of the devil, *aping the Future* more abominably than ever before. That is all. We should not be afraid but should tell ourselves that *this is not it at all*, that the Holy Spirit represented by Our Lady of La Salette will not punish in this way but in a manner worthy of Her, an absolutely unknown, incomprehensible, undivinable manner.

This is not yet "it"! The invaders of France are described as monsters from the pit. What an exaggeration! What a lack of all sense of proportion! They are odious, they deserve to be hated (we shall soon see with what a frenzy of sacred hate) but they are nothing to the fiends that will one day be loosed to ravage the earth, or the angels of vengeance come to chastise man and to kindle souls in the great

ALBERT BÉGUIN

final holocaust of burning love. All that is happening is only a feeble prelude, a simulacrum. A letter dated July 13, 1915, says as much:

> How can one see anything Final in the sorry German farce, horrible and bloody though it be? It is really too paltry, too shamefully fatuous, too nauseating... Finality does not and cannot pertain to such tools of the Devil. In fulfilment of the prophecies which you know as well as I do, Europe is already in flames and it wants but little for the rest of the world to catch fire. Even the blind and the deaf feel the coming of the unknown storm to which no past experience could serve as presage. But a forerunner was needed for this nameless cataclysm, and the lowest of all nations was singled out for this office by the supernatural Disdain of Him whom nobody mentions. When the real Drama has begun, the true inanity of the German colossus will be so evident that it will be difficult to spare it another thought in the infinite convulsion of new terrors...

And Bloy was to add, on August 25, 1915: "The Germans are not frightful enough."

Not that he harbored the least temptation to softness or humanity towards the enemy of the moment! He urged that the invaders should no longer be considered soldiers, that no prisoners should be taken since "we are not at war"; and the vocabulary he reserves for the foe is impossible to quote in these days of censorship... No, indeed! Bloy is not the man for non-resistance to evil. He does not think—as many Christians consider it their duty to do, and as some would fain have made it a watchword in 1939—that war should be waged "without hatred" and the enemy's soldiers considered purely as "creatures who have known salvation." Nor does he think that, however much the crimes of a people cry to Heaven, they should not be judged, on the pretext that all are in some measure to blame for the outbreak of war (though we shall see that a feeling of universally shared responsibility was by no means alien to Bloy). More

LÉON BLOY: A STUDY IN IMPATIENCE

than once he condemns neutrality of judgment, all his allusions to it being prompted by the Church's silence, under which he suffered profoundly, though he could never countenance soldier-priests. He was obviously thinking of the Vatican's non-intervention when in 1916, after one of his books (*Au Seuil de l'Apocalypse*) had been banned by the Swiss censorship, he came out with the amusing sally: "Would that I might prove equally alarming to all neutralities!"

As might be expected, there is nothing ambiguous in Bloy's answer to a certain kind of "evangelism" which takes evading action in the form of an equitable indulgence towards the conquerors and their victims, the oppressors and the persecuted, the warlike and the peaceable; nor to the deplorable attitude of those who preach unconcern in the midst of the general horror and recommend us to "keep cool" for fear of giving way to reprehensible passions which would disturb the lofty composure of a "detached" mind. Bloy was not the man to use the soft pedal, when everything is at stake, and he reminds one of Joan of Arc's dumbfounded rejoinder (when her ecclesiastical judges asked her, with an inimitable air of mealy-mouthed dismay, whether she had not found herself in places where Englishmen were being killed): "How you drop your voices!" It did not seem to her that so many precautions were necessary in speaking of what was a fact, or that it was the proper thing to pretend that the earth was a place of innocence. So Bloy, doubtless recalling various exhortations to universal concord, wrote a eulogy of Hatred well calculated to ruffle the sentimental and the apostles of forbearance, whose agitation it is not unpleasant to imagine. It should not be forgotten that the man who is speaking here is a lover of Justice and that his constant acceptance of it in his own case gives him license, perhaps, to speak of "love's fervent Hatred." As for the little speech which he puts into the mouths of the apostates, ready for every sort of abjuration in the face of victorious might, offering ten times what is demanded of them at the point of the Bayonet, and eager to betray their faith and embrace the paganism of their masters, it must surely be allowed a place among the prophetic writings of Léon Bloy:

ALBERT BÉGUIN

After two years of massacres and atrocities, I am looking for a man sufficiently inspired to tell me exactly what is happening, to give a plausible name to this conflict of all the nations, to this unparalleled loosing of captives from the nethermost pits. Dead silence everywhere. We are so stupid that nobody has anything to say. But now a diabolical sentimentality takes the stage.

There are those who, with a horrible distortion of the Gospel, dare to speak of forgiveness, saying that Hatred is as contrary to Justice as to Mercy, and that it is the duty of Christians to give their enemies everything they ask for and even more. "If anyone would take away thy coat, let him have thy cloak also." That is what Jesus says in the Sermon on the Mount.

You would like half of France, messieurs les Prussiens? Take it all, right up to the Pyrenees. You want to destroy our churches after having profaned them. You must have the souls of our children, to quench their light by corrupting them. Don't stand on ceremony. We have still quite a number of old priests whom you have not had time to murder, and we still have the Body of Christ consecrated by them. If it would amuse you to trample it under foot or throw it to the pigs, we are too good Christians to deny you that little pleasure. We shall thus be fulfilling the law of perfect meekness and mildness which the Redeemer laid down. And don't forget that we have still a lot of women and girls whom it might be enjoyable to rape. Help yourselves. We will give up everything, we will renounce everything, even our Christianity, to please you; and if you would like to turn us into Mohammedans, we are quite ready...

Well, I don't agree to anything. I don't renounce anything and I am convinced that the infinite hatred of all the saints for the devils is precisely what should be offered to the enemies of France. Even in ordinary times, when a war was inflicted upon her, I thought so, and the tocsin of religious awe shook my tower from top to bottom; but, today, how could the first glimmerings of an idea of mercy come into my heart? This is not a war like any other, not even an unjust war, but a wholesale onslaught by cannibals crazed with stupid pride and dead to all human feeling.

To be sure, I remember some of my friends, hideously sacrificed; but what is my private loss in this flood of mourning? How can I locate that pitiful little group among a million victims who have gone groping their way towards God through a red mist? And this great horror, such as mankind had never seen before, what is it compared with the frightful defilement of the Kingdom of Our Lady of Sorrows, unspeakably devastated and polluted by this spawn of the devil?

Oh, sacred Hatred of the children of Light for the children of Darkness, what a refuge you are! What a consolation! What a comfort! Infinite hatred, with no possibility of pardon, with no hope of being sated by anything but the extermination, forever, of that race of Satan's votaries which tried to annex us to its hell!

Waking or sleeping, I always behold this monster born of the basest, the most infamous apostasy, whom the inertia or the blindness of the world has allowed to grow in stature for two hundred years, and who can now be conquered only by the concerted efforts of all the nations. I see it continually and my heart throbs like a bell in the night of All Souls. Then I feel a boundless hate, an absolute hate, a virgin and immaculate hate which announces the presence of God and without which I see clearly that I could not be a Christian. It is the hatred enjoined by the Holy Spirit, the eucharistic hatred, Love's fervent hatred for a swarm of sixty million accursed beings possessed by fiends!

In the anguish of those days of war, Bloy turned towards France, and all that he had ever thought on the subject came back to his mind, now that he felt her existence threatened. It should be recalled that he never speaks of France without in some way using her as an example and an image, but that at the same time it is France herself, in her own person, that is the object of his love.

So long as one remains on the earthly plane of political events, the France of 1914 is, in his eyes, the innocent victim of aggression; and on that plane the war is neither more nor less than an act of brigandage committed upon her. But from a higher viewpoint France is guilty, and the ordeal into which she has been hurled has the value of an atonement.

France is guilty. Oh, not on those counts which have more recently called forth such bitter reproaches from certain Frenchmen and many Pharisees of our acquaintance: that she had neglected to build up her material strength; that she had allowed herself to be badly governed from the standpoint of power; that she had fallen short in social progress or industrial development... Bloy is far removed from that kind of *mea culpa* and mania for self-accusation. He knows only too well that his country's weakness in face of an enemy trained exclusively in warlike virtues is partly the result of her qualities, of her inability to stoop to the level of the others and to live solely with a view to a trial of strength. He would not have been among those who recognize in military victory the sanction of a real superiority and conclude from it that the conqueror ought to be hailed as master or held up as an example. He would have required other proofs.

No. If France is guilty, it is because she is the Eldest Daughter, and for that reason, as Péguy said, any scandal is the more flagrant when it concerns her. She has neglected her supernatural mission by ceasing to live as one who bears witness, by being unfaithful to her Christian tradition, and deaf, more especially, to the solemn warnings of La Salette.

But, needless to say, Bloy's feelings have nothing in common with the lamentations of the right-minded about the "dechristianization of the country districts" or "unbelief among the working class." Though opposed to the French Revolution and to any democratic or "popular" ideology, Bloy, a former royalist, certainly placed more hope in the living soul of the poor, even the free-thinking poor, than in the conventional piety of the bourgeoisie. He would not have hesitated to say, as Bernanos says today, that "it is the *elites* which, claiming to be more Christian than ever, are gradually going over to a pagan order," while the people "have remained true to the more or less dim tradition of the old Christianity"; and that it is quite conceivable that Christian virtues, Christian chivalry and honor, will be reborn first of all among unbelievers rather than under the hard shell of bigotry.

Bloy thinks that, France being a person, a soul within an earthly body, everything that happens to her falls outside the apparent laws of history, because nothing that concerns her is not part of a spiritual drama. In it everything goes back to conflicts between good and evil, France being necessarily either faithful or unfaithful to that in which she has her being and her sole source of strength: the carrying of the gospel message down the generations. It is this that makes her destiny perennially representative of the destiny of every people, of every soul, and linked with the common destiny of the nations by an underlying fellowship.

This being so, Bloy accepted for his country, as for himself, the suffering which means nearness to God. If he sometimes hesitated in his theories of what was going to happen, he rejected no hypothesis, however tragic, pinning all his hopes on finding the most hidden meaning in the misfortunes of war and in its outcome, whatever that was to be.

"There is nothing completely horrible," he wrote to Pierre Termier on July 14, 1915, "when one watches the Hand of God, the invisible Hand which we know to be there and of which our hearts give us glimpses... *We know that there is no suffering without proximity to God.* Because God is drawing near, we shall see the most terrible things that it is possible to see, while waiting for Him to show himself indisputably by extraordinary miracles..."

ALBERT BÉGUIN

Bloy is often led to believe in a temporary atonement, common to all peoples, but in which France, the first to be punished *because* of her primacy, will also be the first to rise again. This kingdom is too valuable to God for him to let it perish, "but it will have to go as far as the threshold of the last door of death," to rise again "from the midst of the dying." But France's sacrifice will then be taken into account "and it may well be that, in the end, a mysterious and incorruptible virginity will be her portion" (August 25, 1915).

At other times, however, Bloy sets aside all hope of earthly recovery and simply holds that the relentless punishment of France must, by its very violence and enormity, be an outward and visible sign of divine favor. A letter dated December 11, 1915, to Emile Baumann expresses this:

> We know that God needs France, that he has an incorrigible love for this harlot, and that in inflicting upon her heavy punishments which are bound to become greater still, *he is actually treating her as a lover would.* The chains which he is now placing on her wrists and round her heart, so that the unclean may outrage her, will one day be seen to have been bonds of mercy and glory...

But there are also times when—believing, in spite of himself, that the apocalyptic cataclysm is at hand—he sees France as the field in which God is about to reveal himself. Thus the most saddening and even the most shocking aspects of the war, the contrast between the bravery of the soldiers and the profiteers behind the lines, with social injustice more glaring than ever, *rejoice his heart.* For, in this division which so sharply separates the good from the wicked, he recognizes a symbol of human nature and its duality. And it seems to him that, for France, *it* is a kind of deeply hidden greatness to be thus chosen by God as a language through which the whole of history is illumined and the mystery of social inequity is brought into the light of day.

LÉON BLOY: A STUDY IN IMPATIENCE

On December 27, 1915, he wrote to Jean Boussac:

I never cease to look at the future beyond the present pain and that vision thrills me with joy. It is in this sense that I am an optimist. Surely no one is better able than I am to see the present evil, which I have so often foretold, and the future evil, now imminent and growing clear enough to blind one. *How could I help rejoicing that God is at last visibly in action upon the earth?* For what is happening is not really of man, and there can be no doubt that we are on the threshold of the Apocalypse.

There are now two Frances: France at the front and France behind the lines, the one almost sublime and the other unspeakably vile. Thus for the first time *the antinomy which, all too often overlooked, is the basis of human history* stands out in stark simplicity. A living wall of poor men who have accepted death and anguish and, behind that protecting wall, those who grub for gold in blood and filth, the profiteers and the pleasure-seekers!...

But, of all Bloy's writings which owe their inspiration to the destiny of France at war—France whose possible defeat he never ceased to imagine and for whom, in a sense, he dreaded a victory which would confirm her in the error of her ways (letters to Maritain dated September 9 and October 12, 1914)—perhaps the most moving is the wonderful conclusion of *Jeanne d'Arc et l'Allemagne*. Identifying the whole country with the saint at the stake, he greets the martyrdom of his people as a hope. It is for this martyrdom that he reserves the name of "victory" and, if he pictures France as saved at the point of death, that is because his love, in spite of all, revolts at the thought that one so beloved could perish. This passage has an extraordinary beauty of language, full of tenderness and simplicity in its last lines, which are—a rare thing in Bloy—a poetic eulogy of French Christendom, of the presence of the Cross in the daily life of France:

The present horrors have an apocalyptic aspect which, it may be predicted, will become clearer still. But in the end the Iron Cross will be conquered by the Wooden Cross, because that Cross is the choice of God and the sign of his dilection. It may be that, in the course of the unimaginable events of which the present war seems but the prelude, France will in her turn be sent to the Heroines stake, condemned like her by the apostate priests who denied the Mother of God when she wept upon the Mountain of La Salette, accusing them. Yes, France, always answerable for her spiritual leaders, might well be condemned, by their criminal infidelity, to perish in dreadful flames. Thus she would be left with the poor Wooden Cross of Joan of Arc, which she will have none of at the moment, but which might save her miraculously at the last hour, so that the human race should not be lost.

The Cross of the needy and the vagrant, the kindly Cross of old country roads, the Cross of welcome for the destitute, the wayworn, those with bleeding feet and weeping hearts, those who have been bitten by the serpents of the wilderness and who, on beholding it, are healed of their wounds, the Cross of misery and of glory!

The war inspired Bloy with other meditations, not confined to the destiny of France. It is true that his heart was entirely hers and that she remained for him the specific reality in which he could discover the ultimate meaning of events. But through and beyond her he sought, as always, understanding of mystery, and this time the mystery to be penetrated was the inexplicable sweep and spread of misery in a universe governed by Providence. Contemplating the facts and asking himself what they meant, Bloy was led to the rediscovery, by new ways and under new symbols, of most of the great truths by which he had always lived. Thus his wartime diary, his letters of the same period and his last books are, as it were, a summary of his doctrine or rather—for it is not, strictly speaking, a

LÉON BLOY: A STUDY IN IMPATIENCE

doctrine—a recrudescence of his love for certain truths of the Faith. Many passages characterized by marvelous lucidity of style and perfect mastery of thought have already been quoted from these great pacific writings, in which his intense ardor had not ebbed but had attained the serenity of a beautiful old age. Thus in the events of the day Bloy rediscovered the meaning of Suffering, of universal Fellowship, of the Communion of the Saints, of personal Identity, of the imminence of Death and Judgment.

In the light of these last researches, Bloy's attitude towards the catastrophe became one which, even at the lowliest level, inspired him with passages rich in salutary lessons for our own times. There is nothing cautious and timorous about Bloy's preachings, which are of a grand robustness. He does not avert his eyes from anything; he seeks no refuge from the torturing thought of human suffering; he preaches neither resignation nor indifference. But, taking a firm grasp of pain, eager like Péguy to "delve deeper into suffering" and to place himself "right on the axis of sorrow," he tries to understand, to fathom the effects which so much misery produces upon souls, and to show what it can create in a truly receptive inward life. A few of these very simple reflections may be noticed once more before we turn, for the last time, to the impatience of Léon Bloy and the supreme expressions of that ardor with which he awaited the Ineffable.

> Why should so much evil be let loose upon the continent of Europe, after centuries of Christian civilization, unless it is that the decadence of modern souls can now be cured only by the violent shock of a brutal warning? When grace comes up against creatures enclosed in a carapace of refusal and indifference, it chooses other ways than its favorite path of gentle penetration, and resorts to force in order to obtain the assent no longer willingly given:
>
> Might it not be said (we read in *Jeanne d'Arc*) that utter misery, the misery that crushes the heart and makes men like

maimed war-horses, is—in the absence of living faith—the sovereign remedy of the Holy Spirit for *supernaturalizing our fallen Christianity*?

The same idea is stamped with a deeper impress in an entry, in Bloy's diary, dated November 10, 1916. This entry is a model of that inner logic to which Bloy attained and that sureness of thought which was his towards the end of his life.

> God created man in his own image in order that we might do what he himself had done. He assumed our nature in order to die for us. We ought to assume his nature in order to give our lives for him, which is our strict and absolute duty.
> But everybody today refuses to do this. *So God takes our lives all the same, in terrible fashion and that sums up contemporary history.*

Thus misery, once again, appears as an act of love on the part of God, who cannot do without the gift of human souls, because He longs for it and He means to be satisfied. How, then, can one fail to rejoice in suffering, since in the life of nations, as of persons, it "means nearness to God, promise, hope? Bloy's hope was certainly confidence in divine mercy, but the whole orientation of his being inclined him more towards adoration of Justice. And it is justice that he invoked in writing to Pierre Termier on July 28, 1915 (the letters of that year are a source of inexhaustible riches):

> I know you are an optimist. I am one too. Only, there are two different kinds: the optimism of Mercy and the optimism of Justice, which certainly meet in the Absolute, but after what a journey!
> You hope for mercy *before* the end of the punishment… My way of looking at things compels me to rejoice at the worst misfortunes (which it is agony to foresee) because I know

LÉON BLOY: A STUDY IN IMPATIENCE

them to be necessary, that is to say willed by God, and consequently calling for worship, because it is a thousand times clear to me that the cataclysms announced are the indispensable prodromes of the Reign of God upon earth, which it is our duty to pray for unceasingly...

And on December 11 of the same year he told Emile Baumann in much the same tone that, if the torments of the present "vision of monstrous injustice" threw him completely "out of gear," he refused to give way to a "merely human" pessimism and persisted in finding his consolation in the thought that "it is God who is in action" through this reign of horror.

Bloy did not fail to ask himself how far mankind was responsible for the unleashing of war. Like all Frenchmen he was convinced that certain major criminals could be singled out, and he foretold their punishment by Providence at the entreaty of one poor child endowed with faith: in answer to her prayer the night will be filled with "a great noise of foot soldiers, horsemen and chariots on the march," conjured up in dreadful fashion by "the movement of the lips of this innocent, whom God will certainly obey." And then "at an enormous distance, beyond the mountains and the rivers, the barbarian chief, the emperor, as savage as he is stupid," hearing this threatening voice, this "feeble breath capable of extinguishing a hundred thousand hearts," will reel before his oncoming doom.

But Bloy quickly passes beyond this plane of simple guilt. He goes beyond it, first of all, in a very proper feeling of compassion for those who have burdened themselves with such enormous crimes and who seem to him the most pitiable victims of his war, the only ones without hope, having pledged and lost their souls. Whereas those subjected to injustice are saved by the miracle of Suffering. On April 5, 1915, Bloy wrote these extraordinary lines:

ALBERT BÉGUIN

Consider the inexpressible affliction, the utter destitution of the mighty who willed this fiendish war, and compare their future fate with that of their innumerable victims.

We are always on the right side when we are with those who suffer persecution and injustice.

Fellowship of suffering, so forcibly expressed here, is one of Bloy's great empirical convictions. But he also comes to assert a fellowship of guilt, which up to then had perhaps been an idea less familiar to him. In a letter dated February 17, 1916, to Jean de La Laurencie—who must have been a truly exceptional person to have more than once aroused the most definite feelings of humility that Bloy ever experienced—he rises to that high level of thought at which all responsibility is shared equally among men. If what is happening is an expiation, it is for all; and if the world is dechristianized, it is not my neighbor's doing but my own, along with the rest:

> You ask God not to let you go "without having been of some use," and those words moved me strangely. That has long been the theme of my constant prayer. You can say what you like, I cannot convince myself that I have been of any use up to the present, unless in trying my neighbor's patience...
>
> Nothing short of self-sacrifice has any reality in this connection, and I am dreadfully far from that. If I had been capable of it, if I had had the soul of a martyr, who knows whether many others might not have been spared the hideous nightmare to which you refer and from which I have been suffering continually for nineteen months? *For each of us is certainly responsible for the present abomination.* That is something to make anyone suffer who is capable of understanding...

Living in this constant worship of divine Justice, and convinced that the war was the punishment sent to men who had set out to

LÉON BLOY: A STUDY IN IMPATIENCE

build their terrestrial city in "the absence of God," Bloy could not, of course, share the optimism of those who believed that a new order would spring from the victory of one side or the other. He did not put his trust in a triumph of democratic progress and of mankind's faith in itself, since they seemed to him the very causes of the disaster. But neither did he revert to his monarchist convictions, deeming the reactionaries, in their ignorance of the course of history, still "more impious" than their opponents. Both were, in his eyes, people who "did not understand," and Bloy, between two camps equally blind, once more felt himself cast out into the prophet's solitude. The last *Meditation d'un Solitaire*, a pendant to the prefatory passage in which he set forth the loneliness of the soul on the threshold of death, voices his lament:

> Once more I am alone—or so it seems to me. Nobody appears to see what I see or to think what I think.... True, I hear sobs and I hear laughter, but at an immense distance. The sobs come from those who are mourning their dead or the loss of their possessions; the laughter is the infamous merrymaking of those who batten on calamities; and the whole forms a strange, remote, concert in which the most attentive ear cannot distinguish one Christian note...
>
> The growing difficulties of daily life have in vain made the dullest realize that the social mechanism is out of gear, and the open fury of the promoters of anarchy has in vain raged more and more loudly around them; they have experts to teach them that *all this is only a passing crisis*, the effect of an excessive strain upon the springs, and that, immediately after the victory of which they are confident, men and things will recover their balance. If it is not exactly the golden age that they promise, it will perhaps be the silver age, or at worst the "paper age," which seems to have begun already. The brazen-browed intellectuals no doubt attach a greater importance to the misfortunes of the age and even go so far as to consider an immediate restoration

of perfect happiness improbable; but *both types have faith in Humanity, which is to work all sorts of miracles.*

How could I help being lonely, having nothing but contempt for this humanity which seeks to supplant its Creator, and regarding all *the catchwords of progress, civilization and, above all, democracy, which have so long replaced trust in God, as clumsy impostures of the Devil?*

How could I endure contact with the Catholics themselves, *the modern Catholics who think it possible to unite the corpse of the past with the carrion of the present and dream of who knows what sort of a restoration of the old royal building, in which a watchdog's kennel would be offered to Our Lord Jesus Christ?...* The foolishness of these predestinates of slaughter seems to me even more impious than the idiot fury of the worst sectarians.

But, if no earthly hope is permissible at the end of the calamities, what does Bloy expect? What prospect does the future offer? The closing lines of the passage just quoted tell us, and reveal once more Bloy's *impatience*, that great impatience of longing for God which runs through his whole life and accompanies him into the war years, giving direction to all that we have already seen of his solitary meditations and coloring them with this one unchanging expectancy:

"Then what is left?" I shall be asked. "Absolutely nothing but to celebrate the Last Supper in the Catacombs and *wait for the unknown Deliverer whom the Paraclete is to send, when the blood of the many who have paid the penalty and the tears of the few elect shall have sufficiently cleansed the earth…*"

"When France has been purified by the scourge of divine Justice," Mélanie wrote in 1892, "when she has been almost destroyed and is nearly dead, then God will give her *a Man.*"

LÉON BLOY: A STUDY IN IMPATIENCE

It is for him and no one else that I have been waiting, in my loneliness, for forty years.

Once more Bloy takes his stand on the prophecies of La Salette. But what exactly is meant by that strange announcement of the coming of "a Man," a Deliverer of France? Countless passages in Bloy's diary and correspondence between 1914 and 1917 revert to these mysterious hopes, sometimes giving concrete details which are nevertheless rather confusing. The allusions to this Figure become more frequent, especially in the closing months of 1915:

> August 25: I am waiting for *a Man so infinitely unknown* that beside him the greatest strangers will seem like first cousins; *a man in rags*, I should imagine; *a barefoot tramp*, I very much hope; but a man specially sent, whose mission is to accomplish all.

> October 25: For my own part, I am waiting for *a man*. I am waiting with unshakable confidence…

> November 1: Yes, a *man coming from God*, and it is the only hope…

> November 12: I am waiting for ONE man from God, and he is long in coming…

> November 20: I am waiting for *the Holy Spirit*, who is the Fire of God, and I have really nothing else to say.

> November 20: I do not know him any more than you do, but I know that he will come, soon perhaps—or rather that he will *appear*, for *I believe he has come already.*

> December 17: I am waiting for a man, a *Leader given by God.*

ALBERT BÉGUIN

My constant, devouring thought is this: All these horrors must end, as always, in *a man sent by God*, and I feel that that man exists. Where is he and why doesn't he reveal himself? This intense preoccupation never leaves me, sleeping or waking; and when I suffer it makes my sufferings ten times as great. In church I weep at the thought of *that Unknown*, without whom nothing seems possible, though I am perhaps the only one to divine or know that he exists. I call upon him *per Deum vivum* and by all the Sacred Names, and I come back, overwhelmed, to read newspapers that drive me to despair.

You will remember one day, my friend, that I told you this, and perhaps you will then be surprised that you were inclined to smile.

And at the end of a volume of his diary called *Au Seuil de l'Apocalypse,* Bloy wrote these lines, printing the last in block letters:

All greatness is exiled in the depths of History and, if God wants to act openly, he will have to take action *Himself,* victoriously, as he did two thousand years ago when he rose from the dead.
I AM WAITING FOR THE COSSACKS AND THE HOLY SPIRIT.

But on Christmas Day 1916 he felt discouraged: "The one I am waiting for does not come and I might well be *tempted to despair."*

It is clear that Bloy sometimes believes that, in the course of history itself, a man sent by Providence will appear and that, *as always,* he will come after the upheavals and disasters—and sometimes he believes in a much more overwhelming miracle which can only be compared to the Resurrection of the Lord. He seems to hesitate between identifying the figure whom he "sees" as a new Joan of Arc or as a new Christ. There is no doubt that very often he had in mind an earthly creature, or a divine messenger who would assume an earthly form. He thought of the "unknown" on whom his heart

LÉON BLOY: A STUDY IN IMPATIENCE

was set as a hero sent by Providence, who would save France from immediate peril, and when he speaks of a "Leader," a "Deliverer" no other explanation is possible: it is a French conqueror whose coming he invokes.

But the expressions he uses in this connection are sufficient evidence that, for the most part, his conception is not such a simple one. When thus invoking, with anguish, the savior of his country, he yields to that earlier temptation to believe that soon, tomorrow, this very day, he, Léon Bloy, will be present at some miraculous happening. Once again the old hope takes possession of him, when he declares that this deliverer has already come, that "he is here or there, a long way off or very, near," that "we have perhaps shaken hands with him without knowing it" (letter of January 28, 1915, to Pierre Termier). Could it be, at last, the fulfilment of Véronique's promises, which were to come to pass during Bloy's lifetime? He trembled at the thought.

There is nothing more natural than that the anguish he felt for France should lead to a fusion in his mind between the deliverance of his country and that other Deliverance which was to put an end to the agonizing slowness of temporal history, and nothing is more consonant with the logic of his inner life: Bloy remains the man who, in every earthly event, recognizes a figure in which the whole of history can be read. And he never experienced a human feeling, a passion like his anxious love for France, without feeding it and justifying it with his highest thoughts and transfiguring it into a symbol representing "something else," while keeping his feet firmly planted in his own concrete and personal reality. How could he help mingling these two earthly and temporal hopes when, at the thought of the battles on the eastern front which might lead to the salvation of France, he invokes in one breath the Cossacks and the Holy Spirit?

Yet this enigmatic Deliverer is to be a man in rags, "a vagabond of the Absolute, of Suffering, of Sleeplessness." We know whom these words point to; they are the words which enabled Bloy to liken wandering Israel to the "Stranger of strangers," to the Paraclete "absent from everywhere," condemned by mankind to be a beggar upon earth, reduced to weeping "with unutterable groans throughout the ages." And Bloy mentions him by name: "I am waiting for the Holy Spirit, who is the Fire of God."

This was Bloy's eternal expectation and the hope which remained to him, since no future built by men seemed any longer possible. But it would be wrong to suppose that it was either a refuge from despair or a recourse to an esoteric doctrine. For Bloy this eschatological imagery—making use of symbols to which, it is true, he sometimes attaches a literal belief, since it is not easy to resist the seduction of words and figures, and because apparent reality, whether it be "visible" or "imaginary," always tends to oust what it represents—this imagery more or less expresses a hope which is not altogether outside time. There is no human hope left; the line of historical evolution has come to a dead end in "absence of God"; men will not rebuild their cities, which they wanted to raise with their own materials and according to an "order" proudly their own. *Therefore* there is only one thing to look forward to: that a devouring flame may kindle souls anew; that love, faith and hope may be reborn in all of them. Then "it will be beautiful beyond all imagining."

Yes! Léon Bloy's expectancy and his impatience are directed towards "last things" and it would be useless to try and deflect his testimony elsewhere. He was saying what he meant to say, when he so often repeated that he cared for nothing but the advent of the Holy Spirit and the End of Time. All his demand for the Absolute pressed forward to this complete fulfilment, and his heart would not tolerate any less perfect object. With this conception of a temporal history in which all moments are simultaneous, he had no difficulty in imagining its end as at hand and in "jumping over" the intervening time. To interpret his words in any other way would be to foist upon them a relative standpoint which was never his, and to reintroduce "successive vision" where his gaze embraced the whole unfolding prospect as an infinitude of contemporaneous things. Do not let us dwarf him for the sake of bringing him back to the

LÉON BLOY: A STUDY IN IMPATIENCE

cautious standpoint of our own mediocrity and saving him from the strictures of the scribes! What is important, what should be recognized, is not so much the imagery which Bloy found, for want of a better, to express his "raging hunger and thirst for the glory of God on earth" as the very insatiability of that love.

At an early stage. Bloy said: "*The Absolute is untranscribable.*" All that he wrote was in some sort intended to take the place of that impossible representation of the Glory of God, loved, desired, invoked, but ineffable. To take its place—not by trying to body it forth in such words as might have a faint chance of approaching the ungraspable reality; nor yet, like the mystics, by going through the whole list of negations which, in saying what God *is not*, enable the mind to close in around that which He is and which cannot be said—but by choosing images which at least compel an awareness of how far beyond all imagining is the invisible Face, and how amazing, strange, unparalleled the sight of it would be—*will be.*

Apart from this continual prompting to *astonishment*, Bloy also expresses—but this time in perfectly tangible and straightforward parlance to which it is impossible to remain deaf—his own fervor and *impatience*. So many images suggestive of fire (from conflagrations and volcanoes to stars; from the ardor of suffering and adoration to the kindling of the whole created world by the flame of the Holy Spirit at last come down from Heaven, at last triumphant) are a cumulative invocation of the longed-for effulgence of Light which will call creation back into itself, of long-awaited Justice flashing down upon the earth, of the Transparence which will reveal to eyes now opened the "identity" of each in the universal fellowship of the saints—and Love entering like a king into all souls. The love which even here below devoured the suffering and unconquerably hopeful soul of Léon Bloy.

He knew, moreover, as no one else knew, that all that he imagined and strove to show forth in glory, the complete empire of God over his creatures and the creatures' gift of themselves to God, was realizable *here and now*: that in this world of sin the Redeemer had come, the Kingdom had begun with Jesus Christ. But he also knew that man remains inexplicably a sinner after Salvation has been brought to him, that he therefore approaches God only through suffering and that his "malady of exile" is the cause of the exile of God himself. That was his great heartbreak—"*There is only one sadness, the sadness of not being saints*"—the source of all his impatience, his grand impatience which was the purest and surest thing about him, his true and unique gift of love.

> So be it, then. I shall wait for the supreme Suffering, the sublime Suffering, the infinite consolation. But what strength I shall need to wait! I shall have to endure everything, put up with everything that is neither true joy nor true suffering…
>
> For it is very certain that I was born to wait continually and to consume myself in waiting. For half a century I have been capable of nothing else.

Saint-Maur—Basle—Geneva—Liddes
July 1942 to October 1943

Author's Bibliographical Note

A complete bibliography of the works of Léon Bloy is to be found in Joseph Bollery's *Un Grand Écrivain français méconnu: Léon Bloy* (La Rochelle, 1929); my own book *Textes choisis de Léon Bloy*, published in the series *Le Cri de France* (Fribourg: Egloff, 1943), contains an abridged list of Bloy's works.

Anyone writing about Bloy owes an immense debt to Stanislas Fumet, whose *Mission de Léon Bloy* (Les Iles, 1935) is a masterpiece of penetration and something far better than a critic's commentary. I owe more than I can say to that book, which is much longer and more complete than my present sketch.

The works of Hubert Colleye (*L'Ame de Léon Bloy* [Paris, 1930]; *L'Homme de l'Absolu* [Brussels, 1943]; *Léon Bloy, Poete* [Brussels, 1943]) are valuable in various ways. The first, which traces the development of Bloy's inner life up to the time of *Le Désespéré*, is an excellent psychological study, containing a wealth of unpublished material on the youth of the "Thankless Mendicant." The second and more systematic work contains some very profound reflections on Bloy's attitude to Joy, his humility and his classicism. In the third book he is at last given his true place among the poets.

ALBERT BÉGUIN

More immediate testimony, by his godchildren and other members of his intimate circle, is to be found in *Quelques Pages sur Léon Bloy* by Jacques Maritain (Cahiers de la Quinzaine, 1929), Raïssa Maritain's reminiscences (*Les Grandes Amitiés* [New York, 1941]), Pierre van der Meer's *Journal d'un Converti* (Paris, 1917), Pierre Termier's *Introduction à Léon Bloy* (Paris, 1930), René Martineau's *Souvenirs d'un Ami* (Paris, 1926), and Leopold Levaux's *Léon Bloy* (Brussels, 1937).

Georges Rouzet's essays (*Dans l'Ombre de Léon Bloy* [Brussels, 1942]), J. Bollery's study of *Le Désespéré* (Paris, 1937), the valuable collection of *Cahiers Léon Bloy* (1922–1938) and especially the profound analyses of the symbolism of *Sueur de Sang* and *La Femme pauvre*, appearing above the signature "Fam," in the latest numbers of that series, have thrown light on important aspects of Bloy's work.

Having ruled out footnotes—for which I have a violent distaste—I cannot acknowledge in detail all that I owe to these various works. I also found a number of suggestions or welcome confirmation of my own views in the manuscripts which I received for the Léon Bloy miscellany about to appear in the *Cahiers du Rhône* (1944), and in particular from the essays by Pierre Emmanual on the symbolism of history, by Hubert Colleye on Bloy's attitude to women, and Georges Cattaui on the destiny of France. This miscellany will contain, *inter alia*, unpublished letters from Pierre Termier regarding his last visits to Bloy, and recollections by his daughter, Jeanne Boussac, and by the great painter Georges Rouault.

My cordial thanks are due to Abbé Charles Journet, who was good enough to let me read, in manuscript, the chapters dealing with *Le Salut par les Juifs* in the book which he is writing on the mystery of Israel; these precise theological notes have helped me to avoid mistakes, although the point of view of the theologian, studying the destiny of the Chosen People in itself and examining Bloy's opinions from that angle, necessarily differs from that of an essay in which those opinions are interpreted as an aspect of Bloy's personality.

In conclusion I should like to express my sincere gratitude to Henri Schubiger, who kindly lent me several of Bloy's works which are no longer obtainable.

I realize that I have cited a great many authorities for a sketch which lacks completeness and finality. They will enable the reader to fill the gaps it has left.

Cluny Media

Designed by Fiona Cecile Clarke, the Cluny Media *logo depicts a monk at work in the scriptorium, with a cat sitting at his feet.*

The monk represents our mission to emulate the invaluable contributions of the monks of Cluny in preserving the libraries of the West, our strivings to know and love the truth.

The cat at the monk's feet is Pangur Bán, from the eponymous Irish poem of the 9th century. The anonymous poet compares his scholarly pursuit of truth with the cat's happy hunting of mice. The depiction of Pangur Bán is an homage to the work of the monks of Irish monasteries and a sign of the joy we at Cluny take in our trade.

"Messe ocus Pangur Bán,
cechtar nathar fria saindan:
bíth a menmasam fri seilgg,
mu memna céin im saincheirdd."

www.ingramcontent.com/pod-product-compliance
Lightning Source LLC
Chambersburg PA
CBHW052053110526
44591CB00013B/2195